THE CATHOLIC BIBLICAL QUARTERLY

MONOGRAPH SERIES

7

JEROME'S *COMMENTARY ON DANIEL:*

A STUDY OF COMPARATIVE JEWISH AND CHRISTIAN INTERPRETATIONS OF THE HEBREW BIBLE

by

Jay Braverman

JEROME'S *COMMENTARY ON DANIEL:*
A STUDY OF COMPARATIVE JEWISH AND CHRISTIAN INTERPRETATIONS OF THE HEBREW BIBLE

BY

JAY BRAVERMAN

The Catholic Biblical Association of America
Washington, DC 20064
1978

JEROME'S *COMMENTARY ON DANIEL:*
A Study of Comparative Jewish and Christian Interpretations
of the Hebrew Bible
by Jay Braverman

© 1978 The Catholic Biblical Association of America
Washington, DC

PRODUCED IN THE UNITED STATES

Library of Congress Cataloging in Publication Data

Braverman, Jay, 1937—
  Jerome's *Commentary on Daniel.*

  (The Catholic Biblical quarterly: Monograph series: v. 7)
  Bibliography: p.
  Includes index.
  1. Hieronymous, Saint. Commentariorum in Danielem prophetam liber. 2. Bible. O.T.
Daniel — Criticism, interpretation, etc. — History — Early church, ca. 30-600. I.
Title. II. Series: The Catholic Biblical quarterly. Monograph series; v. 7.

BS1555.H453B7   244′.5 ′07   78-55726
ISBN 0-915170-06-X

DEDICATED
TO MY WIFE
SANDY
שלי ושלכם — שלה הוא (כתובות סג׳)

AND
TO OUR CHILDREN
DEBBIE, JEFF, ALAN
and
TO THE MEMORY OF
ROCHELLE ע״ה

TABLE OF CONTENTS

ACKNOWLEDGMENTS

"No man is an island" is as valid an aphorism in the field of scholarship as it is in all other areas of human endeavor. The pursuit of knowledge chastens us with the realization that "original research" is merely a metaphor reserved for the unsophisticated and immature. Indeed, we all stand on the shoulders of the giants who preceded us and have them to thank for giving us our vantage point and perspective. The best that I could ever hope to produce is directly attributable to my teachers and advisors.

My debt to the faculty of Yeshiva University, where I attended five schools over the course of fifteen years, is profound. In particular, Prof. Samuel K. Mirsky, of blessed memory, initially guided me along the paths of *midrash* and *aggadah,* and pointed the way to future research. Prof. Louis H. Feldman impressed me with the wisdom of the classics and was instrumental in the choice of this topic, combining the "beauty of Japheth in the tents of Shem." His willingness to spend unlimited time and effort with me during the years it took to produce this work underscores his unique devotion to his students. He has been a constant source of advice and encouragement and has most deeply influenced my academic career.

Several distinguished scholars were gracious in reading the manuscript and offering many learned and valuable suggestions. Prof. Morton Smith of Columbia University suggested detailed emendations that considerably improved both the literary and scholarly tone of this work. The late Fr. Louis F. Hartman of the Catholic University of America encouraged me in the early stages of research and was first to recommend publication. Prof. Saul Lieberman of the Jewish Theological Seminary of America provided me with many references and insights into rabbinic and patristic literature. Prof. Ephraim E. Urbach of the Hebrew University, after reading the manuscript, offered helpful suggestions during an extended interview. Rev. Dr. Stephen Casey, S.J., of Concordia University helped me to clarify contemporary scholarly opinion on various abstruse issues.

The Editorial Board of *CBQMS* have been particularly cordial and understanding. I greatly benefitted from the critique and suggestions of Msgr. Patrick W. Skehan. Fr. Bruce Vawter, C.M., Chairman of the Editorial Board, graciously undertook the arduous task of preparing the manuscript for publication. Fr. Joseph Jensen, O.S.B., Executive Secretary of The Catholic Biblical Association offered valuable practical advice. While I assume all responsibility for whatever errors may be found in the text, I am deeply indebted to all the above for contributing to the possible merit of this work.

The National Foundation for Jewish Culture and the Memorial Foundation for Jewish Culture provided research subsidies which have been greatly appreciated. My students, Irving Mandelbaum and Robert Friedman, were diligent with many technical aspects. Robert also prepared the indices with great care. My secretary, Miss Gladys Urbach, undertook the tedious task of typing the manuscript with unusual devotion and precision.

Constant encouragement and understanding were provided by my family. My mother, Mrs. Ida Braverman, helped me throughout my academic career and enabled me to pursue scholarship. The preparation of this work absorbed much leisure time that rightly belonged to my wife, Sandy; in a real sense, her unselfishness and love form the matrix of my achievements.

To all of the above I dedicate, in appreciation, the fruits of my labor and hope that I have given them a worthwhile return for their investments in time, thought, energy, and love.

PREFACE

The field of midrash, consisting of exegetical and homiletic commentaries and expansions on the Bible, has been systematically and critically explored only during the past century. Jewish rabbinic scholars had generally neglected it, as they often do to this day, because they regarded it as much less important than the legal discussions in the Talmud; and Christian scholars tended to look down upon it as a collection of extravagant legends. Even now the field remains largely uncharted, and debates as to the very definition of midrash, the classification of such midrashic-like works as Pseudo-Philo's *Biblical Antiquities,* the first half of Josephus' *Antiquities,* and the Dead Sea Genesis Apocryphon and *pesher* on Habakkuk, as well as the dating and relationship of the various midrashim, show wide divergences in scholarly opinion.

Inasmuch as the earliest rabbinic midrashim were probably not written down until the end of the Talmudic era in the fifth and sixth centuries, we especially appreciate traditions from any earlier period. Several Jewish scholars, notably Graetz, Krauss, and Ginzberg, recognized the importance of the Church Fathers for this purpose, since a number of the Fathers — notably Origen, Eusebius, Ephraem, Jerome, Tertullian, Lactantius, Ambrose, and Augustine — either studied under or were otherwise directly influenced by Jewish teachers in their Biblical exegesis. The Fathers found such instruction useful and even necessary because they were often engaged in polemics against Jews who frequently charged the Christians with misinterpreting Biblical texts because of their dependence upon the Greek translation of the Septuagint and because of their inability to consult the Hebrew original and the ancient Jewish traditions of exegesis.

Of the Fathers acquainted with Hebrew, easily the most important is Jerome, since he made the greatest efforts — and with a measure of success unmatched by any other Church Father — to master Hebrew and thus was able to approach the Jewish tradition directly. While it is true that the Fathers, including Jerome, often speak disparagingly of the Jewish midrashim as perverted exegesis or old wives' tales, this is largely in line with the ancient practice, seen for example in Livy's attitude toward Valerius Antias, of bitterly criticizing an author from whom one draws heavily. In particular, Jewish scholars and Origen (upon whom Jewish teachers had had the greatest influence before Jerome) exercised an important influence upon Jerome in impressing upon him the authenticity of the Hebrew text of the Bible so that he based his Vulgate translation upon it rather than upon the Septuagint, which had been regarded as divinely in-

spired and which had a special status in the Church. Similarly, under the
influence of Jewish scholarship and of Origen, Jerome refused to recognize
as canonical any book of the Bible rejected by the rabbis.

Dr. Braverman's work presents, for the first time, a systematic comparison of Origen's and Jerome's attitudes toward the Biblical text in the
Hebrew and Septuagint versions and toward the canon of the Scriptures and
traces the stages in Jerome's abandonment of the primacy of the Septuagint. Secondly, and most significantly, it confirms the value of Ginzberg's approach in seeking parallels to existing midrashim and in recovering
traditions, including the juxtaposition of the same apparently unconnected
Biblical verses, long since lost. The fact that that master of midrash and the
most prolific writer on the subject of midrashim in Church Fathers, Ginzberg, failed to utilize Jerome's *Commentary on Daniel* in his *magnum opus,
The Legends of the Jews,* and in his other works except for one passing
reference makes Dr. Braverman's work all the more important. As a result
of the present research we now have external confirmation of two aggadic
traditions previously known to us only through rabbinic literature and
Josephus, two others known only through rabbinic literature, six others
known in part through extant rabbinic texts, and, most important of all, six
cases (including the interpretation of Dan 11:33 as predicting the
destruction of the Temple by Titus and of 11:34 as foretelling the promise
made by the Emperor Julian to rebuild the Temple) where Jerome has
recovered for us previously unknown Jewish traditions.

Inasmuch as the book of Daniel plays such an important role in messianic
speculation both among Jews and Christians, Jerome's comments on Dan
9:24-27, in which he cites his longest midrashic tradition and indeed one of
the longest in all his works, is of particular interest. Here Dr. Braverman
raises a significant question about our text of Josephus, since Jerome cites
Josephus' assertion (unparalleled in the Talmudic literature) that Vespasian
and Titus concluded peace with the Jews for three and a half years, whereas
there is no such passage in our text of Josephus. Again, Jerome's statement
on 11:36 that the Jews look upon this passage as referring to the Antichrist
or false Messiah has no parallel in rabbinic literature; and one is tempted to
think that there might have been such a tradition in early midrashim but
that, like some other such references, it was eliminated by Christian cen-
sorship.

One of Dr. Braverman's most important accomplishments is his
discussion of Jerome's commentary on the story of Susanna and the elders,
one of the apocryphal additions to the book of Daniel. The fact that Jerome
refers to a Jewish tradition giving the names of the elders shows, as Dr.
Braverman has demonstrated, that the apocryphal tradition of Susanna
circulated among the Jews many hundreds of years before it appears in the

earliest extant rabbinic account in the eleventh century.

Dr. Braverman's work is especially valuable because he compares Jerome with earlier (especially Origen), contemporary, and later Church Fathers in their aggadic treatment of Daniel, thus presenting, in effect, a case study in the history of Christian exegesis, as compared with the Jewish exegesis of the Apocrypha, the Pseudepigrapha, Josephus, and rabbinic literature. It is a pioneer study since no systematic work has been done on the treatment of Daniel in patristic literature, and the work on Daniel in Josephus by Rappaport and in the rabbinic literature by Benno Fischer and Ginzberg is far from exhaustive. The present work also sheds much light on the sources and the relationships of the classical medieval Jewish commentators, as well as of that most fascinating eleventh-century Karaite, Jepheth ibn Ali, who sometimes repeats traditions which are not found in extant rabbinic sources but which do occur in Jerome. It also casts light on the identification of the Kittim in the Dead Sea Commentary on Habakkuk, since Jerome says that he follows the Hebrews (as indeed we find in Targumim and in a Midrash) in understanding them as the Romans.

In summary, Dr. Braverman's work is not only an important contribution to the canon and text of the Bible, as well as to rabbinic and patristic literature, but also has significant suggestions for students of the Apocrypha, the Dead Sea Scrolls, and Josephus. Its methodology is a model for future study of aggadic traditions in other works of Jerome, as well as in other Fathers, notably Origen, Ephraem, and Tertullian.

Yeshiva University   LOUIS H. FELDMAN
New York, NY   *24 October 1976*

Acts	Acts of the Apostles
Apoc	Apocalypse
1-2 Apoc. Bar.	*1-2 Apocalypse of Baruch*
Apoc. Mos.	*The Apocalypse of Moses*
Am	Amos
Aristeas	*The Letter of Aristeas*
Asc. Isa.	*The Ascension of Isaiah*
Ass. Mos.	*The Assumption of Moses*
Bar	Baruch
1-2 Chr	1-2 Chronicles
Ct	Canticle of Canticles
Col	Colossians
1-2 Cor	1-2 Corinthians
Dt	Deuteronomy
Dan	Daniel
Eccl	Ecclesiastes
Eph	Ephesians
Esth	Esther
Ex	Exodus
Ezek	Ezekiel
Gal	Galatians
Gen	Genesis
Hab	Habakkuk
Hag	Haggai
Heb	Hebrews
Hos	Hosea
Isa	Isaiah
Jas	James
Jdt	Judith
Jer	Jeremiah
Jgs	Judges
Jn	John
1-2-3 Jn	1-2-3 John
Jon	Jonah
Jos	Joshua
Jub.	*The Book of Jubilees*
1-2 Kgs	1-2 Kings
Lam	Lamentations

Lev	Leviticus
Lk	Luke
1-2-3-4 Mac	1-2-3-4 Maccabees
Mal	Malachi
Mic	Micah
Mk	Mark
Mt	Matthew
Nah	Nahum
Neh	Nehemiah
Num	Numbers
Ob	Obadiah
1-2 Pet	1-2 Peter
Phil	Philippians
Phlm	Philemon
Pr	Proverbs
Ps	Psalms
Ps. Sol.	*The Psalms of Solomon*
Rom	Romans
Ru	Ruth
1-2 Sam	1-2 Samuel
Sib. Or.	*The Sibylline Oracles*
Sir	Wisdom of Jesus, Son of Sirach (Ecclesiasticus)
1-2 Thes	1-2 Thessalonians
1-2 Tim	1-2 Timothy
Tit	Titus
Tob	Tobit
Test. Levi	*The Testament of Levi*
Test. Naph.	*The Testament of Naphtali*
Test. XII Patr.	*The Testaments of the Twelve Patriarchs*
Wis	Wisdom
Zech	Zechariah
Zeph	Zephaniah

ABBREVIATIONS OF JOURNALS, SERIES, AND STANDARD REFERENCE WORKS

APOT	R.H. Charles (ed.) *Apocrypha and Pseudepigrapha of the Old Testament*
Bib	*Biblica*
BJRL	*Bulletin of the John Rylands Library*
BS	*Bibliotheca sacra*

BWANT	*Beiträge zur Wissenschaft vom Alten und Neuen Testament*
CBQ	*Catholic Biblical Quarterly*
CCSL	*Corpus Christianorum: Series Latina*
CSEL	*Corpus Scriptorum Ecclesiasticorum Latinorum*
FC	*Fathers of the Church*
HTR	*Harvard Theological Review*
HTS	*Harvard Theological Studies*
HUCA	*Hebrew Union College Annual*
ICC	*International Critical Commentary*
IDB	G. A. Buttrick (ed.) *Interpreter's Dictionary of the Bible*
JAAR	*Journal of the American Academy of Religion*
JBC	R. E. Brown et al. (eds.) *Jerome Biblical Commentary*
JBL	*Journal of Biblical Literature*
JBR	*Journal of Bible and Religion*
JQR	*Jewish Quarterly Review*
JTS	*Journal of Theological Studies*
LCL	*Loeb Classical Library*
MGWJ	*Monatsschrift für Geschichte und Wissenschaft des Judentums*
PEQ	*Palestine Exploration Quarterly*
PG	J. Migne, *Patrologia graeca*
PL	J. Migne, *Patrologia latina*
RB	*Revue Biblique*
RBen	*Revue Bénédictine*
Rech	*Recherches bibliques*
RevScRel	*Revue des sciences religieuses*
RQ	*Revue de Qumran*
RSR	*Recherches de science religieuse*
RTP	*Revue de théologie et de philosophie*
SC	*Sources chrétiennes*
SPB	*Studia postbiblica*
TLZ	*Theologische Literaturzeitung*
TU	*Texte und Untersuchungen*
VC	*Vigiliae christianae*
VT	*Vetus Testamentum*
VTSup	*Vetus Testamentum, Supplements*
ZAW	*Zeitschrift für die alttestamentliche Wissenschaft*

CHAPTER 1

INTRODUCTION

The Church Fathers and Rabbinic Tradition

The relationship between the writings of the Church Fathers and Rabbinic tradition has only begun to be recognized about a century ago. Beginning with H. Graetz's pioneer article in 1854, "Haggadische Elemente bei den Kirchenvätern"[1] and continuing sporadically with the work of D. Gerson, Moritz Rahmer, A. H. Goldfahn, Carl Seigfried, S. Funk, Samuel Krauss, M. J. Lagrange, Louis Ginzberg, V. Aptowitzer, W. Bacher, A. Condamin, F. Stummer, Frank Gavin, M. G. Bardy, and E. F. Sutcliffe, we find that this field has just begun to be tapped.[2] The two men who have contributed most to this investigation have been Samuel Krauss and Louis Ginzberg: the former for recognizing the importance of this research and charting its course, and the latter for devoting a good part of his lifetime to investigation of the areas indicated by Krauss. And yet they only touched the surface, leaving room for others to search and discover.

Krauss offers us a practical introduction to this field in his articles in the *Jewish Quarterly Review* and the *Jewish Encyclopedia*.

> The contemporaries and, in part, the co-workers of those men who are known from the Talmud and the Midrash as the depositaries of the Jewish doctrine, were the instructors who transmitted this doctrine to the Church Fathers also. Hence such a mass of haggadic material is found in the work of the fathers as to constitute an important part of Jewish theological lore.[3]

These traditions were so generally accepted that many times their Jewish origins were forgotten. "Therefore modern Jewish learning turns, although not yet with sufficient eagerness, to the investigation of the works of the Church Fathers."[4] "This Midrash treasure has unfortunately not yet been fully examined; scholars have only recently begun to investigate this field."[5]

Louis Ginzberg's six-part series of *Die Haggada bei den Kirchenvätern* as well as his monumental *The Legends of the Jews* remain, until the present

---

[1]   Throughout this study reference is made by abbreviated title or by author's name only to works which will be found cited in full in the Bibliography at the end of the book.

[2]   The most comprehensive bibliography of works in this area has been compiled by E. Lamirande, "Etude bibliographique sur les pères de l'Eglise et l'Aggadah." His annotations are quite helpful.

[3]   "Church Fathers," *Jewish Encyclopedia* 4, 80.

[4]   Ibid., 86.

[5]   Samuel Krauss, "Jerome," *Jewish Encyclopedia* 7, 117.

1

day, the most significant studies in tracing Jewish traditions in the works of the Church Fathers. In Volumes 5 and 6 of the latter work he quotes approximately eight hundred passages from patristic literature together with their parallels in rabbinic writings. Ginzberg gives us a good idea of the scope of this field.

> Not only the Church Fathers, Origen, Eusebius, Ephraem and Jerome, of whom it is well known that they studied the Bible under the guidance of Jewish teachers, have appropriated a good deal of Jewish legendary lore, but also Tertullian, Lactantius, Ambrosius, Augustine and many other teachers and leaders of the Church have come under direct influence of Jews. . . . The large material culled from the writings of the Church Fathers to illustrate their dependence upon Jewish tradition will be, I hope, of some value to the student of the patristic literature.[6]

Jerome and the Antiochian and Alexandrian Schools

Before analyzing the relationship of Jerome (331?[7]-420 C.E.) to rabbinic tradition, it is important to assess his qualities, method and educational background which made him such a successful exegete. The scope of his erudition was indeed most unusual. His contemporary, Sulpicius Severus, says of him: "In universal knowledge no one would dare to compare himself with him."[8] His theological background matched his secular one. Augustine, his famous contemporary whom he never met face to face, also remarks that Jerome "had read all or almost all the authors of both parts of the world who had written anything before his time on the teaching of the Church."[9] Augustine's praise is even more significant in light of his opposition to Jerome's new Vulgate translation on the grounds that it would (as indeed it did) upset the faith of the Christian masses in the *Vetus Latina,* the current Latin version of the Hebrew Scriptures.[10]

Despite his erudition, Jerome states quite clearly that "the prime concern of an exegete is not to show off his own eloquence but to help the reader understand the sense of the original author."[11] Indeed Jerome was in-

---

[6]   *Legends* 5, ix.

[7]   J. N. D. Kelly, *Jerome: His Life, Writings, and Controversies* 1, 337-339, prefers this date but notes, as well, the more commonly accepted date of 347, with an analysis of the entire matter.

[8]   *Dialogus* 1.8 = *PL* 20:189. In 1868, fire destroyed Migne's presses and molds. Unfortunately, when they were subsequently reprinted, the numbering of the columns was changed, although the text (except for typographical errors) remained the same. Unless otherwise noted, the edition prior to 1868 is cited in this work.

[9]   *Contra Julianum* 1.34 = *PL* 44:665.

[10]   *PL* 22:833, 952.

[11]   Letter 36.3.

fluenced by three different schools of exegesis. The Antiochian school stressed that any interpretation of Scripture, even its "higher" or "spiritual" sense, had to be founded on the words of the text and the meaning intended by its inspired author. Thus they were known as the school of *literal* interpretation. The Alexandrians, on the other hand, under the strong influence of Philo, stressed that the Divine Author of the Bible did not tie his intentions rigorously to the words of the text: a passage often is to be interpreted figuratively (or "spiritually," "tropologically," or "allegorically") to arrive at its fuller, higher meaning. Thus they were known as the school of *spiritual* interpretation. The Antiochian method was more scientific, while the Alexandrian method lent itself better to homiletics, preaching and the inculcation of faith and religious values. Jerome studied under representatives of each of the above schools: Apollinaris of Laodicea, of the Antiochian school, and Didymus of Alexandria.[12] In his exegetical method, Jerome borrowed from each school, stressing their merits and trying to avoid their excesses.[13] Usually Jerome begins with the literal interpretation, and he speaks of the literal sense as the *secundum historiam* ("according to history," i.e., literal meaning) or the *historiae veritas* ("the truth of history"), or just *historia*. Then he expounds the spiritual message, according to the style of the Alexandrians. From a quantitative point of view, he spends much more time on the latter method of exegesis. His eulogy dedicated to Paula perhaps best sums up his philosophy of biblical exegesis:

> The Holy Scriptures she knew by heart, and though she loved their literal meaning (*historia*) and said that it was the foundation of truth, yet she still preferred to follow the spiritual meaning, and with this roof she protected the edifice of her soul.[14]

Jerome and Rabbinic Tradition

Jerome had another most important exegetical influence upon his career—direct Jewish tradition and rabbinic exegesis. It is most significant to note that in the same letter where he describes his education and in-

---

[12] Letter 84.3.

[13] Jerome has been accused of an inconsistent approach in his eclectic exegetical method. It should be remembered, however, that although he quotes various opposing opinions from various schools and thus seems to be inconsistent, he does not adopt all of these explanations. Many times he is rendering the invaluable service of recording these traditions which would otherwise have been lost. Often he records verbatim, and with respect, the interpretations which he opposes. A good example of this is Porphyry's interpretation of Dan 11. See Chapter 15, n. 3.

[14] Letter 108.26 (*PL* 22:902).

fluential teachers, together with Apollinaris and Didymus he mentions a Jewish teacher, Bar-anina,[15] from whom he learned "with what trouble and at what a cost!"[16]

As we will presently show, Jerome was the Church Father most conversant with Jewish traditions. He surpasses all others in his erudition as well as in his importance for Judaism. There were several other Jewish scholars, whom he does not identify, who served as his teachers. He studied with them mainly in order to master the Hebrew text, so as to be able to translate it. Jerome worked with his Jewish teachers to master the Hebrew biblical text even before he began to compose his Vulgate translation. In his preface to his revision of Chronicles (composed in 389) based on the Old Latin Version (*Vetus Latina*) he wrote:

> I procured a former teacher of the Law from Tiberias, who was held by the Hebrews[17] in admiration and I conferred with him from the top of the head to the bottom toenail, so to speak.[18]

Jerome adopted this procedure even in translating the Aramaic book of Tobit (done between 386-390).

> Inasmuch as the language of the Chaldees [i.e., Aramaic, the language of his text of Tobit] is allied to the Hebrew, I procured the help of the most skillful speaker of both languages I could find, and gave to the subject one day's hasty labor; whatever he expressed to me in Hebrew words I, summoning a secretary, explained in Latin.[19]

This clearly shows us Jerome's ability of oral comprehension of the Hebrew language. In his preface to the translation of Job from the Hebrew, he recalls the help given to him by a Jewish teacher in translating this very difficult Hebrew text:

> I remember that in order to gain an understanding of this book, I hired, for no small sum of money, a certain teacher from Lydda, who was considered by the Jews to be first-rate. Whether I advanced any by his teaching I do not know. But this one thing I do know — that I would not have been able to interpret something if I had not first understood it.[20]

---

[15] For the attempted identification of this Bar-anina see S. Krauss, "Church Fathers," *Jewish Encyclopedia* 4, 81. He claims that Bar-ḥanina (Jerome's Bar-anina) is not identical with R. Ḥama bar Ḥanina as Rahmer insists.

[16] Letter 84.3. Jerome tells us that Bar-anina surreptitiously removed books from the synagogue in order to instruct him.

[17] See Chapter 15, n. 1.

[18] *PL* 29:401.

[19] *PL* 29:25-26. Cf. Chapter 3, n. 54.

[20] *PL* 28 (ed. 1845): 1081; (ed. 1889) 1140. Cf. n. 8 above.

Interestingly enough, the first one to teach Jerome Hebrew was a converted Jew, a Hebrew-speaking monk in the desert of Chalcis, from 376-380 C.E. Jerome tells us quite vividly of his trials and tribulations in learning Hebrew.

> . . . I learned the [Hebrew] alphabet and practised both the hissing and panting words.[21] What labor I spent there! What difficulty I went through! How often I despaired! How often I quit in despair, and then, in my eagerness to learn, began again. This can be attested to both by myself, the subject of this misery, and by those who then lived with me. But I thank the Lord that from a bitter seed of learning I now pluck sweet fruits.[22]

Jerome lived in Palestine for approximately thirty-five years (from 386 until his death in 420) and apparently continued to study with his Hebrew teachers all during this period.[23] Although he was severely criticized by his opponents[24] for his associations with Jews, he steadfastly maintained the necessity for this.

> Shall I not be permitted to inform the Latins in the work of my commentaries of what I have learned from the Hebrews? . . . I would now show you how useful it is to tread on the threshold of the Masters and to learn the art from the artists.[25]

Jerome was criticized by his opponents, and even admitted himself, that his Latin style and rhetoric suffered from his intensive pursuit to master the Hebrew language.

> I entreat you, reader, to forgive me for expressing [myself] with swift speech; do not look [in my writings] for charm of eloquence. I lost it long ago by my study of the Hebrew language.[26]

[21] Jerome here refers to the pronunciation of certain aspirate and guttural sounds in Hebrew, difficult for a non-native to master. He writes of similar difficulties in his *Preface to Daniel* (*PL* 28:1291-2). Cf. E. F. Sutcliffe, "St. Jerome's Pronunciation of Hebrew," and J. Barr, "St Jerome's Appreciation of Hebrew." Jerome seems never to have been able to speak Hebrew as a native Palestinian. In his *Commentary on Titus* 3:9 (*PL* 29:594) he tells us that the Jews laughed at his quaint accent and his faulty pronunciation of the sibilants and gutturals of Hebrew.

[22] Letter 125.12 (*PL* 22:1079). We also find in this letter that one of the reasons Jerome undertook the study of Hebrew was to discipline his passions and rid himself of impure thoughts.

[23] *Commentary on Nahum* 2:1.

[24] He was even accused of attempting to Judaize the Church of Christ. Out of malice, Rufinus changed Jerome's Hebrew teacher's name from Bar-anina into Barabbas, the criminal who was released instead of Jesus before Passover. Cf. Mt 27:16, Mk 15:7, Lk 23:19, Jn 18:40 and Acts 3:14.

[25] *Apology Against Rufinus,* 1.20 (*PL* 23:414).

[26] *Commentary on Haggai,* end. See the latest edition, *CCSL* 76A, 746, 11. 744-746.

Indeed, we find Jerome's writings replete with Hebrew idioms turned into Latin as well as biblical metaphors, allusions and figures of speech.

We see ample evidence in Jerome's works of his specific reliance upon Hebrew authorities for his novel translations of Hebrew Scripture. "Ask any Hebrew and he will tell you" is a phrase that recurs quite often. For example, in his *Commentary on Amos* 3:11 we find: "The Hebrew who gave me instructions in the sacred Scripture told me this."[27] It is most likely to assume, whenever Jerome's translation radically departs from the older versions that preceded him, especially in the identification of the biblical *flora* and *fauna,* that he is following current Jewish interpretation. There is a surprising number of similarities between his Vulgate and the Targumim and Rabbinic exegesis.[28]

Thus far we have pointed out the influence of the Jews upon Jerome's Latin translation of the Bible and the principles which affected it. Indeed, this itself is a subject worthy of intensive study and analysis. However, rabbinic tradition influenced Jerome to a much wider extent than mere grammatical exposition and translation of the text. We find hundreds of Jewish traditions preserved in his commentaries referring to all aspects of biblical interpretation. In his *Commentary on Zechariah* 6:9-15, we find a clear statement which points out vividly the importance of a study of Jerome's writing for Jewish scholarship:

> I once proposed to make available for Latin listeners the secrets of Hebrew erudition and the recondite teachings of the Masters of the Synagogue, as long as the latter is in keeping with the Holy Scriptures.[29]

These traditions are not limited to those current in his time but also preserve the opinions of rabbis who lived centuries before him. In his *Commentary on Ecclesiastes* 4:13-16 we find:

> When my Hebrew friend, to whom I often refer, was reading Ecclesiastes with me, he testified that Barakiba (Baracchiba), whom alone or especially they esteem, had transmitted this concerning the present passage.[30]

There is no doubt that this is the famous Rabbi Akiba ben Joseph, the second century *tanna*.[31] Jerome again refers to Akiba in his *Commentary on*

---

[27] *PL* 25:1019.
[28] See A. Condamin, "L'influence de la tradition juive dans la version de S. Jérôme," F. Stummer, "Beiträge zu dem Problem Hieronymus und die Targumim," and C. H. Gordon, "Rabbinic Exegesis in the Vulgate of Proverbs."
[29] *PL* 25:1455 = *CCSL* 76A, 796, ll. 172-175.
[30] *PL* 23:1048 = *CCSL* 72, 288, ll. 179-182.
[31] Jerome's contemporary, Epiphanius, also mentions "Bar-akiba" in *Against Heresies* 15, and "Akiba" in *Against Heresies* 33.

Isaiah 8:14,[32] where he gives a list of the leading rabbis of the first two centuries C.E., including Shammai, Hillel, Johanan ben Zakkai and Meir. In his Letter 121.10 we find:

> [The Jews say] 'Barachibas and Simeon [i.e., Ben Gamaliel] and Hellel [*sic*], our masters, have handed down to us that we may walk two miles on the Sabbath' and other such things, preferring the teachings of men to God's teachings.[33]

Jerome was also well aware of the technical phrases of rabbinic literature. In the same Letter 121 cited above, Jerome informs us that the Jews call their tradition *deuterōsis*[34] (literally, "repetition") which is equivalent to the Hebrew word משנה, meaning repetition. He also writes that

> Their teachers are called *sophoi,* that is, "wise men," and whenever on given days they set forth their traditions, they have the custom of telling their disciples *hoi sophoi deuterōsin,* that is, "the wise men teach the traditions."[35]

The Greek phrase *hoi sophoi deuterōsin* is equivalent to the Hebrew שנו חכמים and the Aramaic תנו רבנן. In Jerome's *Commentary on Habakkuk* 2:15-17 we read:

> At Lydda I once heard a certain one of the Hebrews, who was called a wise man and a *deuterōtēs* among them, telling a story of this sort.[36]

The Greek word *deuterōtēs* (literally, "repeater") is equivalent to the Aramaic word תנא (*tanna*), a scholar who memorized texts of the Mishna and recited them in the colleges before the Rabbis.[37]

Krauss has pointed out[38] other technical terms of the midrash that recur in Jerome's works: *Hoc Scriptura nunc dicit* = זה שאמר הכתוב, *Hoc est quod dicitur* = הדא הוא דכתיב, and *Non debemus legere* or *non legi potest* = אל תקרי.[39]

---

[32] *PL* 24:119.

[33] *PL* 22:1033-4.

[34] Justinian's *Novella* 146.1.2 contains the prohibition of Jews' teaching the *deuterōsis*.

[35] Letter 121.10, *PL* 22:1034.

[36] *PL* 25:1301 = *CCSL* 76A, 610, 11. 578-580.

[37] Saul Lieberman, *Hellenism in Jewish Palestine,* 88.

[38] "The Jews in the Works of the Church Fathers," 251-252.

[39] Jerome's *Commentary on Nahum* 3:8, and his *Commentary on Haggai* 1:1. Saul Lieberman, *Hellenism in Jewish Palestine,* 73 points out that the methods called "notarikon" and "gematria" are also found in non-Jewish exegetical works and thus do not constitute evidence of Jewish influence. "The use of letters as numerals is apparently a Greek invention which was adopted by the Semites at a much later time" [73, n. 211]. Jerome in using these is therefore following a current Graeco-Roman custom.

Krauss sums up the importance of the Jewish traditions cited by Jerome:

> Jerome's opinion of these traditions is immaterial at the present time. The important point is that he quotes them; for thereby the well-known traditions of the Midrash are obtained in Latin form, and in this form they are sometimes more concise and comprehensible—in any case they are more interesting. Moreover, many traditions that appear from the sources in which they are found to be of a late date, are thus proved to be of earlier origin. Jerome also recounts traditions that are no longer found in canonical Jewish sources, as well as some that have been preserved in the Jewish and Christian apocrypha. It is, furthermore, interesting to note that Jerome had read some of these traditions; hence they had been committed to writing in his time.[40]

We have an interesting example of Jewish traditions which Jerome saw in writing. In his Letter 36.1, written at Rome in 384 to Pope Damasus, he writes concerning his acquiring copies of certain Hebrew books.

> . . . there suddenly came a Hebrew carrying not a few volumes which he had received from the synagogue as if he intended to read them. "Here you have right now what you have been asking for," he said. And while I was hesitating and wondering what to do, he so frightened me by his haste that I laid everything else aside and flew to transcribing them.[41]

What were these books? They certainly were not books of the Hebrew Bible, for these he already had. They were most probably certain *midrashim*.[42]

We should not be misled and conclude that Jerome accepted all Jewish interpretations and traditions. To give one mild example of his rejection of Jewish interpretation we cite his *Commentary on Zechariah* 10:11-12.

> Just as these things have been handed down to us by the Hebrews, we have expressed them for the men of our own tongue, but as far as the reliability of these stories is concerned, we refer to those by whom they were spoken. For the rest, we who are enrolled under Christ's name, leave the letter that kills [i.e., the literal interpretation] and follow the spirit [i.e., the spiritual interpretation] that gives life.[43]

Some Jewish traditions he considers worthless and even scandalous. In his Letter 121.10 we find:

> I cannot recount how numerous are the traditions of the Pharisees, which they today call *deuterōseis* [literally, "repetitions"] nor how old-womanish are

---

[40] "Jerome," *Jewish Encyclopedia* 7, 117.
[41] *PL* 22:452.
[42] Cf. Krauss, "The Jews in the Works of the Church Fathers," 251.
[43] *PL* 25:1496 = *CCSL* 76A, 846, 11. 315-319.

their tales. For the size of this book would not permit it, and very many of them are so improper that I would be ashamed to tell them.[44]

At times we find Jerome's position regarding Jewish traditions quite inconsistent. For example, in his *Commentary on Titus*[45] he ridicules the Jews for discussing so minute a subject as King Solomon's age at the time of his marriage, and yet several years later, in his Letter 72, he devoted an entire letter to this matter. The same Jerome who described Jewish learning as "belching and nausea"[46] and Jewish Scriptural interpretation as "foolish tales, inept inventions and anile fables"[47] at times proudly proclaims his debt to Jewish interpretation even when he is in fact not citing it.[48]

Jerome's use of the Hebrew Scriptures in polemics against the Jews is quite understandable.[49] However, despite Jerome's great erudition and his openly acknowledged debt to his Hebrew teachers and rabbinic tradition, he occasionally falls prey to the caustic and vituperative anti-Jewish remarks that characterized his patristic predecessors Tertullian, Cyprian, Eusebius, Origen, and Ephraem Syrus as well as his particularly caustic contemporary, John Chrysostom. However, Jerome's statements "the Jew's mourning is the Christian's joy"[50] and "If it is expedient to hate any men and to loathe any race, I have a strange dislike for those of the circumcision"[51] are mild in comparison with others he made.[52]

---

[44] *PL* 22:1033.

[45] *PL* 26:631.

[46] Preface to the *Book on Hebrew Names, PL* 23:816.

[47] *PL* 25:356 and 1411. Indeed, as noted in Chapter 8, n. 4 it is remarkable that in Jerome's *Commentary on Daniel* we find only one, comparatively mild, criticism of Jewish interpretation.

[48] See G. Bardy, "Saint Jérôme et ses maîtres hébreux."

[49] See Chapter 3.

[50] Letter 60.6.

[51] Letter 84.3.

[52] On this point see David Wiesen, *St. Jerome as a Satirist,* 188-195. He cites examples of Jerome's harsher invectives against the Jews. Jews are lascivious (Letter 59.8); have foul and foolish customs like the observance of the Sabbath (Letter 121.10); produce sons and grandsons like little worms (*Commentary on Isaiah = PL* 24:479); are gluttonous (Ibid., *PL* 24:559), avaricious (Ibid., *PL* 24:49 and 52), and arrogant (*Commentary on Ezekiel, PL* 25:346). Their prayers resemble the grunting of pigs and the braying of asses (*Commentary on Amos = PL* 25:1054). Jerome, in summing up his bitter hostility, characterizes the Jews, together with heretics and pagans, as "the most foul dregs" (*spurcissimae faeces*) [*Commentary on Joel = PL* 25:956] and, in typical patristic fashion, says: "If they have suffered terrible oppression, they have deserved it" (*Commentary on Zechariah = PL* 25:1051). It should be kept in mind that Jerome did not direct his harsh invectives solely against the Jews. He was often vitriolic against anyone who opposed him, and made many unkind and unwarranted remarks towards Christians and non-Christians alike.

In the final analysis, the most important influence which the Jews had on Jerome was in impressing him with the authenticity of the Hebrew text of the Bible. In all of his writings we find one important recurring phrase describing the Hebrew text as the *veritas hebraica* or "Hebrew truth." Jerome's attitude towards the Hebrew text strongly influenced his revolutionary decision to base his Latin translation of the Old Testament (the Vulgate) on the Hebrew text and not on the Septuagint or *Vetus Latina*. His remarks in the *Preface to the Books of Samuel and Kings* (the famous "prologus galeatus") sum up his approach in preparing the Vulgate.

> If you are not happy [with the translation], you can call me a paraphraser; although I am not conscious at all of having changed anything from the Hebrew truth.[53]

His respect for the *veritas hebraica* also influenced his attitude toward the canon of the Old Testament: any book, or even part of a book, that was not included in Hebrew Scriptures should not be part of the Christian Bible as well.[54]

Jerome's Commentary on Daniel

Now that we have noted the relationship of Jerome's works in general to rabbinic tradition, we wish to point out the place that his *Commentary on Daniel* has among his exegetical works. During the last fifteen years of his life (406-420) Jerome's biblical works were of much greater length and more carefully written. It was at this time that he composed his *Opus Prophetale,* the masterful commentaries on the following: Daniel in 407, Isaiah in 408-410, Ezekiel in 410-415, and Jeremiah in 415-420.

Jerome's *Commentary on Daniel,* coming as it does near the end of his exegetical activity, shows the fruits of his many years of previous diligent study of the Bible. His new Latin text, which was later to become the Vulgate, had already been established.[55] In writing his *Commentary on Daniel* he could also draw upon traditions and interpretations gathered during a lifetime. It is not surprising, therefore, that in this work he cites sixteen Hebrew interpretations. These traditions make up the basis for the present work.

---

[53] *PL* 28 (ed. 1845): 557-8; (ed. 1889): 603.

[54] The attitude of Jerome toward the biblical text and canon will be analyzed in detail in Chapters 2 and 3.

[55] There is proof that Jerome had finished his Vulgate translation of Daniel well before he wrote his *Commentary on Daniel*. In the Preface to his *Commentary on Daniel* we find: "For this same reason, when I was translating Daniel many years ago. . . ." (*PL* 25:493 = *CCSL* 75A, 774, 1. 58ff.).

With the abundance of research available on all facets of Jerome's exegetical activities, it is indeed remarkable how little research has been devoted to his *Commentary on Daniel* in general and the Jewish traditions found therein, in particular. The only study that has been written on this commentary is a twenty-page article by J. Lataix. Concerning the Hebrew traditions, he merely cites them verbatim in two and one-half pages (275-277) offering little comment. Nor have any of the long list of scholars who during the past century have written on the relationship between rabbinic and patristic literature explored this scholar's gold mine. Siegfried made an inadequate attempt in his article in 1883, citing only five traditions and giving the barest of rabbinic parallels. Krauss in his article in *JQR*,[56] does cite the "eunuch tradition" mentioned in Jerome's *Commentary on Daniel* 1:3 and gives several sources in rabbinic and patristic literature, but admittedly, he only touched the surface since he was primarily interested in pointing this out as an *example* of a rabbinic tradition in the works of the Church Fathers. In the present work, we have developed this "eunuch tradition" into a lengthy chapter.[57] But most amazing of all, Louis Ginzberg, the most prolific writer in this field, did not cite any of the Hebrew traditions in Jerome's *Commentary on Daniel* in his *Kirchenvätern* series, and only one in his *Legends*.[58] When Ginzberg does discuss the "eunuch tradition" regarding Daniel and his three friends in patristic tradition[59] he cites Jerome's *Commentary on Isaiah* 39:7 (where indeed it is also found) rather than the most obvious place, his *Commentary on Daniel* 1:3. Montgomery points out the dependence of Jerome's *Commentary on Daniel* upon rabbinic tradition. "His commentary is intrinsically valuable for its constant dependence upon the tradition of the rabbis under whom he studied, and the work is a monument to the early stages of the Jewish exegesis, as appears from its frequent agreement with the Mediaeval representatives of the latter."[60] This is presumably in large part because Jerome, as well as the Jewish medieval commentaries, frequently relies on

---

[56] 5 (1893) 154-156.

[57] See Chapter 4.

[58] In the index to *The Legends of the Jews,* Boaz Cohen cites the following number of references made by Ginzberg to Jerome's works: 38 to his *Quaestiones in Genesim,* 24 to his *Commentary on Isaiah,* 4 to his *Commentary on Jeremiah,* 5 to his *Commentary on Ezekiel,* 29 to his *Commentary on the Minor Prophets,* 3 to his *Commentary on Ecclesiastes,* and 9 to his letters and other writings. The one time Ginzberg cites Jerome's *Commentary on Daniel* is on Dan 8:16 in vol. 5, 71, n. 13. (Ginzberg's text, by error, reads "Dan 8:*10*".) Boaz Cohen did not cite this reference in his index.

[59] *Legends* 6, 368, n. 88.

[60] James A. Montgomery, *Commentary on the Book of Daniel,* 107.

ancient rabbinic traditions.[61]

The Purpose, Methodology, Scope and Available Sources of Data for this Work

In approaching the task of tracing the Hebrew traditions of Jerome's *Commentary on Daniel* in rabbinic and patristic literature, we have taken note of the advice of our learned predecessors in this area of research, especially the words of Krauss in criticizing Rahmer's work:

> Rahmer does not compare other Church Fathers with Jerome; he even omits to place the parallel expressions side by side, nor does he seem to have any idea that several of these Agadas are already to be found in the so-called Hellenistic literature. The Jewish sources are also treated uncritically. The Jalkut and Midrash Rabba are not enough; the Babli, Jerushalmi, Sifre, Sifra, and Mechilta, finally the Targum, have also some connection with the subject.[62]

The purpose of this investigation is to evaluate Jerome as a biblical exegete: 1) To show his relationship to his *predecessors*—the Apocrypha and Pseudepigrapha, Hellenistic Jewish Literature, including Josephus, Pseudo-Philo's *Biblical Antiquities,*[63] the Rabbis, and earlier patristic commentators on Daniel (Philo, who usually must be carefully studied when analyzing Jewish traditions found in the Church Fathers, does not refer to the Book of Daniel). 2) To show his relationship to his *contemporaries*. 3) To show his influence on his *successors*.

As a result of this study we shall be in a position to point out how much Jerome relied on Jewish traditions quoted by previous Church Fathers, how much of Jewish tradition he knew directly and the extent of his own exegetical creativity in this area. One important aspect of this work will be to analyze the Jewish sources cited by Jerome and compare them with extant rabbinic literature, pointing out variations and revealing earlier and later versions of the same tradition, wherever possible. If Jerome cites a Jewish tradition which we cannot find in extant rabbinic literature we will be rewarded by recovering a "lost" tradition. Another by-product of this research will be to show the relationship of various patristic commentaries, one to the other, with regard to common and contrasting traditions and interpretations.

---

[61] The question of the extent to which medieval Jewish exegetes knew and used Jerome has not been investigated.

[62] "The Jews in the Works of the Church Fathers," 252-253.

[63] One passage, Pseudo-Philo 6.17, by implication compares Abraham in the furnace and Daniel in the furnace. Thus it is clear that the author was aware of the book of Daniel.

The following, in addition to Jerome (331-420), are the most important early Christian commentators on Daniel that were consulted (arranged chronologically):

1) Hippolytus (140-235) *On Daniel* (written *c.* 202), in Greek;
2) Origen (185-254), originally composed in Greek, extant only in fragments, mostly as quoted in Latin translation by Jerome;
3) Ephraem Syrus (308-373), in Syriac;
4) Aphraates (mid-fourth century), *Homilies,* in Syriac;
5) John Chrysostom (347-407), in Greek;
6) Theodoret (393-457), *Commentary on Daniel* in Greek;
7) Polychronius (first half of 5th century), fragments of *Commentary on Daniel,* in Greek.

The following are the most important Medieval Jewish commentators on Daniel that were consulted (arranged chronologically):

1) Jepheth ibn Ali (*c.* 1000), Karaite;
2) Rashi (1040-1105);
3) Pseudo-Saadia (12th century) printed in standard Rabbinic Bibles as "Saadia";[64]
4) Abraham ibn Ezra (1092-1167);
5) Rabbi Levi ben Gershon = Gersonides (1288-1344);
6) Isaac Abrabanel (1437-1508);
7) Joseph ibn Yaḥya (1494-1539).

Benno Fischer's *Daniel und Seine Drei Gefährten in Talmud und Midrasch* and Louis Ginzberg's *The Legends of the Jews* are helpful in providing a large number, though not an exhaustive listing, of rabbinic references to Daniel. There are, however, no similar works devoted to Daniel in patristic literature; lack of these makes research in this area more difficult. In his *Commentary on Daniel* Jerome cites Josephus many times, and whenever possible points out whether he is in agreement with the Hebrew tradition or not. Rappaport's work *Agada und Exegese bei Flavius Josephus* was not very helpful in tracing Josephus' relation to rabbinic tradition on Daniel since Rappaport investigates only nine traditions with regard to Daniel (pp. 66-68), and these but briefly. Further research in this direction has therefore been conducted by the present writer.

The critical edition of Jerome's *Commentary on Daniel,* volume 75A of *CCSL,* is the basic text for this work unless otherwise indicated. This supersedes the century-old text of Migne[65] which is not critical and contains numerous typographical errors.

[64] See S. Posnanski, *Hagoren* 2 (1900) 92-103.
[65] *PL* 225:401-584.

We have read Gleason L. Archer's translation of Jerome's *Commentary on Daniel,* but have, in most cases, adopted our own translations, differing from his in various degrees, so as not to necessitate citation of his work in each case. In certain cases, the Latin translations were checked for accuracy by Professor Louis H. Feldman of Yeshiva University.

All Jewish Scriptural passages quoted in this work are according to the Jewish Publication Society Translation (Philadelphia, 1917), unless a commentator has himself translated a passage in which case his translation is given.

CHAPTER 2

JEROME AND THE SEARCH FOR THE AUTHENTIC BIBLICAL TEXT
IN LIGHT OF ORIGEN'S SCHOLARSHIP

The two dominant themes which run through all of Jerome's exegetical activity are the search for the authentic text and the establishment of the canon. This is particularly true of the Jewish Scriptures. In order to appreciate his monumental work in these two areas and to understand fully his comments on the Jewish traditions in the *Commentary on Daniel* we must first thoroughly acquaint ourselves with the achievements of the man who most influenced his scholarly career, the Greek Father, Origen (*c.* 185-*c.* 254 C.E.). A study of Origen becomes even more important when we note that Jerome's comments on Susanna constitute a paraphrase of the tenth book of Origen's *Stromata*. Although almost ninety years elapsed from Origen's death until Jerome's birth, the profound effect of the former upon the latter is clear.[1]

The impetus behind Origen's and Jerome's search for the correct text and canon was the controversy between Christians and Jews which frequently was based on Scriptural texts and their interpretation.[2] The Alexandrian Septuagint (LXX) which, according to tradition, had originally been translated by Jews *c.* 270 B.C.E.[3] and was later accepted by Christianity in its infancy, became a source of contention in the second century C.E. Jews in Palestine began to doubt its accuracy[4] and claimed that it had become corrupt, while at the same time Christian writers cited it with increased authority and devotion. In the beginning of the third century, Origen began to concern himself with this problem. It must be stressed that throughout his life

---

[1] To the author's knowledge, hitherto no systematic comparison of Jerome's and Origen's attitudes toward the biblical text and canon has been presented.

[2] H. Swete, *Introduction to the OT,* 30, 462.

[3] According to tradition, the translation took place during the reign of Ptolemy II Philadelphus (285-246 B.C.E.). See E. J. Bickerman, "The Septuagint as a Translation." The first few pages of this article refer to the ancient data concerning this tradition. See also n. 5.

[4] Alfred Rahlfs, *Septuaginta* 1, xxiii-xxiv, gives three main reasons for this: 1) phrases cited by Christians in disputations which were quotations from the LXX but not found in or borne out by the Hebrew text; 2) the closing of the Jewish canon in Palestine towards the end of the first century C.E., excluding the "apocryphal" books found in the LXX and thus undermining the latter's authority; 3) the influence of Rabbi Akiba's school of Rabbinic interpretation at the beginning of the second century C.E. according to which every letter of the *Hebrew* text was important for hermeneutic conclusions. Cf. n. 5 for the conflicting rabbinic sources in Megillah and Soferim regarding the evaluation of the LXX.

Origen, as did the Church itself, accepted the ultimate authenticity as well as the divine inspiration[5] of the LXX.

[5]   In order to appreciate the patristic attitude toward the LXX, we must be aware of the elements of the legend concerning its genesis and its chief embellishments. The basic textual source is the *Letter of Aristeas* which Hadas dates *c.* 130 B.C.E. (*Aristeas to Philocrates,* 54). The request for the translation was made by King Ptolemy, who is never directly referred to as Philadelphus in the *Letter,* but who has been thus indirectly identified by most subsequent writers (cf. Hadas, 112, n. 35). Ptolemy requested the High Priest Eliezer to send him seventy-two competent translators (*Letter,* 39) to translate the Hebrew Pentateuch. They began their work ". . . making all details harmonize by mutual comparisons. The appropriate result of the harmonization was reduced to writing under the direction of Demetrius." (*Letter,* 302; Hadas, 219). The Greek term for "harmonize" is *antiballein* which is a technical term for the collation of manuscripts. This technique was used by Alexandrian scholars to arrive at the text of Homer (see below). The author of the *Letter of Aristeas* seems to be pointing out this analogy regarding the production of the texts of the LXX and Homer. Thus it is clear here that the translation was not divinely inspired, but the result of careful scholarly teamwork. Philo's account of the origin of the Septuagint in *De Vita Mosis* 2.25-44 introduces the important element of divine inspiration. ". . . they [the secluded translators] became as it were possessed, and under inspiration, wrote, not each scribe something different, but the same, word for word, as though dictated to each by an invisible prompter" (Philo, *De Vita Mosis* 2.37 [tr. F. H. Colson; *LCL,* Cambridge: Harvard University Press, 1935] 467). It is important to refer to the Greek original for two important terms: *enthousiōntes* = "having God within them, possessed," and *proephēteuon* = "prophesied, under inspiration."
   The above citation from Philo could very well have been the source for Origen's opinion of the divine inspiration of the additions and discrepancies in the LXX text, when compared with the Hebrew text. Philo's account identifies Ptolemy as Philadelphus, does not mention Aristeas by name, does not specify the number of translators, and presents certain differences. This leads Hadas (pp. 22, 26, n. 33) to conclude that although Philo probably read Aristeas' account, he may well have used an independent tradition as well. Josephus in *Antiquities,* 12.12-118, gives a close paraphrase of a large part of the *Letter of Aristeas.* On Josephus' use of *Aristeas* see André Pelletier, *Flavius Josèphe adaptateur de la lettre d'Aristée.* He also identifies Ptolemy as Philadelphus (*Antiquities* 12.11). Interestingly, he not only avoids the issue of divine inspiration, but also does not even mention the comparison of translations at the end of the day, and says: "Thereupon they set to work as ambitiously and painstakingly as possible to make the translation accurate. . . ." (*Antiquities* 12.104, in Josephus, *Jewish Antiquities* XII-XIV [tr. Ralph Marcus; *LCL,* 1943] 51-53). With regard to the number of translators, *Antiquities* 12.39, 49 and 56 mention 72 (six from each tribe); 12.57 however, mentions "Seventy Elders."
   Rabbinic tradition regarding this legend goes back to tannaitic times wherein we find a new embellishment: the translators worked in isolated cells. "It happened that King Ptolemy assembled seventy-two elders and placed them in seventy-two cells. . . . God put counsel into the heart of every one of them, that they were all of one mind, and they wrote out for him . . . ." [Baraitha in Megillah 9a. Cf. parallels in Massekhet Soferim 1:8, Mekilta Exodus 12:40, Midrash Rabba Exodus 5.5, Tanḥuma Exodus 22]. Some rabbinic sources give the number of translators as seventy, others give seventy-two. In Massekhet Soferim 1:7, we find the important variant that *five* translators worked for Ptolemy. The source for Soferim 1:7 seems to be Aboth de Rabbi Nathan ch. 37, second version (ed. S. Schechter; New York: P. Feldheim, 1945) 94. Schechter's n. 1 *a.l.* cites a variant referring to *ten* translators. The

This can be clearly seen in an interesting comment in his *Commentary on the Song of Songs*. In Book 1.3 Origen cites Song of Songs 1:2b as follows: "For thy breasts are better than wine," and then proceeds to give an involved allegorical interpretation of this verse. After citing the next verse

---

tradition of *five* translators probably assumes one for each book of the Pentateuch. It is interesting to note the diametrically opposing views concerning the LXX in Megillah 9b (the Bible itself authorized the Greek translation as seen in Gen 9:27 "God enlarge Japheth and he shall dwell in the tents of Shem" since Javan [Greece] is a son of Japheth [Gen 10:2]) and Sopherim 1:7 (the day the Septuagint was translated was as calamitous to Israel as the one on which the Golden Calf was made). Cf. Hadas, *Letter,* 81, n. 110, inserted by S. Zeitlin.

The elements of insulation of the translators and divine inspiration of the translation were the basis for further embellishments on the part of patristic writers. The earliest reference is made by Justin Martyr (died *c.* 165), in his *Apology* 1.31 and *Dialogue with Trypho* 68, 71. He refers to Ptolemy with no surname, avoids implication of divine inspiration, but introduces other embellishments. The most significant departure is reference to the books of *prophecies* as the texts translated. Until now all sources referred to the Pentateuch alone. The legend has spread to include the entire Bible and it remained so until Jerome intervened. Bickerman, "The Septuagint as a Translation," p. 5, notes the reason for the expansion of the LXX to include the entire Bible. "But for the Christians, the prophets and hagiographa were much more important than the Law, obsolete under the new dispensation." Next we have the account of Pseudo-Justin (second and third century, C.E.) in *Exhortation to the Greeks,* 13. After mentioning that the seventy translators were each put in separate cells, "Ptolemy charged the attendant ministers . . . to keep them from communicating with each other, in order that their agreement might afford further proof of the accuracy of the translation. When he found that the seventy men . . . had employed the very same phraseology . . . he held the books to be divine. . . ."(*The Letter of Aristeas* [tr. H. St. J. Thackeray; London: SPCK, 1917] 102-103). Pseudo-Justin then refers to Philo and Josephus as authorities who have written about this episode. Pseudo-Justin is the first patristic writer to mention the isolated cells. Philo's account indeed stresses the seclusion of the translators. The embellished legend continued with Irenaeus (died *c.* 202) in his *Against Heresies* 3.212. He identifies the Ptolemy as son of Lagus (Philadelphus' father and predecessor) and describes the isolation of the translators as well as the inspiration of the translation. "God was indeed glorified, and the Scriptures were acknowledged as truly divine. For all of them read out of the common translation [which they had prepared] in the very same words and the very same names, from beginning to end, so that even the Gentiles present perceived that the Scriptures had been interpreted by the inspiration of God" (*The Writings of Irenaeus* I [tr. A. Roberts and W. H. Rambaut, *Ante-Nicene Christian Library* 5; Edinburgh: Clark and Co., 1868] 353). Clement of Alexandria (died before 215) in his *Stromateis* 1.149 gives an account similar to that of Irenaeus, although he is unsure if it was Ptolemy son of Lagus or Ptolemy Philadelphus. " . . . and all the translations being compared together, they agreed both in meaning and in expression. For it was the counsel of God carried for the benefit of Grecian ears. It was not alien to the inspiration of God, who gave the prophecy, also to produce the translation" (*The Writings of Clement of Alexandria* [tr. W. Wilson, *Ante-Nicene Christian Library* 4] 448). Tertullian (born *c.* 160) interestingly does not include the miraculous or divine embellishments (*Apology,* 18) and he is the first writer since Josephus to specifically mention "Aristaeus." This brings us to Origen whose statements concerning the LXX can now be appreciated in their patristic milieu.

(Song of Songs 1:3a) and commenting upon it, Origen, as an afterthought, returns to 1:2b and makes the following comment:

> We must not, however, overlook the fact that in certain versions we find written "for thy sayings are better than wine," where we read "for thy breasts[6] are better than wine." But although it may seem that this gives a plainer meaning in regard to the things about which we have discoursed in the spiritual interpretation, we ourselves keep to what the Seventy interpreters wrote in every case. For we are certain that the Holy Spirit willed that the figures of the mysteries should be roofed over in the Divine Scriptures,[7] and should not be displayed publicly and in the open air.[8]

Another example of Origen's attitude toward the LXX is found in his famous letter to Julius Africanus (*c.* 240), which fortunately has been preserved in the original, and to which we shall refer many times. After pointing out that he is well aware of the many discrepancies between the LXX and the Hebrew text, he emphatically states that this Greek version has the sanction of the Church and to reject it would be tantamount to conceding to the Jews.

> And, indeed, when we notice such things [the many discrepancies between the Septuagint and the Hebrew text], we are forthwith to reject the copies in use in our Churches, and enjoin the brotherhood to put away the sacred books current among them, and to flatter the Jews, and persuade them to give us copies which shall be pure and free from forgery! . . . In all these cases

---

[6] The Hebrew Masoretic text has: "for thy love (דֹּדֶיךָ) is better than wine" (Song of Songs 1:2b). Obviously the Septuagint reading "breasts," which Origen cites, is based on an alternate Hebrew reading דַּדַּיִךְ. This word literally means nipple and it is found in the Hebrew Bible three times in Ezekiel 23 and once in Proverbs 5:19. This alternate Hebrew reading was well known to the Rabbis, cf. Mishna Avoda Zora 2, 5, Tosefta Para, 10 and S. Lieberman, *Tosefeth Rishonim,* 3 (Kelim-Niddah), (Jerusalem, 1939) 248-249. See also Reuven Kimelman, *Rabbi Yochanan of Tiberias* (unpublished doctoral dissertation, Yale University 1977), the chapter "Origen and Rabbi Yohanan on Canticles."

[7] There is a striking parallel to this comment in Jerome's *Preface to Isaiah:* "And so I surmise that the Seventy Interpreters were in their day unwilling to disclose the mysteries of their faith clearly to the gentiles, lest they should 'give what is holy to the dogs and pearls to the swine' — for when you read the edition [i.e., Jerome's new translation of Isaiah] you will see that they hid these mysteries." We also find a similar remark in Jerome's preface to his *Hebraicae Quaestiones in Genesim:* "The fact is that they [the seventy interpreters], since their work was undertaken for King Ptolemy of Alexandria, did not choose to bring to light all the mysteries which the sacred writings contain. . . ."

[8] R. P. Lawson, *Origen:* The Song of Songs, Commentary and Homilies (*Ancient Christian Writers* 26; London: The Newman Press, 1957) 74.

consider whether it would not be well to remember the words "Thou shalt not remove the eternal boundaries[9] which thy fathers have set" (Pr 22:28).[10]

Indeed, some of the *additions* and *discrepancies* which Origen found in the current LXX when he compared it with the Hebrew text were regarded by him as divinely inspired![11] For example, in his *Homily on Leviticus* 12.5, he states that the Jews say that their text lacks the phrase "of his own people" in Lev 21:14.[12] Origen claims that it is by divine providence that the Hebrew text omits this while the LXX has it, since the Jews rejected Christ by their own disobedience. But only *some* of the additions and discrepancies in the LXX were divinely inspired according to Origen. Others were corruptions. Indeed, sometimes Origen finds it difficult to determine whether a phrase is a "divine device" or a scribal error.[13] More often than not in these cases, he solves the problem in typical Origenist fashion: he expounds both alternatives.

Thus, unlike Jerome, Origen did not attempt a new translation of the OT since he accepted the divine inspiration of the LXX. However, early in life, he did recognize the need to study the Hebrew Bible in the original,[14] an

---

[9]   Although Jerome does not quote this verse, his remarks in his preface to the translations of Proverbs, Ecclesiastes and Song of Songs carry the same intent as Origen's words: "For it is not our aim in producing a new edition to destroy the old." Both Origen and Jerome follow in the spirit of the rabbinic interpretation of Pr 22:28, cf. Midrash Mishle (ed. Buber) 93 and Sifre Deuteronomy 188 (ed. Finkelstein) 227 and variants.

[10]   "Letter from Origen to Africanus" 4-5 (tr. Frederick Crombie, in *The Ante-Nicene Fathers* 4, 387) = *PG* 11:57-60.

[11]   A parallel to Origen's views on this matter is found in Jerome's early work, *Preface to Chronicles* where he characterized the additions made by the seventy translators "either for the sake of ornament or on the authority of the Holy Spirit."

[12]   Origen most probably refers to the Masoretic text of Lev 21:13 which lacks the phrase "of his own people" that appears in the LXX.

[13]   For example, in *Commentary on Psalms* 2:12 (*PG* 12:1116) the word "right" in the phrase "lest you perish from the right way" appears in the LXX version of Ps 2:12. The Hebrew text does not have it. Unsure which is correct, Origen expounds both alternatives. This example, as well as the previous one, along with others are found in R. P. C. Hanson's *Allegory and Event*, 164.

[14]   Hanson in *Allegory and Event* 167-172, summarizes scholarly opinion on the extent of Origen's knowledge of Hebrew. "He certainly knew *some* Hebrew; he could not have compiled the Hexapla unless he had at least a working knowledge of the language . . ." [p. 167]. ". . . Origen certainly knew considerably more than merely the letters of the Hebrew alphabet, and could venture occasionally to expound the Hebrew text, even though he often made mistakes in doing so. He does not in fact pretend to know much Hebrew; he is modest about his knowledge and more often than not will refer the reader to the experts in Hebrew" [p. 171]. In addition to the references cited by Hanson concerning Origen's knowledge of Hebrew, see also C. J. Elliot, "Hebrew Learning Among The Fathers," 855-860. This article, however, is over harsh in evaluating Origen's knowledge of Hebrew. See also R. P. C. Hanson, "In-

undertaking which both Eusebius[15] and Jerome[16] imply was almost unknown at that time among Christian scholars of non-Jewish origin. This led him to realize that the current LXX text had undergone change.[17] He wished to point out its additions and deletions, and this led him to his *magnum opus,* the *Hexapla* or six-fold Bible.[18] He arranged in six parallel columns the following texts of the OT: 1) the Hebrew, in Hebrew letters; 2) the Greek transliteration of the Hebrew text, in order to fix the pronunciation; 3) the Greek translation of Aquila, a Jewish proselyte who wrote *c.* 130 C.E.; 4) the Greek translation of Symmachus, who wrote at the end of the second century; 5) the Greek translation known as the Septuagint; 6) the Greek translation of Theodotion, a proselyte or possibly a Jew by birth, who lived at the end of the second century.[19] Origen would thus be able to

---

terpretations of Hebrew Names in Origen," *VC* 10 (1956) 103-123, and P. E. Kahle, *The Cairo Geniza* (New York, 1959) 240-241. With reference to the rabbinic influence on Origen's exegesis, see Y. Baer, "Israel, the Christian Church, and the Roman Empire from the Time of Septimus Severus to the Edict of Toleration of 313" in *Scripta Hierosolymitana* 7 (Jerusalem, 1961) 79-149; E. E. Urbach, "The Homiletical Interpretations of the Sages and the Expositions of Origen on Canticles, and the Jewish-Christian Disputation" in *Scripta Hierosolymitana* 22 (Jerusalem, 1971) 247-275; and R. Kimelman, *Rabbi Yochanan of Tiberias,* in the chapter "Origen and Rabbi Yochanan on Canticles."

[15] *Historia Ecclesiastica* 6, 16.

[16] *De Vir. Illustr.* 54.

[17] In modern terminology we would say that the text had become *corrupt* through these changes and that he worked to restore it to its *authentic original state.* But taking into consideration Origen's conservative attitude toward the traditional LXX during his entire life, the above statement might be misleading. Indeed, as we have just pointed out, some of these additions and discrepancies in comparison with the Hebrew text were regarded by Origen as divinely inspired. Therefore, not all were "corruptions."

[18] According to R. P. C. Hanson, *Origen's Doctrine of Tradition* 15, n. 3 and p. 26, Origen began work on his Hexapla before 212 and finished it by 243, thus working on it for more than 30 years.

[19] It is important to note the general characteristics of each of the three Greek versions of the OT in addition to the LXX. (Cf. Alfred Rahlfs, ed., *Septuaginta* 1, xxiv-xxvii; and Swete, *Introduction,* 31-53; and P. Skehan *et al.,* "Texts and Versions," *JBC* 2, 571-2. The first version, that of Aquila, was based on the "proto-Theodotionic" recension (see below), directed against the Christian interpretations in the LXX; it was extremely literal and was influenced by the Palestinian rabbis. (Cf. A. E. Silverstone, *Aquila and Onkelos* [Manchester, 1931], especially the sources for the life of Aquila and his system of exegesis, pp. 161-163.) The second, Theodotion's, was basically a free revision of the LXX primarily according to the standard Hebrew text. It was superior to Aquila's in style and it did not depart from the LXX as much as the latter. It was this version that Origen most often used to supply *lacunae* in the LXX which were present in the Hebrew text. This version was more highly valued by the Christians than the other two. In fact, the Theodotion version of Daniel displaced the LXX version in the Church even before Origen's time. See p. 31, n. 61. The latest scholarly opinion in light of D. Barthélemy, *Les devanciers d'Aquila* (*VTSup* 10; Leiden, 1963) is that Theodotion actually wrote very little of the version which bears his name. Most of it was

restore to the Church the original Greek version of the OT without displacing entirely the time-honored Alexandrian version of the LXX. The textual criterion was basically the Hebrew text; all critical work was done in the fifth column, the LXX text. Differences of order in various verses and sections were easily changed by generally transposing the Greek order to fit the Hebrew. Corruptions in words, especially proper nouns, were easy to correct. The main problem was the additions and omissions in the LXX text. Origen did not wish to tamper with this text to such an extent as to remove the former; nor did he wish to add the latter indiscriminately. He therefore resorted to a system of two basic critical signs which had been used by earlier Greek scholars, first employed in critical editions of Homer in the third century B.C.E. The obelus (÷) was placed in the LXX text before words or lines which were lacking in the Hebrew; the asterisk (∗) called attention to words or lines lacking in the LXX, but present in the Hebrew.[20] Origen usually supplied these *lacunae* from one of the other versions, most often Theodotion's. To close the word or passage begun by an obelus or asterisk Origen marked a metobelus (✓). In Origen's own words:

> When I found a passage that was not in the Hebrew, I marked it with an obelus, as I did not dare to omit it altogether. In other cases, I added an asterisk to show that the passage was not in the Septuagint but had been added from the other Greek versions that were consonant with the Hebrew. He who wishes may pass over these words. If such a method offends you,[21] you may accept or reject it as you think fit.[22]

Origen is ever wary of displacing the old with the new by removing ancient landmarks.

------

composed earlier in the first century C.E., and is now referred to as the "proto-Theodotion recension." Cf. P. Skehan *et al.,* "Texts and Versions," *JBC* 2, 570-2. The third translator, Symmachus, seems to have worked with "proto-Theodotion," as well as with the LXX and the Hebrew text. He seems mostly to follow the Hebrew text and was not as literal as Aquila, but much more concerned with a polished Greek style. On the relationship between Symmachus and Rabbi Meir, and his possible identification with Sumchos, pupil of Rabbi Meir, cf. D. Barthélemy, "Qui est Symmaque," *CBQ* 36 (1974) 451-465.

[20] Jerome also used these critical signs when he revised the *Vetus Latina* version of Psalms.

[21] Jerome was similarly concerned lest he shock his readers. In his *Commentary on Ecclesiastes,* the first original Latin commentary to make use of the Hebrew text, he attempts to soften the effect of his departure from the LXX text by referring to the other Greek versions as well as to the Hebrew original: "I have occasionally referred also to the versions of Aquila, Symmachus and Theodotion so as not to discourage the reader's interest by too many novelties. . . ."

[22] *Commentary on Matthew* 15, 14 (*PG* 13:1294). Compare this with Origen's *Letter to Africanus* 4, where the obelus and asterisk method is mentioned again. Eusebius, *Historia Ecclesiastica* 6, 16, also mentions it.

Having established a critical text of the LXX, Origen now provided a more reliable basis for Christian polemics with the Jews.

> . . . I paid particular attention to the interpretation of the Seventy, lest I might be found to debase something for the Churches which are under heaven, and give occasions to those who seek such a starting point for gratifying their desire to slander the common brethren. . . . And I make it my endeavor not to be ignorant of their readings, lest in my conversations with the Jews I should quote to them what is not found in their copies, and that I may make use of what is found among them, even though it should not be in our books. For if we are so prepared for them in our investigations, they will not, as is their manner, scornfully laugh at Gentile believers for their ignorance of the true reading[23] as they have them.[24]

One instance of this is found in Origen's work *On Prayer* 14 where he gives examples from Scripture for the term "prayer." He quotes first a verse from the Prayer of the Three Children found only in the LXX and Theodotion (Dan 3:25). Then Origen cites Tob 3:1,2 and immediately afterward states

> But since "they of the circumcision" [i.e., the Jews] have obelized[25] the passage in Daniel, as not found in the Hebrew, and since they reject the book of Tobit as uncanonical, I will quote from the First Book of Kingdoms [i.e., 1 Samuel] the passage about Hannah. . . .[26]

But Origen's new text was more than a polemic device. He made use of it in his massive exegetical works even when he was not directly addressing himself to Jews.[27] He is considered the first Christian scientific exegete.[28]

---

[23] Jerome gives a similar statement in his preface to the translation of Isaiah: ". . . I have sweated over the learning of a foreign tongue [i.e., Hebrew] to this end, that the Jews may no longer mock our churches for the falsity of our Scriptures."

[24] Origen's *Letter to Africanus* 5 (*PG* 11:60-61).

[25] This of course refers to Origen's use of the obelus in the LXX column of the *Hexapla* to note portions which were lacking in the Hebrew text. Origen here used the expression "to obelize" in the metaphorical sense, meaning "to reject as spurious."

[26] Translation taken from *The Library of Christian Classics 2: Alexandrian Christianity,* translated and annotated by John E. L. Oulton and Henry Chadwick (London: SCM Press, 1954) 267-268 (*PG* 11:461).

[27] Ample evidence of this fact is given both by F. Field, *Origenis Hexaplorum quae Supersunt: Prolegomena* 1 (Oxford: Clarendon Press, 1925) liv and lxi, and R. P. C. Hanson, *Allegory and Event,* 165-166.

[28] R. P. C. Hanson in *Allegory and Event,* 360 clearly points this out. "In this sense we may say that Christian biblical exegesis begins with Origen; he is the first professional, because though Hippolytus had written works which we might call commentaries and Melito (and no doubt many others) had written homilies on Scripture, and Clement of Alexandria had in his rambling way dealt with individual passages, none of these efforts could be called methodical or profound. In contrast to these, Origen brought the whole weight of contemporary scholar-

He wrote in various literary forms: the *scholia* are brief explanations of difficult passages; the homilies are sermons on select chapters or passages of the Bible, for popular edification; the commentaries are the basis of his scientific exegesis.

Daniélou clearly points out the dual loyalties which Origen held toward the authority of Church Tradition on one hand and the pursuit of textual criticism on the other.

> Origen's attitude is quite clear: he recognizes a twofold authority, the authority of Scripture and the authority of Tradition.[29]

According to Hanson's view, Origen did not regard the tradition of the Church or "rule of faith" fixed and infallible in all cases, and was willing at times to uphold his own independent opinion.[30] But, as will soon be shown, in most cases tradition predominated.

Dual loyalties forced Origen into most difficult positions, especially when he tried to maintain both views. For example, Daniélou[31] points out that in his *Homilies on Jeremiah,* which we have in the original Greek, Origen brings two readings for Jer 15:10. The first is the more common reading; the second, the more accurate since it is closer to the Hebrew.[32] Despite the fact that he realizes a scribal error in the more popular LXX text, he writes:

> We must therefore explain that which is in use [but textually incorrect] and is read in the Church, but that does not mean that one found in the Hebrew manuscripts should be passed over untouched.[33]

He then proceeds to give the exegesis of both readings!

---

ship — linguistic, critical, and philosophical — to bear upon the task of making the biblical commentary a permanent literary form for Christian writers, and he succeeded brilliantly. In fact all writers of commentaries today owe a debt to Origen as in this sense the great Founding Father of their activity." Here again it becomes evident that no study of Jerome as a biblical exegete can begin without a thorough understanding of Origen's contributions.

[29] Jean Daniélou, *Origen,* 136.

[30] In *Allegory and event,* 373, he puts it as follows: "It seems to me, therefore, both accurate and honest to conclude that the chief restraining influence upon Origen's interpretation of Scripture was the Church's rule of faith. He did not, it should be added, regard this rule as infallible. On the contrary, he was ready to encourage his pupils to ignore it in certain cases." Hanson defines the 'rule of faith' as "the version of Christianity which was preached, lived, and witnessed to by the church of his [Origen's] day, so far as he knew it" [p. 373]. Hanson warns us, however, that "it is exceedingly difficult to determine at any moment in church history what the 'tradition of the church' is" [p. 372]. Compare also Hanson, *Origen's Doctrine of Tradition,* p. 111.

[31] *Origen,* 136.

[32] Origen's exact words are: "but in the most accurate ones [readings], those closest to the Hebrew. . . ."

[33] *Homilies on Jeremiah* 14.3 (*PG* 13:405).

But, alas, we must admit that although Origen spent over thirty years in correcting the LXX text in the *Hexapla* on the basis of the Hebrew original, the majority[34] of the scriptural references in all of his other works[35] are to the unedited LXX text.[36] In most of these cases no mention is even made of the conflicting Hebrew text. One striking example is found in his *De Principiis* 1, 5.2 (written between 225 and 230, while he was working on the *Hexapla*), in Homily 8, 2 on Ex 20:3-6 (composed between 246 and 254, well after the *Hexapla* was completed), and in *Contra Celsum* 4, 8 and 5, 29 (composed *c.* 246). In all these places he cites Dt 32:8 as "according to the number of angels of God" which is the LXX reading, while the Hebrew text has "according to the number of the children of Israel."[37] Despite a lifetime

---

[34] Hanson in *Allegory and Event,* 162, uses the term "vast majority." Perhaps, however, we should be more conservative in our estimation, keeping in mind two points: 1) Most of Origen's extant work is preserved not in the original Greek, but in Latin translations, chiefly done by Rufinus and Jerome. Both of them, as Hanson himself points out (*Origen's Doctrine of Tradition,* 40) took liberties in their translation, and Rufinus especially "allowed himself peculiar license in translating" (*Allegory and Event,* 163). We thus cannot be sure when Rufinus might have substituted the more traditional LXX version of a text for Origen's edited one. Admittedly, in the case of Jerome, this would be far less likely. 2) We have today, including Latin translations, only a mere fraction of Origen's total literary output. According to Jerome (*Adv. Ruf.* 2, 22) his treatises numbered two thousand; according to Epiphanius [*Haer.* 64, 63] they totalled six thousand. Jerome in his Letter 33 gives the titles of eight hundred! Out of 291 commentaries which Origen is known to have written, 275 have been lost in Greek and very few are extant in Latin translation. Thus, any generalizations which we make about Origen's works must be viewed in light of the above points.

[35] Even in the *Hexapla* itself Origen conservatively clings to the traditional LXX text refusing to edit with an obelus *all* additional words not found in the Hebrew text. See F. Field *Origenis Hexaplorum quae Supersunt: Prolegomena,* lxi-lxii, and Hanson, *Allegory and Event,* 163. The latter brings the following interesting comment which Origen makes in the Hexapla to a sentence found in the LXX version at the end of Job but lacking in the Hebrew: "We accept these words also, even if they are not entirely in continuity with what precedes, yet (we accept them) on the grounds that one of the holy men attached them to the book: yes, in spite of this we accept it all, since we have received the book in this form from the Fathers." In this case Tradition clearly supersedes Scripture.

[36] Hanson makes this point quite clear in *Allegory and Event,* 162. "He follows his tradition faithfully, even in its mistakes. In his *Commentary on Hosea* [which was written between 246-249, at least three years after the *Hexapla* had been completed] he said that it is wrong to try to emend the text of the LXX even when the literal meaning seems to make nonsense. . . . On several occasions he treats a word in the LXX text as if it were in fact the original word written by the author of the book concerned. . . . And he regards the headings to the Psalms in the LXX version, some of which seem to bear little reference to the Hebrew original, as inspired." See also pp. 163-164 of Hanson's work. Several other examples of this are given in "Hebrew Learning among the Fathers" in *A Dictionary of Christian Biography,* Smith and Wace, 857-858.

[37] It is interesting to note that Justin Martyr, who died (*c.* 165) twenty-one years before Origen was born, and who certainly did not approach Origen in Biblical scholarship, notes the

devoted to textual criticism, in the final analysis Origen remained loyal to Church Tradition.

We are now prepared to evaluate the work of Jerome in establishing the authentic biblical text and canon. Our point of departure is the following: Jerome stood on the shoulders of the giant Origen, taking full advantage of the achievements of the latter in the above two areas, thereby gaining perspective for his own work. He was faced with the similar problem of dual loyalties, and in many respects, his solution of this problem parallels, and then supersedes, the solution of Origen.

As with Origen, the impetus for Jerome's work in both text and canon resulted from his attitude toward the LXX and its relationship to the Hebrew text. Jerome inherited much the same patristic attitude concerning the authenticity and divine inspiration of the LXX as did Origen.[38] In Jerome's case however, we can clearly chart the metamorphosis of his views concerning the LXX which led to quite radical conclusions especially with respect to the canon, some of which were never accepted by the Roman Catholic Church.

Jerome's first major work as translator and editor involved the *Chronicle* of Eusebius of Caesarea (d.*c.* 340), known as the "father of church history." While in Constantinople, *c.* 378, Jerome translated this work from Greek into Latin, making numerous insertions and adding a lengthy

---

difference between the Masoretic text and the LXX on this same verse in his *Dialogue with Trypho* 131.

[38] See n. 5 above. In order to bring this account up to date until Jerome's time we should note that Cyril of Jerusalem in his *Catechetical Lectures* 4, 33-5 (*PG* 33:493-500) once again refers to the inspiration of the LXX and the miracle of the identity of the seventy translations. He extends the embellishment recorded by Justin Martyr and states that the translation was made of the twenty-two books of the Hebrew canon, which according to Cyril constituted the Christian canon as well. (Note that the otherwise careful account of the LXX legend in patristic sources compiled by Moses Hadas in *Aristeas to Philocrates,* 73-80, lacks the above citation to Cyril's work.)

Next we have the highly fanciful and embellished tale of the LXX written by an older contemporary of Jerome in the Eastern Church, Epiphanius (*c.* 315-403). In his *Weights and Measures* 3-11 (composed in 392) he describes how the seventy-two translators were locked in thirty-six cells and each pair given all the canonical and apocryphal books to translate so that each book was translated thirty-six times. "When the work was completed, the king took his seat on a lofty throne, and thirty-six readers sat at his feet having the thirty-six reproductions of each book while one held a copy of the Hebrew volume. Then one reader recited and the rest dilligently attended; and there was found no discrepancy. . . . where they added a word they all added it in common, and where they omitted, the omission was made by all alike" (Hadas, *Aristeas to Philocrates,* 77). For a discussion of Epiphanius' account see Sidney Jellicoe, *The Septuagint and Modern Study,* 45. This work brings up to date, on many points, the standard work, which is Swete's *Introduction.*

supplement. In his preface Jerome makes one of his earliest references to the LXX and the three other Greek versions.

> . . . the content even of the divine volumes testifies to the difficulty of the matter [its translation], which produced by the Septuagint translators does not keep the same flavor [as the Hebrew] in the Greek tongue. Aquila, Symmachus and Theodotion, having been spurred on for this reason, produced in the same work almost a different work; while one was striving to express a literal translation, another to follow rather the sense, and the third differing not much from the ancients [Septuagint]. . . . hence it gets to the point that the sacred literature seems to be less elegant and sonorous because learned men, unaware that they [the Scriptures] have been translated from the Hebrew, look at the surface and not at the marrow, so that they shudder more at the sordid cloak of oratory [in their translations] rather than to discover the beautiful core of the matter.[39]

The first stage of Jerome's Scriptural translations was carried out during his stay in Rome, 382-385 C.E. Pope Damasus asked him to *revise* (not re-translate) the Latin NT by comparison with the best available Greek manuscripts, and to revise the Old Latin Psalter by comparison with the LXX. The current Latin Bible texts, the *Vetus Latina,* had been made by unknown authors from the Greek of the LXX in the second century C.E.,[40] and were obviously corrupt. In his *Preface to the Four Gospels,* his first important biblical work (384) he again refers to the LXX and the three other Greek versions.

> I am not discussing the Old Testament, which was turned into Greek by the seventy elders, and has reached us by a descent of three steps.[41] I do not ask what Aquila and Symmachus think, or why Theodotion takes a middle course between the ancients and moderns. Let that be the true translation which had apostolic approval.[42]

We will soon point out that "apostolic approval" played an important role in Jerome's replacing the LXX with the Hebrew text. His first revision of

---

[39] R. Helm, ed. *Eusebius Werke: Die Chronik des Hieronymus, Griechischen Christliche Schriftsteller,* 47 (Berlin, 1956) 2. See n. 19 above for the general characteristics of the Greek versions of Aquila, Symmachus and Theodotion.

[40] W. Schwarz, *Principles and Problems of Biblical Translation,* 26.

[41] From the original Hebrew, translated into Greek (LXX) and then into Latin (*Vetus Latina*). It is thus clear that the *Vetus Latina* was not at all based on the Hebrew text. W. Schwarz, p. 28, correctly stresses that at this stage of his career, Jerome was not as yet aware of the *extensive* differences between the Hebrew Scriptures and the LXX.

[42] *PL* 29:527.

the Old Latin Psalter at this time did not take Origen's *Hexapla* into consideration.[43]

The second stage of Jerome's Scriptural work took place immediately after his settlement in Bethlehem (386). In this period he undertook a revision of the *Vetus Latina* of the OT according to the LXX text of Origen's *Hexapla* which he had consulted at Caesarea. Since the *Vetus Latina* had not been based on Origen's text, he felt he could improve on it.[44] He used the same basic technique as did Origen. In his *Preface to Psalms* he states:

> Let everyone observe for himself where there is placed either a horizontal line or radiating marks, that is, either obeli or asterisks. And wherever he sees a little twig [i.e. an obelus] preceding, he is to understand that from this mark up to the two stops [:] which I have introduced, the Septuagint translation contains superfluous matter. But where he sees the likeness of a star [i.e., an asterisk], he should know that something has been added from the Hebrew books, which also goes as far as the two stops.[45]

In his *Preface to Chronicles* written in the same period (*c.* 389), he still maintains the authenticity and divine inspiration of the LXX, attributing readings in the LXX and *Vetus Latina* which differed from the Hebrew text to the errors of copyists.

> In the Greek and Latin manuscripts, this book of names is so corrupt that one would think that it was compiled less of Hebrew than of barbarian and Samaritan names. This, however, is not to be ascribed to the Seventy Translators, who, filled with the Holy Spirit, transcribed the true text, but to the fault of the copyists.[46]

Jerome then describes the function of the obelus as introducing what the seventy translators have added to the Hebrew text "either for the sake of ornament or on the authority of the Holy Spirit."[47]

---

[43] Jellicoe, *Septuagint,* 252, points out that this "Roman Psalter" was "carried out in only a cursory manner, a number of serious discrepancies between the Old Latin and the Septuagint being left untouched." In 387 Jerome made a further revision of Psalms which was accepted in Gaul and is known as the "Gallican Psalter."

[44] Unfortunately most of this work of Jerome was stolen (Epistle 134.2); only Job and Psalms remain in full.

[45] *PL* 29:119-120.

[46] *PL* 29:402.

[47] *PL* 29:402. This reminds us of Origen's attitude of divine inspiration toward some of the additions and discrepancies in the current Septuagint text when compared with the Hebrew. W. Schwarz, *Principles,* 29-30, further clarifies Jerome's phrase, "either for the sake of ornament [i.e., stylistic reasons] or on the authority of the Holy Spirit." If the translators worked "on the authority of the Holy Spirit," what room was left for changes "for the sake of style?"

As Jerome worked on the above project, he simultaneously improved his knowledge of Hebrew. Soon he was ready to take one step further than Origen had ever dared, and work directly from the Hebrew text. He never did abandon the LXX completely, but as his work progressed he began to rely more and more on the *veritas hebraica,* the Hebrew truth. His *Commentary on Ecclesiastes* (389) is a most important work in the history of biblical exegesis in that it is the first original Latin commentary based on the Hebrew text. In its preface, Jerome gives us a good insight into his method of translation.

> I would briefly warn that I have not followed anyone's authority [i.e., text], but, translating from the Hebrew, I have adjusted myself more to the custom of the Seventy interpreters, but only in those places in which they did not diverge far from the Hebrew. I have sometimes referred also to Aquila, Symmachus, and Theodotion, so as not to deter the reader's interest by too much novelty,[48] nor, on the other hand, to follow the rivulets of opinions, omitting, against my conscience, the source of truth [the Hebrew text].[49]

This was the first indication that Jerome was abandoning the primacy of the LXX.

Jerome now entered the third stage of Scriptural translation. While in the midst of *revising* the Latin OT, he decided (*c.* 390) to make a *new translation* of the OT on the basis of the Hebrew or Aramaic original. This immense project continued until 406, and later became known as the

---

Jerome could well have had two types of additions in mind. The first was where there was no corresponding Hebrew text at all to the Septuagint's words — these were "on the authority of the Holy Spirit," reminiscent of Origen, as we have seen. These additions were indeed inspired. The second type of additions were for stylistic reasons — idiomatic and syntactic — and these were not the result of inspiration. We can better understand the justification for these stylistic changes when we note the remark of pseudo-Longinus, "On the Sublime," in Theodore Reinach, *Textes d'auteurs grecs et romains relatifs au Judaisme* (Paris, 1895) 114-115, praising the style of the Septuagint as sublime, and a parallel passage by Cleomedes regarding the style of the Hebrew Scriptures [212-213] accusing the Jews of low language with no sense of style. Jerome thus departs from the definition of inspirational translation delineated by Philo (cf. above n. 5). (Regarding Jerome's knowledge of Philo, see P. Courcelle, *Les lettres grecques en occident de Macrobe à Cassiodore,* 70-71.) The translator is not the instrument of God who writes as if the words "were dictated by an invisible prompter." He is inspired as regards the rendering of truth, but he has the liberty to choose his style. While Philo leaves no room for the human element in inspired translation, Jerome does.

[48] Jerome was well aware that he was displacing the old with the new and in preferring the Hebrew text to the LXX, was guilty, in the words of Origen in his *Letter to Africanus* 5, of transgressing Prov 22:28 "Thou shalt not remove the ancient landmarks which thy fathers have set." Jerome thus attempts to soften the effect of his departure from the Septuagint text by referring to the other Greek versions as well as to the Hebrew original.

[49] *PL* 23:1009 (*CCSL* 72, 249, 11.11-18).

Vulgate. Jerome's attitude toward the LXX continued to change, in stages. His very important work *Hebraicae Quaestiones in Genesim* (c. 390) is a series of notes made on passages from Genesis while he was studying the Hebrew text in preparation for his new Latin translation. In its preface, he cannot help referring again to the LXX. This time, he elaborates upon his theory why the *original* LXX did not exactly follow the Hebrew text.

> I do not, indeed, as hostile men rail, accuse the Seventy interpreters of errors, nor do I think my own labor a disparagement of theirs. For they were unwilling to report to Ptolemy, the king of Alexandria, all the mysteries which the sacred writings contain,[50] and especially those that promised the advent of Christ, in order that the Jews might not seem to be worshipping also a second god: he, a follower of Plato, had a high regard for them for this reason, because they were said to worship one God. But the evangelists, and also our Lord and Saviour, and the Apostle Paul, also bring forward many citations as coming from the Old Testament which are not contained in our [Septuagint] manuscripts. . . . But it is clear from this fact that those manuscripts [of the Old Testament] are more true which are in harmony with the authority of the New Testament. Add to this that Josephus also, who gives the story of the Seventy interpreters, reports them as translating only the five books of Moses,[51] and we also acknowledge that these are more in harmony with the Hebrew [texts] than the rest. But also those who afterward came into the field as translators—I mean Aquila and Symmachus and Theodotion—have a version very different from the one that which we read.[52]

In his *Preface to Isaiah* written about three years later (c. 393) Jerome again stresses that in preparing his new Latin version of the OT based on the Hebrew text he does not wish to displace the LXX, but rather presents an alternate Latin text (his Vulgate) in addition to the *Vetus Latina,* just as Aquila, Symmachus, and Theodotion presented alternate Greek texts in addition to the LXX.

Nevertheless, as the Greeks read Aquila, Symmachus and Theodotion after the

---

[50] Compare this statement with the second citation from Jerome's *Preface to Isaiah,* quoted below. This seems to be a departure from Jerome's previous position stated in his *Preface to Chronicles* (c. 389) where the additions to the LXX text are regarded as inspired (cf. n. 47). Although in his preface to *Quaestiones in Genesim* he does not specifically state that the translators were *not* inspired, his recognition of their omissions shows that Jerome already placed more reliance on the Hebrew text than any of his patristic predecessors.

[51] Cf. *Antiquities* 12.11, 56, 107, 108. In truth, the *Letter of Aristeas* 39 itself mentions the Pentateuch specifically. Jerome was indeed aware of the *Letter of Aristeas,* as seen from his *Preface to the Pentateuch* which will be cited shortly. In Jerome's *Commentary on Ezekiel* 2. 5 (Ezek 5:12) he states: "Yet Aristeas and Josephus and the whole Jewish school assert that only the five books of Moses were translated by the Seventy."

[52] *PL* 23:985-986 = *CCSL* 72, 2 (Lagarde 2.16-3.5).

Septuagint, either out of a desire for their teaching or so as to understand the Septuagint the more by comparison with them, so I ask my fastidious readers that they too will deign to have at least one interpreter [i.e., Jerome's Vulgate] after their earlier ones [i.e., the *Vetus Latina*].[53]

It is clear from this work that Jerome still held that the LXX translation was divinely inspired:

And so I surmise that the Seventy Interpreters were in their day unwilling to disclose the mysteries of their faith clearly to the gentiles,[54] lest they should "give what is holy to the dogs, and pearls to the swine": when you read this edition [i.e., Jerome's new translation of Isaiah] you will notice that they hid these [mysteries].[55]

In his preface to the translations of Proverbs, Ecclesiastes and Song of Songs (written c. 393) we find an echo of the same conflict of Scripture *vs.* Tradition which pervaded Origen's works:

If anyone is better pleased with the edition of the Seventy interpreters, he has it formerly corrected by us. For we do not hammer out new things in order to destroy the old.[56]

We are reminded of Origen's use of Proverbs 22:28 in this connection: "Thou shalt not remove the ancient landmarks which thy fathers have set,"[57] as well as the choice he apologetically offers his readers in his *Commentary on Matthew* 15:14: "He who wishes may pass over these words [i.e., the additions in the Hexapla text based on the Hebrew text]. If such a method offends you, you may accept or reject it as you see fit."[58]

In his prefaces to Ezekiel and Daniel (composed at approximately the same time as Isaiah, c. 393), however, we encounter Jerome's first critical remarks regarding the LXX which, within ten years, led to his utter rejection of its divine inspiration. In the *Preface to Ezekiel* we find:

The current [Septuagint] edition of it is not very different from the Hebrew. Therefore I rather wonder what was the reason, if we have the same translators in all the books,[59] for their translating the same elements in some books dif-

---

[53] *PL* 28 (ed. 1845):772-773; (ed. 1889):826-827.

[54] See n. 7 above for a parallel statement by Origen.

[55] *PL* 28 (ed. 1845):772; (ed. 1889):826.

[56] *PL* 28 (ed. 1845):1243; (ed. 1889):1308.

[57] See n. 10 above.

[58] Cf. n. 21 above. It should be noted how conservative Origen was, in comparison with Jerome, in displacing the old with the new, even though Origen did not outright emend the LXX text in his Hexapla, but resorted only to the use of the obelus and asterisk as critical signs.

[59] Jerome previously specifically mentioned that the same translators did not translate all the books of the Bible. In his preface to *Hebraicae Quaestiones in Genesim* he had previously

ferently than in other books.[60]

In the *Preface to Daniel* we find:

The Churches of our Lord, the Saviour, do not read the prophet Daniel according to the Seventy interpreters. They use Theodotion's version,[61] but why this came to pass I do not know. Whether it be that the language is Chaldee [i.e., Aramaic], which differs in certain peculiarities from our speech and the Seventy interpreters were unwilling to preserve the same lines of language in a translation; or that the book was published in their name by someone or other not familiar with Chaldee; or if there be some other reason, I know not. This one thing I can affirm: that it differs widely from the truth, and has been by a correct judgment rejected.[62]

Notwithstanding his criticisms of the LXX expressed in the prefaces to Ezekiel and Daniel, Jerome retained his faith in the authority of the original LXX which he had previously expressed in the Preface to his *Quaestiones in Genesim* with his famous Letter 57 (395 C.E.), *On the Best Method of Translating.* After referring to the many additions and omissions in the current Septuagint texts, he nevertheless speaks respectfully of the primitive LXX, giving two reasons for its primacy in the Church.

Still the Septuagint edition has rightly kept its place in the Churches, either because it is the first and made before the coming of Christ, or else because it

---

stated, on the authority of Josephus, that the Seventy Translators worked only on the five books of Moses: ". . . and we also acknowledge that these are more in harmony with the Hebrew [i.e., with the Apostles' citations of the Old Testament found in the New Testament] than the rest [i.e., the other books of the Bible]." This would imply that the Greek versions of the other books of the Bible, such as Ezekiel, would be inferior to the LXX on the Pentateuch, a point which Jerome now rejects.

[60] *PL* 28 (ed. 1845):938; (ed. 1889):995-996.

[61] Before Jerome's time, the Theodotion version of Daniel had superseded that of the LXX so completely that the latter was lost for centuries and is now extant only in two Greek manuscripts [Jellicoe, *Septuagint,* 84]. Jerome mentions that the Theodotion version of Daniel displaced that of the LXX, not only in his *Preface to Daniel* cited above, but also in his *Commentary on Daniel* 4:6, where he notes that Origen, in his *Stromata,* already preferred Theodotion's edition of Daniel since the LXX on Daniel "greatly differs from the Hebrew original" (*PL* 25:514). Jellicoe, *Septuagint,* 86, notes that Origen was indeed instrumental in causing Theodotion's text of Daniel to displace that of the LXX. Jerome also notes the use of Theodotion in the prologue to his *Commentary on Daniel* (*PL* 25:492) as well as in his *Apology Against Rufinus* 2.33. Saul Lieberman, *Greek in Jewish Palestine,* 55, notes that "the Greek version of Daniel used by the Rabbis in Palestine during the third century was close to that of Theodotion." The latest scholarly opinion is that the "Theodotion" Daniel is really a pre-Christian Greek recension, now referred to as "proto-Theodotion." See n. 19 above.

[62] *PL* 28 (ed. 1845):1291; (ed. 1889):1357.

has been used by the Apostles (among whom, nevertheless, it does not disagree with the Hebrew).[63]

In the above parenthetical remark, we find, for the first time, Jerome's claim that apostolic citations of the LXX were limited *only* to the places where it follows the Hebrew. It is indeed true, as was noted above in Jerome's *Preface to Quaestiones in Genesim,* that the apostles did cite *some* OT verses which were found only in the Hebrew text and not in the LXX. However, even a cursory examination of all the OT passages cited in the NT clearly shows that the LXX and not the Masoretic Hebrew text is the principal source for these quotations.[64] In fact, Justin, almost 250 years before, had employed the direct opposite of Jerome's argument. Based on the available LXX text, he had accused the Jews of removing many words and phrases from the Hebrew text.[65] Jerome must have been aware that his argument was sheer rationalization, necessary in order not to offend the Church in its sanction of the LXX. The only proof the Church would accept concerning the validity of the Hebrew OT would have to be based on the NT. Jerome thus brought the apostles to bear testimony for him concerning the Hebrew OT text.

This theme of apostolic citations is found as well in his *Preface to Ezra and Nehemiah* (composed 394/5) where he notes the mutilation of the Septuagint text.

Now, should anyone appeal to the Seventy interpreters . . . the copies of whose work prove by their diversity that they have been mutilated and disordered (for what is in discord surely cannot be declared true), send him to the Gospels, in which many passages are cited as from the Old Testament which are not contained among the Seventy interpreters. . . .[66]

---

[63] Letter 57.11 (*PL* 22:577). The original Latin text of the important parenthetical remark is "in quibus tamen ab Hebraico non discrepat."

[64] Swete, *Introduction,* 392.

[65] *Dialogue with Trypho* 68.71-73.

[66] *PL* 28 (ed. 1845):1403-4; (ed. 1889):1472-1473. A more complete citation of this text will appear below. In his *Preface to Chronicles* (composed 395) Jerome gives specific examples of citations in the Gospels from the Hebrew Scriptures not found in the LXX text. After citing several such passages from the Gospels, he says: "Where is it written down? The Septuagint does not have it, and the Church does not recognize the apocrypha. Therefore, we must go back to the [books of the] Hebrews of which also the Lord speaks and the examples of the disciple [John] presume" (*PL* 28 (ed. 1845):1326; (ed. 1889):1394). We find much of the same approach in his *Apology Against Rufinus* 2 composed in 402: ". . . in the authoritative publications of the evangelists and apostles we read much from the Old Testament which is not found in our [i.e., the Septuagint] manuscripts." After giving examples from Mt 2:5, Jn 19:37 and 1 Cor 2:9 he continues (echoing the above citation from his *Preface to Chronicles* composed seven years earlier): "Let me ask our opponents then where these things are written, and when they are unable to tell, let us produce them from the Hebrew" (*Apology Against Rufinus* 2.25 = *PL* 23:449).

In the *Preface to Chronicles* (composed 395) he goes further and attacks the myth of the seventy separate cells.

> If then it was lawful for others not to hold to that [the Septuagint] which they had once received, and if, after the seventy cells which are popularly tossed about on no one's authority,[67] they have each opened cells of their own, and this is read in the churches which the Seventy did not know, why should not my Latin [brethren] receive me, who without doing any violence to the old version have so prepared my new one that I can guarantee my labour on the authority of the Hebrews, and, what is more, of the Apostles. . . . One must, therefore, go back to the Hebrews, whence also speaks the Lord.[68]

It is in his *Preface to the Pentateuch (Genesis)* (*c.* 403) that we find Jerome's most critical evaluation of the Septuagint's divine inspiration.

> I do not know who was the first author who through his lie built seventy cells in Alexandria in which they [the translators] were separated and yet all wrote the same words; whereas Aristeas . . . and long after him Josephus have related nothing of the sort, but write that they were assembled in a single hall and conferred together, not that they prophesied. For it is one thing to be a prophet and another to be an interpreter;[69] in one case the Spirit foretells future events, in the other erudition and command of language translate those things which it understands, . . . or the Holy Spirit has woven testimonies from the same books one way through the Seventy interpreters and another way through the Apostles, so that these latter falsely declare to be written what the others have passed over in silence. What then? Do we condemn the old texts? By no means; but we work in the Lord's house as best we can after the endeavors of our predecessors.[70]

It should be made clear, however, that Jerome continued to cite the LXX version both as a basis for oral instruction as well as in his scholarly works even until the end of his career. In the *Preface to Chronicles* (395) cited above, where he is critical of the divine inspiration of the LXX, he nevertheless mentions that his instructions and sermons in his own

---

[67] Moses Hadas, *Aristeas to Philocrates,* 83, is of the opinion that the tradition of the insulation of the translators goes back to tannaitic times (Megillah 9a. See above, n. 5). If this is so, Jerome could be attacking a Jewish tradition in his *Preface to Chronicles* above. It does seem odd, however, that he does not make use of this opportunity to mention the Jews by name. We are thus safe in concluding Jerome was not aware that he was criticizing a Jewish tradition.

[68] *PL* 28 (ed. 1845):1325-6; (ed. 1889):1393-4.

[69] Jerome thus departs one step further from Philo's definition of inspirational translation. See above, n. 47. Despite Jerome's severe and accurate criticism of the Septuagint legend, not many years later, Augustine, in his *City of God* 18.42 repeats the legend of the separate cells and the miraculous consensus of the inspired translators.

[70] *PL* 28 (ed.1845):150-1; (ed. 1889):181-3.

monastery were based on the LXX. In his last major effort devoted to biblical scholarship, his commentaries on the Prophets, he regularly cites the LXX in addition to his new Vulgate version. Often the LXX is the basis of his spiritual application of the text.

We thus clearly see that Jerome's scholarly career, devoted to the establishment of the authentic biblical text, closely paralleled Origen's career. While it is true that Jerome went one step further than Origen and produced a new translation of the OT based directly on the Hebrew text, not only did he refuse to abandon the LXX, but, on the contrary, he continued to cite it and interpret it until his last day.

CHAPTER 3

JEROME AND THE SEARCH FOR THE AUTHORITATIVE BIBLICAL CANON
IN LIGHT OF ORIGEN'S SCHOLARSHIP

In the previous chapter, we have discussed Origen's and Jerome's attempts at establishing an authentic text of the OT. The second theme which concerned them was one of canon: which books were to be officially included in the OT, to be regarded as inspired and to be read in church services? Here too, in order to appreciate Jerome's work in this area, we must first acquaint ourselves with his patristic predecessors, especially Origen.

It should be made clear at the outset that in Origen's time there was no official list of OT books held authoritative by all the provinces of the Church; the Greek word "canon" had not yet assumed that meaning. In discussing Origen's use of this term, Hanson writes as follows:

> He never uses it to mean what we mean by the phrase "Canon of Scripture." Indeed, according to H. Oppel, who has written a monograph upon the word,[1] *Kanōn* does not occur with the meaning "the list of writings acknowledged by the Church as documents of the divine revelation" until we reach Athanasius[2] [of Alexandria, 295-373 C.E.].[3]

Jepsen[4] has pointed out that in Origen's time, each province had its own list of accepted OT books. One of the main reasons for this diversity was that Christianity had already become to a large extent separate from Judaism before the Hagiographa was canonized by Palestinian Jews about the close of the first century C.E.[5] Therefore, the "extra-canonical" religious litera-

---

[1] "Kanōn, zur Bedeutungsgeschichte des Wortes und seiner lateinischen Entsprechungen (Regula-Norma)," in *Philologus,* Supplement-band 30, Heft 4 (Leipzig, 1937) 70-71.

[2] Cf. n. 27 below.

[3] Hanson, *Origen's Doctrine of Tradition,* 133.

[4] "Kanon und Text des Alten Testaments," 65 ff.

[5] A. Sundberg, *The Old Testament of the Early Church* 82, 113-114. It is the commonly held view that the Jewish canon was closed at the end of the first century C.E. at the Council of Jabneh, established by Rabbi Joḥanan ben Zakkai. This view is based on, among other things, the rabbinic discussions regarding the canonical status of Ezekiel, Proverbs, Song of Songs, Ecclesiastes, and Esther (all being accepted) and Sirach and all other books written after it (not being accepted). Cf. Tosefta Yadaim 2.13 and Tosefta Shabbat 13 (14).5. Solomon Zeitlin, in his article "An Historical Study of the Canonization of the Hebrew Scriptures," provides all of the relevant rabbinic sources. He challenges the view that canonization was completed at Jabneh, and points out that as late as 132 C.E. the entire Hagiographa had not yet been canonized [p. 135].

ture flowed freely among the Christians, and it was not circumscribed and canonized formally until the Council of Laodicea (between 343-381 C.E.) in the East, and the Councils of Rome (382), Hippo (393) and Carthage (397 and 419), in the West.[6]

Admittedly the canonization process was a gradual one, beginning informally well before the Council of Laodicea. Origen played an important role in its early history. With this in mind we are prepared to evaluate Origen's contributions to the circumscription of the OT canon during the first half of the third century, almost a century prior to the Council of Laodicea.

The earliest OT list of definite date in the Church is that of Melito, bishop of Sardis (c. 170).[7] His list is essentially the Hebrew canon minus Esther[8] and Lamentations.[9] Next we come to Origen, who introduces his only extant list as the twenty-two[10] books of the Hebrew canon. It is cited by

[6]   Even these councils did not represent the entire Church, but were called by local bishops.

[7]   Preserved in Eusebius, *Historia Ecclesiastica* 4, 26.14. The list is contained in a letter to his brother who had requested such information from him. Melito says that he journeyed to the East [Palestine] in order to ascertain the answer, reflecting the fluidity of the OT canon in his time.

[8]   See n. 28 below.

[9]   This could very well have been included in Jeremiah, as Origen specifically shows.

[10]   According to rabbinic literature, there are twenty-four books composing the Hebrew canon: the five Books of Moses, four books of Former Prophets, four of Latter Prophets, and eleven books of Hagiographa. Samuel, Kings, Ezra-Nehemiah, Chronicles, and The Minor Prophets were each counted as single books. See the baraitha in Baba Bathra 14b which lists the order of books in the Prophets and Hagiographa; although it does not use the number "twenty-four," it implies it. In fact, no Tannaitic source cites this number; it is found, however, in later Midrashic and Talmudic sources. (See the *Jewish Encyclopedia* 3 [1903] 143, *s.v.* "Bible Canon" by Nathaniel Schmidt.) In 4 Ezra 14:46 we find the number 24, although there are variant readings. Josephus in *Contra Apionem* 1.38 however, mentions the number of books in the canon as twenty-two. He further subdivides them into Five Books of Moses, thirteen of Prophets and four of hymns and moral precepts. Most scholars maintain that he counted Ruth and Lamentations as appendices to Judges and Jeremiah respectively, as did both Origen and Jerome in their canon lists. Solomon Zeitlin, on the other hand, pp. 132-134, strongly maintains that during Josephus' time the Jewish Bible consisted of only twenty-two books; Ecclesiastes and Esther were added later (not until the second or third centuries, respectively).

Zeitlin correctly warns us (p. 134, n. 53) that concerning the Hebrew Canon, the Church Fathers' "testimony must, however, be taken with a grain of salt as they were outsiders and most likely they followed the order of the Septuagint." This is definitely true of most of the patristic OT canon lists. However, Jerome, in his *prologus galeatus (Preface to the Books of Samuel and Kings, c.* 393) follows Hebrew tradition most conscientiously, since, here alone among all of patristic canon lists of the Old Testament, do we find the tripartite Hebrew grouping of Torah, Prophets, and Hagiographa. (Origen, on the other hand, although influenced by Jewish tradition, several times refers only to the Law and the Prophets as making up the OT [cf. Homily 12 on Numbers]. All scholars agree that the Hagiographa were

Eusebuis[11] as follows:

> But it should be known that there are twenty-two canonical books[12] according to the Hebrew tradition; the same as the number of the letters of their alphabet.

The books are then enumerated as follows: Genesis, Exodus, Leviticus, Numbers, Deuteronomy, Joshua, Judges and Ruth combined in one book, Kingdoms I and II combined in one book — Samuel, Kingdoms III and IV combined in one book — the Kingdom of David, Chronicles I and II, Esdras I and II combined in one book — Ezra, Psalms, Proverbs, Ecclesiastes, Song of Songs, Isaiah, Jeremiah with Lamentations and the Epistle combined in one book — Jeremiah, Daniel, Ezekiel, Job and Esther. He then states "and outside these there are the Maccabees," showing that these are definitely outside the canon.[13]

---

canonized by Origen's time, the beginning of the third century.) There he cites both the tradition of 22 and 24 books and clearly points out that the number 22 was arrived at by combining Ruth and Lamentations with Judges and Jeremiah respectively. This would seem to support the view that Josephus, three centuries earlier, refers to this same grouping. Jerome again refers to the tripartite grouping in his *Preface to Daniel* (*c.* 393), this time citing only the Hebrew tradition of 24 books. However, in his Letter 53 (394 C.E.), he is entirely oblivious of the tripartite division. In the Greek prologue to the Book of Sirach, written by Ben Sirah's grandson (*c.* 130 B.C.E.) [*APOT* 1, 293], we find for the first time, the tripartite division of Jewish Scripture: "Law, Prophets, and the others who followed after them." He also refers to the third category as "the other books of our fathers." Cf. *APOT* 1, 316, n. 1, regarding the vagueness of this third category which had not yet been delineated. In Lk 24:44 we find the only New Testament passage which refers to the tripartite division in Hebrew Scripture: "Law of Moses, Prophets, and the Psalms."

There is a difference of opinion among modern scholars as to which number, 22 or 24, was the original. See Otto Eissfeldt, *The Old Testament: An Introduction*, 569, for the literature on this matter. Both canonical numbers of 22 and 24 were prevalent among ecclesiastical writers, but the former predominated, especially in the East, e.g. Melito, Origen, Eusebius, Cyril of Jerusalem, Epiphanius as well as Jerome and Augustine. (See S. Schultz, "Augustine and the Old Testament Canon.") When another canonical number was cited, an explanation usually accompanied it to show that it was not a true departure from the number 22. Thus, it was this number that Origen cites, with the additional note that this is the same number as the number of letters in the Hebrew alphabet.

[11] *Historia Ecclesiastica* 6, 25.2 quoted from Origen's lost *Commentary on Psalms.*

[12] The Greek word here is *endiathēkos,* literally "committed to writing," and not "canon."

[13]Athanasius (295-373) of Alexandria was even more persuaded than Origen that the Christian OT should conform to the Jewish canon. It is significant that he does not introduce his canonical list, as Origen did, with the qualifying phrase "according to the Hebrew tradition." Thus he went one step further than Origen in setting the Jewish canon as the guide for OT recognition by the Church. The list is found in his *Letters on the Paschal Festival* 39.3-4 (*PG* 26:1436-8) where he states: "There are, then, of the Old Testament, twenty-two books in number; for, as I have heard, it is handed down that this is the number of the letters among the Hebrews." The list that follows is identical with Origen's, except that Judges and Ruth are

There are two obvious problems with Origen's list: the omission of the book of the Twelve Minor Prophets and the inclusion of two books never recognized by the Jews as canonical[14] — the first book of Esdras[15] and the Epistle of Jeremiah. Sundberg[16] deals with both these problems, and offers plausible solutions, although there is not enough definitive evidence for positive conclusions. The Twelve Minor Prophets are absent through error,[17] and not design, since Origen's list of *Hebrew* names adds up to twenty-one books. It should here be clarified that in Origen's list cited by Eusebius, first the Greek name of the book is given, then the Hebrew name in Greek transliteration, and then the meaning of the Hebrew name follows in several cases.[18] Sundberg maintains that Origen received from the Jews only the Hebrew names of the books and their meanings and not the corresponding Greek titles. Origen then correlated the twenty-two-book Hebrew canon with the equivalent Greek names of Septuagint-Christian use. Several times he includes more than one Greek name equivalent to one Hebrew title — e.g., Jeremiah, Lamentations and the Epistle equivalent to Jeremiah. If it be true that Origen was responsible for the correlation, then

---

counted as two books, Baruch is added to the group of Jeremiah, Lamentations and Epistle, Esther is missing (see n. 28), and the Twelve [Minor Prophets] is included. The books of the "Apocrypha" are given in a special list (see n. 27). According to H. Oppel (see n. 1) he was the first to use the Greek word *Kanōn* (Canon) in the modern sense. The correspondence of the 22 books of the canon to the number of letters in the Hebrew alphabet, first pointed out by Origen and then by Athanasius, was repeated by Gregory of Nazianzus, Hilary of Poitiers, and Epiphanius, as well as Jerome (Ryle, *Canon of the Old Testament,* 232). Thus, irrespective of the fact that the alphabet sum of twenty-two does not seem to have affected the fixing of the Jewish canon, this numbering certainly influenced the Jewish canonical list adopted by the Church, especially in the East. There is also an interesting alternate counting by Epiphanius of Salamis (a younger contemporary of Jerome, d. 403) [*Weights and Measures* 23 = *PG* 43:277 and *Against Heresies* 1.1.8 = *PG* 41:213] of twenty-seven books, by counting double books twice (1-2 Chronicles, 1-2 Kings, 3-4 Kings, 1-2 Esdras) and Judges-Ruth as two. The number 27 equals the number of letters in the Hebrew alphabet, plus the five special final forms.

[14] Swete, *Introduction,* 222.

[15] In the most important manuscripts of the Septuagint "1 Esdras" refers to the apocryphal work, the "Greek Ezra." It was accepted in the early Church without suspicion by, among others, Clement of Alexandria, Origen, and Cyprian. Jerome in his *Preface to Ezra* (*PL* 28:1403) rejects this book and subsequently, in the Vulgate, it is called 3 Esdras, while 1 and 2 Esdras in the Vulgate refer to the two parts of Ezra-Nehemiah. Cf. Swete, *Introduction,* 266-267. In the Protestant Apocrypha it is still listed as 1 Esdras. "2 Esdras" in Origen's list would therefore refer to the canonical books Ezra-Nehemiah.

[16] *The Old Testament of the Early Church,* 135.

[17] Note also that Athanasius' list (n. 13) includes the Twelve Minor Prophets. Ryle, *Canon of the Old Testament,* 218, points out that Eusebius or some copyist could have made the error as well as Origen.

[18] For example: "Deuteronomy, Elle Addebareim, 'These are the words.'"

his inclusion of 1 Esdras and the Epistle of Jeremiah was only his conjecture as to which books the Jews included under the title Ezra and Jeremiah.[19]

It should also be noted that the order of books in Origen's list shows definite influence of the Alexandrian tradition since it does not follow the Hebrew tripartite division of Torah, Prophets, and Hagiographa.[20] But Origen does not mention all the other works which the Alexandrian school recognized as canonical:[21] the books of the Maccabees are specifically excluded, and no mention is made of Judith, Tobit, Wisdom of Solomon, Ecclesiasticus, Baruch, the additions to Esther and the additions to Daniel. It is thus clear what Origen's conception of the Hebrew canon was.

Origen's equivocal position regarding the correct text of the OT, analyzed previously, is certainly analagous to his position regarding the canon. Again we find the dual loyalties, Church tradition and textual criticism. It has been noted previously[22] that in his Hexapla, Origen was careful to compare the Greek texts of the OT with the Hebrew text then current in Palestine, and to note the differences. However, there was no Hebrew text for those books which the Jews considered outside the canon! This one fact, more than anything else, must have influenced Origen's critical opinion. But he could not leave these books out just as he could not tamper extensively with the LXX text by making indiscriminate additions and omissions based on the Hebrew. After all, these books were present in the Alexandrian tradition and some of them were read throughout the Church![23] As a result, Origen accepted as inspired a group of books not included in the Jewish canon. Since we have no definitive list of this group, we must piece it together from Origen's extant writings. His chief criterion for this recognition was use in the Church.

An important source for this investigation is Origen's *Letter to Africanus,* portions of which we have quoted previously with regard to

---

[19] There must have been some reason, however, that prompted Origen to include only the above two books. Perhaps he was reporting a local practice of which we have no other record.

[20] Cf. n. 10, regarding Jerome's recognition of this grouping.

[21] Robert H. Pfeiffer, *Introduction to the OT* 68-69, suggests that the conspectus of the Hellenistic Jewish Bible was that of the Vatican Manuscript (Codex Vaticanus, Gr. 1209) or Codex B of the middle of the fourth century. Most printed editions also follow its order and contents.

[22] See above pp. 20-21.

[23] Hanson in *Origen's Doctrine of Tradition* puts it somewhat less precisely: "In his attitude to the Canon of the Old Testament, then, Origen seems to us to-day to attempt to have it both ways, that is, he acknowledges the right of the Jews to decide their own Canon, and yet he also recognizes the authenticity of any tradition outside the Jewish Canon that appeals to him. But in fact this only means that Origen is adopting the very loose attitude to canonicity which he inherited from Clement, and modifying it by the respect for the Hebrew Bible which his biblical scholarship — so much sounder than Clement's — taught him" [p. 137].

Origen's attitude toward the LXX.²⁴ This letter was basically an answer to
Africanus' challenge of the canonicity of Susanna. Africanus called attention to the fact that Origen had cited an incident from Susanna in a
disputation. But, claimed Africanus, this work was not found in the
Hebrew text of the book of Daniel, and there were several indications from
its language and style that seemed to prove that it did not originally belong
to Daniel. How, then, could it be canonical? Origen defends its authenticity, as well as that of Bel and the Dragon, the Prayer of Azariah, and the
Song of the Three Children. These passages, although lacking in the
Hebrew, are present in the LXX and Theodotion's version. As we have
indicated above, Origen stresses most the fact that they are read throughout
the Church, and in the final analysis, the Church defines the acceptability of
the books of the OT. He uses the same argument later in the letter²⁵
regarding the book of Tobit. The status of Judith is not as clear, but it
seems to be in the same category as Tobit.²⁶ Elsewhere, Origen seems to
employ another criterion: the didactic character of a book. In Homily 27.1
on Numbers he recommends various books for moral instruction of
youngsters:²⁷ Esther,²⁸ Judith, Tobit, and Wisdom.²⁹ In his *Letter to
Africanus* 3, he characterizes two additions to the book of Esther, the
Prayers of Mordecai and Esther, as "both fitted to edify the reader"³⁰ even

---

²⁴ See n. 10 and n. 24 in Chapter 2.

²⁵ *Letter to Africanus* 13.

²⁶ The books of Maccabees may also have been included in this group, as Origen cites 2 Mac
7:28 as having "the authority of holy scripture" in *De Principiis* 2, 1.5.

²⁷ Athanasius in his *Letters on the Paschal Festival* 39:7 (*PG* 26:1437ff.), after giving the
list of OT books (cf. n. 13) adds the following: ". . . there are other books besides these, on
the one hand not canonical, but appointed by the Fathers to be read by those who newly join us
and who wish for instruction in the word of godliness: the Wisdom of Solomon, and the
Wisdom of Sirach, and Esther and Judith, and Tobit, and the so-called Teaching of the
Apostles, and the Shepherd. But the former [list of the OT books, cf. n. 13], my brethren, are
included in the canon, the latter being read; nor is there in any place a mention of the
apocryphal writings." This three-fold division of Scripture will be discussed shortly, cf. n. 36.

²⁸ The inclusion of Esther in this grouping of otherwise non-canonical books according to
the Jews is of great interest. The late date of the acceptance of Esther into the Jewish canon is
well known. Solomon Zeitlin [134] believes that Esther was added as late as the middle of the
second century, at the Synod of Usha. In Origen's case, however, the list of the twenty-two
books of Hebrew Scriptures from his *Commentary on Psalms* (begun c. 224), preserved in
Eusebius *H.E.* 6, 25, specifically includes Esther. It is interesting to note, however, that
Athanasius (295-373), who lived a century after Origen, in his Hebrew canon list did not include Esther! It is also missing in the list of Gregory of Nazianzus, of a generation later than
Athanasius (*Carmen* 1, 12, 5 = PG 37:472-4).

²⁹ This is most probably Wisdom of Solomon. In Homily 18.3 on Numbers he cites Ecclesiasticus as "Wisdom of Jesus, son of Sirach."

³⁰ Note that Jerome used a similar term, "for the edification of the people" as the reason
the Church reads the books of the Wisdom of Solomon and Sirach.

though they are not found in the Hebrew text. It is still not clear, however, whether all of the above books enjoyed the same status as those in the Hebrew canon, or whether they were regarded by Origen as less authoritative. The latter is clearly the case with Athanasius[31] and, much later, Rufinus.[32]

Next we come to another category of Scripture for Origen. In his prologue to the *Commentary on The Song of Songs* he states:

> . . . in the case of those writings that are called apocrypha—because many things were found in them that were corrupt and contrary to the true faith, our predecessors did not see fit for them to be given a place, or admitted among those reckoned as authoritative. . . . We must not overpass the everlasting limits which our fathers have set[33] [cf. Prov 22:28].[34]

Again we find in Origen's *Commentary on Matthew* 17:35:[35] "They who have recourse to apocryphal books will take a method not approved by the faithful." As Daniélou has pointed out, by "apocrypha" Origen does not here refer to "the deutero-canonical books, but the apocrypha in the modern Roman Catholic sense of the term [i.e., pseudepigrapha],[36] i.e., Jewish works like the Testaments of the Twelve Patriarchs and the Book of Enoch."[37]

But here again, Origen does not furnish us with a definitive list as to

---

[31] See n. 27.

[32] See n. 36.

[33] Note that this is the same verse cited by Origen in his *Letter to Africanus* 5, in support of those books read in the Church although not accepted by the Jews.

[34] Translation taken from *Origen: The Song of Songs, Commentary and Homilies,* translated and annotated by R. P. Lawson (Westminster, Maryland: The Newman Press, 1957) 56. We do not have the original Greek text, only Rufinus' Latin translation.

[35] *PG* 13:1593 on Mt 22:29.

[36] A clearer tripartite division of Scripture into canonical, deutero-canonical, and apocryphal categories was given more than a century later by Rufinus (d. 410) in his *Commentarius in Symbolum Apostolorum 38* (*PG* 21:374). After enumerating the inspired books of the Old and New Testaments, he adds: "However, it ought to be observed that there are also other books, which are not canonical, but have been called by our forefathers ecclesiastical: as the Wisdom of Solomon; and another, which is called the Wisdom of the Son of Sirach, and among the Latins is called by the general name of Ecclesiasticus, by which title is denoted not the author of the book, but the quality of the writing. In the same rank is the book of Tobit and Judith, and the books of the Maccabees. In the New Testament is the book of the Shepherd or of Hermas which is called the Two Ways, or the Judgment of Peter. All which they permit to be read in the Churches, but not to be alleged by way of authority for proving articles of faith. Other scriptures they called apocryphal, which they would not have to be read in the Churches."

[37] *Origen,* 137.

which books are in the category of unreliable apocrypha.[38] In fact, the statement in his *Commentary on Matthew,* Series 28 (written in 246) best characterizes his ambivalent attitude toward the apocrypha which only two years previously he had totally rejected in his *Commentary on the Song of Songs.*

> We ought therefore, to use caution[39] that we neither accept all the apocryphal writings which are circulated under the names of the holy men on the authority of the Jews, who perhaps have forged some writings in order to overthrow the truth of our scriptures, supporting false teachings;[40] nor should we reject all [apocryphal writings] which help to confirm our scriptures.[41]

Although Origen continues with the warning that only a great man can distinguish between the true and false apocryphal statements,[42] and hence the general rule should be: "let no one employ in support of his religious view books which are outside the Church's list of scriptures," evidently he felt himself released from following his own rule. Throughout his extant writings, he cites as genuine, apocryphal traditions from the Martyrdom of Isaiah, the Ascension of Moses, the Assumption of Moses (which he refers to, but does not name), the Prayer of Joseph, the Testaments of the Twelve Patriarchs, and a work on the life of Asenath (Joseph's wife).[43] The majority of apocryphal references in Origen's works, however, are not identified by the name of the apocryphal book, and we cannot identify them today.

Hanson interestingly points out that with regard to the Book of Enoch "we can actually observe Origen's judgment altering in the course of

---

[38] An exhaustive analysis of all apocryphal references in Origen's works is found in Ruwet's "Les Apocryphes dans l'oeuvre d'Origène."

[39] Jerome echoes the same idea, a bit more picturesquely in his Letter 107.12 which contains the books of Scriptures to be read by a child dedicated by her parents to a life of virginity: "But let her avoid all apocrypha; and if she will read them occasionally not for the truth of their teaching, but to show respect for the miracles they describe, let her know that they were not composed by those whose names are given in the titles, there is much mixed in with them that is faulty and it is a task for great prudence to seek gold in the mud."

[40] Compare his *Letter to Africanus* 9, where he accuses the Jews of deliberately inserting false phrases in otherwise valid apocryphal writings, in order to discredit the entire work. Contrast this with the above citation from his *Commentary on Matthew,* where the Jews are reported to accept and circulate apocryphal writings in order to confound Christian Scripture.

[41] Extant in Latin translation, *PG* 13:1637.

[42] Compare Origen's *Prologue to the Commentary on the Song of Songs* (tr. R. P. Lawson) 59, where a similar statement is found: ". . . The apostles and evangelists being filled with the Holy Spirit, knew what was to be taken out of those writings and what must be rejected."

[43] Hanson, in *Origen's Doctrine of Tradition,* 135ff. gives the passages in Origen's works where the above are cited.

time."[44] He quotes it three times in *De Principiis*[45] (begun in the year 225) without comment. In the *Commentary on John*[46] (begun in the same year) he again refers to it, adding "if anyone cares to receive the book as holy." In *Contra Celsum*[47] (written in 248) he supposes that Celsus took some idea from the book of Enoch, not being aware that "the books which bear the name Enoch do not at all circulate in the Churches as divine." In the next chapter of the same work[48] Origen terms a certain citation from Enoch "a thing never mentioned or heard in the Churches of God." Finally, in the *Homilies on Numbers*[49] (written between 246 and 254, the last nine years of his life), he refuses even to quote Enoch regarding a certain matter "since these books do not appear to have recognized authority with the Hebrews." It is particularly significant to note that this last reference did not at all deal with polemics against the Jews and yet Origen gave the lack of Jewish acceptance rather than the lack of Christian authority as a reason for Enoch's dismissal.

The above citations and remarks concerning Enoch best sum up Origen's attitude toward the canon of the OT. As we have pointed out regarding the text of Scripture, Origen was well aware of the importance of the Hebrew text and Jewish tradition. However, the tradition and current practice of the Church, as well as the utility of a passage in substantiating his own point of view, prevented him from adopting a strict and consistent attitude toward the canon, as it similarly affected him with regard to the text of Scripture.[50]

We are now prepared to evaluate the work of Jerome with regard to the authoritative biblical canon of the OT. Jerome's views concerning this are integrally related to his views concerning the text. Since he accepted the

---

[44] *Origen's Doctrine of Tradition,* 136.

[45] Once in 1.3.3, and twice in 4.35. In the latter place he even cites Enoch as a prophet!

[46] 6, 42.

[47] 5, 54 = *PG* 11:1268a.

[48] *Contra Celsum* 5, 55.

[49] 28.2 = *PG* 12:802.

[50] Just as Origen cites from books not found in his list of the twenty-two books of Hebrew Scriptures, so do other patristic authorities who followed him. Athanasius, who, it will be remembered, listed an even stricter Jewish canon than Origen (n. 13), nevertheless cites non-canonical books intermingled with citations from the books of his Jewish list "with no indication of any difference of status" (Sundberg, *The Old Testament,* 140, n. 28). The same is true of other Fathers of the eastern church who published OT lists: e.g., Gregory of Nazianzus and Cyril of Jerusalem. This leads Sundberg (ibid., 147) to conclude: "the restriction of the Christian Old Testament to the names of the Jewish canon, even in the Greek recension [i.e., according to the Septuagintal inclusion of more than one book under a single name in the Jewish canon, as with Baruch and the Epistle of Jeremiah together with Jeremiah], was not a long established tradition in the East but was an innovation in the throes of gaining acceptance."

veritas hebraica or Hebrew truth with regard to the text, he also refused to accept as inspired or authoritative works not preserved in Hebrew. As we have shown with regard to the biblical text, in the first part of his scholarly career Jerome was completely uncritical towards the OT canon. He frequently refers to texts and narratives from books and passages which he later excludes from canonical writings, and he makes none of the qualifying statements that he does later in his career. At times he quotes the texts themselves; sometimes he merely refers to an episode or character of a story, or the title of an apocryphal work in order to illustrate or substantiate a point. To take the story of Susanna as an example, he refers to it in particular in the first of his Letters (1.9, written *c*. 374), along with the episodes of the three children singing in the furnace and Daniel in the lions' den. He refers to the heroes of these as characters in situations; he does not speak of the titles of the books, nor does he cite any passages. In his Letter 14.9 (376-7 C.E.) he certainly refers to Susanna, although not by name, when he remarks: "Daniel was but a child when he judged the elders."[51] Next, in *Contra Helvidium* 4 (383 C.E.) he refers to "the case of Susanna" who was condemned as an adulteress.

Howorth[52] points out that the years 390-391 mark the dividing line between the uncritical and critical attitude of Jerome towards the canon. He notes that Jewish influence was partly responsible for this change.[53] It should be clearly pointed out, however, that no one year represents a radical change for Jerome. His metamorphosis is gradual. Moreover, considering his entire life's work, his practice with regard to the canon is similar to his practice regarding the text: throughout his life he continues to cite passages from books which he considers non-canonical. However, he certainly cites them comparatively less after 390, and often with critical reservations.

Sometime after his settlement in Bethlehem, between 386-390, he translated the books of Tobit[54] and Judith from Semitic texts. In his preface to

---

[51] In Susanna 45, Daniel is described as a young man when he interceded in the judgment.

[52] "The Influence of St. Jerome on the Canon of the Western Church," 493.

[53] Howorth thinks that Jerome's conflict with the supporters of Origen's views, later considered heretical, also affected his attitude towards the canon. Patrick W. Skehan, "St. Jerome and the Canon of the Holy Scriptures," 263, points out two objections to the above hypothesis. The first is chronological, since ". . . the outbreak of the Origenistic controversy for St. Jerome dates to A.D. 393." The second is a more essential point: ". . . Origen's direct formulation of the canon of the Old Testament is actually the narrow, Jewish one which St. Jerome now comes to accept."

[54] In its preface we find the famous statement of Jerome that, with the aid of a Jew who spoke both Hebrew and Aramaic, he translated Tobit into Latin in "one day's hasty labor; whatever he expressed . . . " (See n. 19 in Chapter 1.) M. M. Schumpp points out in *Das Buch*

these works he recognized that the books are apocryphal. The obvious question is then: why did he translate them? The answers which he gives us in the preface are the keys to Jerome's attitude toward the Apocrypha: while his scholarship on the one hand forced him to reject them, the tradition of the Church propelled him towards them. Regarding Tobit, he gives his *apologia* "judging it better to displease the judgment of Pharisees and to obey the behests of bishops."[54a] As to Judith, he notes: "because the Nicene Synod is alleged to have counted this book among the Holy Scriptures."[55]

We can chart in detail a gradual turn in the course of Jerome's scholarship. In his commentaries on the Pauline Epistles Philemon, Galatians, Ephesians, and Titus (*c.* 386-7) he cites no less than eleven apocryphal verses from the books of 1 Maccabees, 2 Maccabees, Wisdom of Solomon, Sirach (Ecclesiasticus), and the Additions to Esther. This practice is continued in his *Commentary on Ecclesiastes* (*c.* 389), the first original Latin commentary to take cognizance of the Hebrew text. Despite this advance in Jerome's scholarship, he continues to cite a considerable number of apocryphal works including the book of Tobit. For example, in his first series of commentaries on the Twelve Minor Prophets: Nahum, Michah, Zephaniah, Haggai, and Habakkuk (*c.* 392), he cites apocryphal verses ten times. At the same time, however, in his prologue to the *Commentary on Habakkuk,* the canonicity of the narratives Bel and the Dragon (Dan 14, Vulgate) is questioned: ". . . although among the Hebrews this story is not read. Therefore if someone accepts this Scripture or if he doesn't. . . ."[56]

During this time, Jerome began work on the Vulgate. In the preface to the books of Samuel and Kings (composed before 393)—the *prologus galeatus* or "helmeted preface," as he calls it, Jerome set forth the principles which he adopted in all his translations from the Hebrew. Before listing the books of the Hebrew canon he makes it quite clear that this canon should be accepted by Christians as being that by which "the still tender and nursing infancy of a just man is instructed in the teaching of God."[57] Thus

---

Tobias xxix-xxxiii that Jerome checked the translation with the previously extant Latin text. On the Vulgate version of Tobit, see also Frank Zimmerman, *The Book of Tobit* (New York: Harper & Bros., 1958) 132.

[54a] *PL* 29:25.

[55] *PL* 29:39. However, in the preface to his translation of Proverbs, Ecclesiastes, and Song of Songs (*c.* 393), he seems to contradict this statement: "As, then, the Church reads Judith, Tobit, and the books of Maccabees, but does not admit them among the canonical Scriptures" (*PL* 28 [ed. 1845]: 1242-3; [ed. 1889]: 1308).

[56] *PL* 25:1274.

[57] *PL* 28 (ed. 1845):552; (ed. 1889):593.

Jerome went beyond Origen in that he accepted the Hebrew texts as the canon binding upon *Christians*.[58]

Jerome then lists the books of the Hebrew canon as follows: Genesis, Exodus, Leviticus, Numbers, Deuteronomy. "These are the five books of Moses, which they properly call *Thorath,* that is, laws. The second class is composed of the Prophets": Joshua, Judges — Ruth, Samuel, Kings, Isaiah, Jeremiah [-Lamentations], Ezekiel, Twelve Prophets. "To the third class belong the *Hagiographa*": Job, Psalms, Proverbs, Ecclesiastes, Song of Songs, Daniel, Chronicles, Ezra [-Nehemiah] and Esther. Jerome tells us that some counted these books as 22 and some as 24,[59] depending upon whether Ruth and Lamentations were counted separately. He then continues:

> This prologue to the scriptures may serve as a helmeted preface, as it were, to all the books which we have turned from Hebrew into Latin, so that we may be able to know that whatever is outside these must be placed among the apocrypha. Wisdom, therefore, which commonly bears the name of Solomon, and the book of Jesus the Son of Sirach, and Judith and Tobias and the Shepherd are not in the canon. The first book of Maccabees, I have found to be Hebrew,[60] the second is Greek, as can be proved from the very style also.[61]

In the preface to his translations of the books of Solomon: Proverbs, Ecclesiastes, and Song of Songs, published shortly thereafter (*c.* 393), he further qualifies his position regarding the Apocrypha and defines its proper use. After writing of the books of the Wisdom of Solomon and Sirach, he states:

> As, then, the Church reads Judith, Tobit and the books of the Maccabees, but does not admit them among the canonical Scriptures, so let it read these two

---

[58] Origen, it will be remembered, cited the twenty-two books "according to the Hebrew tradition," but it is clear from his works that he defined the Scriptures of the Church to include more books than those in the Hebrew canon. Jerome later again affirms the Hebrew texts to be the actual copies of Scriptures in his *Apology Against Rufinus* 3.25 = *PL* 23:498 (composed in 404).

[59] See n. 10 for a discussion of the canonical numbers 22 and 24 as well as the tripartite division of Hebrew Scriptures in rabbinic and patristic traditions. Previously, in this preface, Jerome noted that the 22 basic letters of the Hebrew alphabet correspond to the 22 books of the canon, and that the five letters in Hebrew which are written differently when they occur at the end of a word ("Caph, Mem, Nun, Phe, Sade") correspond to five double-books: Samuel, Kings, Chronicles, Ezra-Nehemiah, and Jeremiah-Lamentations.

[60] Despite this, Jerome did not include it in his canon, for reasons he does not specify.

[61] *PL* 28 (ed. 1845):555-557; (ed. 1889):600-603. Admittedly, Jerome here is not concerned with listing all of the apocryphal books. For example, although he does not mention Baruch by name, we are told in the preface to Jeremiah written during the same period (*c.* 393) that the Hebrews do not have the book of Baruch.

volumes also for the edification of the people (*ad aedificationem plebis*), not to confirm the authority of Church doctrines.[62]

Thus again we see Jerome's attraction to the Apocrypha on the basis of popular Church tradition, the key phrase being *ad aedificationem plebis*. This brings to mind a similar statement made by Origen concerning two additions to the book of Esther—the Prayers of Mordecai and Esther— which he qualified as "both fitted to edify the reader" even though they were not found in the Hebrew text.[63] Skehan[64] advances an interesting theory concerning this phrase: ". . . he [Jerome] uses the term by contrast to [canonical] books which can be used as authority in establishing the truth of Christian doctrine for the Jews in particular." This becomes more feasible in light of two similar statements by Jerome. In his preface to the translation of Psalms from the Hebrew, he says: "It is one thing to read Psalms in the Churches of those who believe in Christ, but another thing to reply to the Jews who cavil at each separate word."[65] In the preface to his translation of Isaiah, we find: ". . . I have sweated over the learning of a foreign tongue [i.e., Hebrew] to this end, that the Jews may no longer mock our churches for the falsity of our Scriptures."[66] Jerome thus agrees to adopt the Hebrew text in his polemics so that the Jews "may be smitten most effectively by their own spears."[67]

The dual loyalties of Jerome, to both Hebrew Scripture and Church Tradition, become even more apparent when we note that while he was composing the above Vulgate translations based on the *veritas hebraica*, in *Adversus Jovinianum* and its companion Letters of apology, numbers 48 and 49 (composed in 393), he continues to quote verses from apocryphal works (Wisdom and Ecclesiasticus) as well as to cite Job extensively in *Adversus Jovinianum* according to the LXX although in Letter 49 it is quoted according to the Vulgate following the Hebrew.[68]

In his *Preface to Ezra and Nehemiah* (composed 394/5), we find Jerome's most forceful statement accepting the Hebrew canon and rejecting

[62] *PL* 28 (ed. 1845):1242-3; (ed. 1889):1308.

[63] *Letter to Africanus* 3.

[64] "St. Jerome and the Canon," 271.

[65] *PL* 28 (ed. 1845):1126; (ed. 1889):1186. In his *Letter to Africanus* 4, Origen similarly cites Jewish polemics as the incentive for his intensive study of the biblical text: "And I make it my endeavor not to be ignorant of their various readings, lest in my controversies with the Jews I should quote them what is not found in their copies, and that I make some use of what is found there, even though it should not be in our Scriptures" (*PG* 11:60).

[66] *PL* 28 (ed. 1845):774; (ed. 1889):828. Origen was concerned with the same matter in his *Letter to Africanus* 4-5.

[67] *Apology* 3.25 = *PL* 23:498.

[68] Skehan, 270.

the canon of the LXX.

> And let no one be disturbed because we bring forth this [Ezra-Nehemiah] as a single book, nor let anyone be delighted by the dreams of third and fourth [Ezra] of the apocrypha [i.e., the apocryphal books we now call 1 and 2 Esdras], for among the Hebrews, too, the speeches of Ezra and Nehemiah are confined to a single scroll; and what is not contained among them or numbered among the twenty-four elders,[69] is to be cast far away. Now, should anyone appeal to the Seventy interpreters against you [i.e., that in the Septuagint we find the books of Ezra and Nehemiah separated], the copies of whose work prove by their diversity that they have been mutilated and disordered (for what is in discord surely cannot be declared true) send him to the Gospels, in which many passages are cited as from the Old Testament which are not contained among the Seventy interpreters . . . .[70]

We are well aware however, that the above exhortation on the exclusive authority of the Hebrew canon existed for Jerome more in theory than in practice.

Jerome gives two lists of the OT canon in addition to the one found in his *prologus galeatus* to Samuel and Kings. One is found in Letter 53.8[71] (395 C.E.) where we find essentially the same list of the Hebrew Scriptures cited in his *prologus galeatus* with the following exceptions: no mention is made of the tripartite division of Hebrew Scripture; after Deuteronomy we find Job;[72] the Twelve Minor Prophets (in the internal order found in Hebrew Scripture, adopted later in the Vulgate) precede Isaiah; Daniel appears after Ezekiel;[73] and Esther appears before Chronicles. No specific mention is made of apocrypha. The above list gives the same number of books as in the *prologus galeatus,* assuming that Jeremiah includes Lamentations as well. It is clear, however, that this list in his Letter 53.8 was more affected by the Septuagint tradition in two aspects: the place of the Minor prophets before the other Prophets and the inclusion of Daniel at the end of the Prophets, ostensibly as one of them.

Another list is found in Letter 107.12 (*c.* 402), which contains the books of Scriptures to be read by a child dedicated by her parents to a life of

---

[69] A fanciful allusion based on Apoc 4:4 which Jerome suggests refers to the twenty-four books of the Hebrew canon. This representation is first found in the *prologus galeatus* to Samuel and Kings.

[70] *PL* 28 (ed. 1845):1403-4; (ed. 1889):1472-3.

[71] *PL* 22:545-8.

[72] Cf. Baba Bathra,. 14b where Moses is mentioned as one possible author of the book of Job, thus explaining its place after the Pentateuch.

[73] Ostensibly, Jerome here considers Daniel to be a prophet. Cf. Ginzberg, *Legends* 6, 413, n. 76; 416, n. 83; 436, n. 18, concerning the rabbinic views whether Daniel was a prophet or not. Cf. Chapter 4, n. 33.

virginity. The order he gives is not canonical but didactic. There is specific mention of apocrypha:

> But let her avoid all the apocrypha; and if she will read them occasionally not for the truth of their teaching, but to show reverence for their miracles, let her know that they were not composed by those whose names are given in the titles: there is much mixed in with them that is faulty, and it is a task for great prudence to seek gold in the mud.[74]

As we have already pointed out, despite Jerome's clear pronouncement excluding apocrypha as early as 393 in his *prologus galeatus,* he continues his earlier practice of quoting verses from apocryphal works for the rest of his life. Sometimes verses are quoted with no comment; other times Jerome makes some qualifying remark. For example, after referring to the book of Judith in his Letter 54.16 (394-5) he remarks parenthetically: ". . . if anyone is of the opinion that the book is to be received as canonical." In his Prologue to the *Commentary on Jonah* (396), Tobit is cited "because, though it is not in the canon, it is made use of by churchmen." In the Prologue (sec. 2) to his *Commentary on Jeremiah,* his last work (composed between 415-420), Jerome explicitly tells us that he had resolved not to comment on Baruch or on the Letter of Jeremiah which he calls a *pseudepigraphon.* Yet Baruch had been quoted as late as 400 in his Letter 77.4. It thus seems quite evident that Jerome's statements implying the exclusive authority of the Hebrew canon differed from his practice of citing apocryphal works, especially, those read by the Church and popularly accepted.

Just as with apocrypha in general, we find a similar attitude of Jerome toward the non-canonical parts of Daniel: the prayer of Azariah and the Song of the Three Children, Susanna, and Bel and the Dragon. In the preface to his translation of Daniel (*c.* 392) he notes quite clearly that the above three sections are not to be found in the Hebrew.

> Because they have been scattered in the entire world, we have subjoined them,[75] prefixing to them an obelus, and thus cutting their throat so that we

---

[74] *PL* 22:877. The above should be compared with a similar statement made by Origen who blamed the Jews for the corruption of the apocrypha. "We ought therefore, to use caution, that we neither accept all the apocryphal writings which are circulated under the names of the holy men on the authority of the Jews, who perhaps have forged some writings in order to overthrow the truth of our scriptures, supporting false teachings" (*Commentary on Matthew* [Series 28], *PG* 13:1637).

[75] In truth, the Prayer of Azariah and the Song of the Three Children are not presented as an appendix, but are inserted as Dan 3:24-90, with a note *both* at the beginning and end of the section that they are not to be found in the Hebrew but have been translated from Theodotion.

may not seem to the untrained to have cut off a large portion of the volume.[76]

He then quotes the objections of one of the Jewish *praeceptores* or teachers to each of these sections.[77] "By these and similar arguments he used to refute the apocryphal fables in the Church's book. Leaving this for the reader to pronounce upon as he may think fit. . . ."[78] Within about one year (*c.* 393), in *Adversus Jovinianum* Jerome refers to the freeing of Susanna as a possible reason why Daniel, as a young man, was already well-known to Ezekiel.[79] But in *Adv. Jov.* 2, 15, we find the episode of Habakkuk bringing food to Daniel (Bel and the Dragon, 33ff.) with the added parenthetical comment: "although we do not find this in the Hebrew Scriptures."[80] From Jerome's *Preface to Daniel* cited above, the conclusion of the reader regarding the non-Hebrew-canonical portions of Daniel seems quite evident. However, when Jerome was accused of being too much the scholar, Jerome the traditionalist answers in the *Apology Against Rufinus* 2, 33 (composed in 402):

> For I have not been relating my own personal views [about the canonicity of the additions to Daniel] but rather what they [i.e., the Jews] are wont to say against us. If I did not reply to their views in my preface, in the interest of brevity, lest it seem that I was composing not a preface but a book, I believe I immediately added the remark, for I said:[81] "This is not the time to discuss such a matter."[82]

This is certainly a weak answer on Jerome's part. The truth is that he never did later make time to defend the canonicity of these sections of Daniel,

---

Susanna and Bel and the Dragon, however, *are* presented as appendices, Dan 13 and 14 respectively. Cf. n. 84. In all Greek and Latin Bibles prior to Jerome, they were placed in the beginning of the book of Daniel. Hence the importance of Jerome's placing them at the end.

[76] *PL* 28 (ed. 1845):1292-3; (ed. 1889):1359.

[77] The objection concerning Susanna which Jerome here notes is identical with the objection which Africanus brought against Origen (*Letter to Origen* 7) and is, curiously enough, cited in the Prologue to Jerome's *Commentary on Daniel* in the name of Porphyry: Susanna can be shown to have been composed in Greek in view of two word-plays (paronomasia) found in it which are peculiar to the Greek language.

[78] *PL* 28 (ed. 1845):1294; (ed. 1889) 1360.

[79] 1, 25. See Chapter 4, pp. 63-65.

[80] *PL* 23:308. Note the peculiar contradiction that in the same work Jerome at one point seems to accept one addition to Daniel (Susanna) while at another point he rejects an addition to Daniel (Bel and the Dragon).

[81] We do not find this phrase in Jerome's *Preface to Daniel*. We do find the phrase cited above: "Leaving this for the reader to pronounce upon as he may think fit." Jerome probably referred to this.

[82] *PL* 23:455.

even in his *Commentary on Daniel* (407). In fact, he there indicates the opposite, as will next be pointed out.

In Jerome's *Commentary on Daniel,* the three sections referred to above are placed in the same position as in his previous translation of Daniel, showing little change of mind in this matter. If anything, he seems apologetic in his commenting upon these portions in the first place; his remarks are very sparse, except those on Susanna. The Prayer of Azariah and the Song of the Three Children (Dan 3:24-90) are again marked off by Jerome, both at the beginning and end, with phrases indicating that this section is not to be found in the Hebrew [i.e., Aramaic] but was translated from Theodotion. Before this section in the *Commentary,* however, we have the added apologetic phrase: "Lest we seem to pass over them altogether, we must make a few observations."[83] With regard to Susanna (Dan 13) and Bel and the Dragon (Dan 14) we find at the end of chapter 12 in the Vulgate translation: "Thus far we have been reading Daniel in the Hebrew edition; but the remaining matter to the end of the book has been translated from Theodotion's edition."[84] In his *Commentary on Daniel* 13 Jerome prefaces his comments on Susanna with the following remarks: "Having expounded to the best of my ability the contents of the book of Daniel according to the Hebrew, I shall briefly set forth the comments of Origen concerning the stories of Susanna and of Bel contained in the Tenth Book of his *Stromata.* These remarks are from him and one may observe them in the appropriate sections [of Origen's work]."[85] Origen's *Stromata* were preserved only through Jerome's translation. We wonder how much liberty Jerome took in translating Origen's remarks.[86] Certainly the last one, the sole comment on Bel and the Dragon (v. 18), seems more indicative of Jerome's attitude than that of Origen, who supported the Church tradition concerning Susanna (as clearly seen in his famous letter to Africanus). In answer to an exegetical problem concerning Bel and the Dragon we find: "This objection is easily solved by asserting that this particular story is not contained in the Hebrew of the Book of Daniel. If, however, anyone should be able to prove that it belongs in the canon, then we should be obliged to seek out some answer to this objection."[87] The Dragon narrative (Dan 14:22 ff.) is not commented on at all.

In the prologue to his *Commentary on Daniel* we find an attack on the validity of Susanna and Bel and the Dragon which is much more definite

[83] *PL* 25:509 = *CCSL* 75A, 803, 1. 620 ff.

[84] *PL* 28 (ed. 1845):1319; (ed. 1889):1386.

[85] *PL* 25:580 = *CCSL* 75A, 945, 1. 698ff.

[86] See Chapter 19, n. 4.

[87] *PL* 25:584 = *CCSL* 75A, 950, 1. 844ff.

than his remarks in the prologue to the translation of Daniel, and which definitely contradicts Jerome's defense in his *Apology Against Rufinus* 2.33 quoted above. Jerome makes an original point attacking their validity in addition to the oft-quoted one that these additions are not found in the Hebrew canon and the two cases of Greek paronomasia.[88]

> Just as we find in the title[89] of that same story of Bel, according to the Septuagint: "There was a certain priest named Daniel the Son of Abda, a table-companion of the King of Babylon," though Holy Scripture testifies that Daniel and the three [Hebrew] children were of the tribe of Judah.[90]

Jerome continues three lines later: "And I am surprised that certain fault-finders are indignant with me as if I have truncated the book."[91] This is indeed a much different answer from the one found in his *Apology Against Rufinus* 2, 33, given only five years before.

Jerome's loyalty to the tradition of the Church remained paramount in all of his endeavors, and many times accounts for his departure from the theories he evolved with regard to both biblical text and canon. His statement in Letter 119.11 written in 406, fourteen years before his death, sums up his commitment to Christian tradition:

> I made it my resolve to read all the men of old, to test their individual statements, to retain what was good in them, and not to depart from the faith of the Catholic Church.[92]

---

[88] See n. 77 above.

[89] Bel 1:2. See Chapter 4, n. 85.

[90] *PL* 25:492 = *CCSL* 75A, 773, 1. 55; 774, 1. 58. We find this repeated in his *Commentary on Daniel* 2:25: "And note that Daniel is of the sons of Judah, rather than being a priest as the story of Bel contains at the end." See Chapter 4, n. 87.

[91] *PL* 25:493 = *CCSL* 75A, 774, 1. 61-62.

[92] *PL* 22:980.

CHAPTER 4

JEROME'S *COMMENTARY ON DANIEL* 1:3

ויאמר המלך לאשפנז רב סריסיו להביא מבני ישראל ומזרע המלוכה ומן
הפרתמים . (דניאל א':ג')

And the king spoke unto Ashpenaz his chief officer, that he should bring in certain of the children of Israel, and of the seed royal, and of the nobles (Dan 1:3).

In Jerome's *Commentary on Daniel* 1:3 we find:

From this passage the Hebrews think that Daniel, Hananiah, Mishael and Azariah were eunuchs, thus fulfilling that prophecy which is spoken by the prophet Isaiah to Hezekiah: "And they shall take of thy seed and make them eunuchs in the house of the King [of Babylon]" (Isa 39:7). If, however, they were of the seed royal, there is no doubt but that they were of the line of David, unless by chance the following words are opposed to this interpretation: ". . . lads (or youths), in whom there was no blemish . . ." (Dan 1:4).[1]

The Tradition that Daniel, Hananiah, Mishael, and Azariah were Eunuchs

The rabbinic tradition that Daniel and his three associates were eunuchs is well known.[2] The midrash does look upon the captivity of Daniel and Hananiah (=H), Mishael (=M), and Azariah (=A) as the fulfillment of the verse cited by Jerome in the above passage, namely, Isa 39:7,[3] spoken by the prophet to King Hezekiah: "And of thy sons that shall issue from thee, whom thou shall beget, shall they [the Babylonians] take away; and they shall be eunuchs (סריסים) in the palace of the king of Babylon."[4]

---

[1]   *PL* 25:496 = *CCSL* 75A, 779, 11. 51-59.

[2]   It should be here noted that there exists a short resumé of sources in rabbinic and patristic literature on this topic compiled by S. Krauss in his article "The Jews in the Works of the Church Fathers." This served as the starting point for our investigation. There were, however, several mistakes in the references to various sources which we have corrected. We have also added many sources to his. We wish to note as well that the substance of Krauss' material was taken verbatim from a long footnote (no. 7) by P. D. Heut to Origen's *Commentary on Matthew* 15:5, *PG* 13:1264-6.

[3]   This verse is identical with 2 Kgs 20:18. The translation of Isa 39:7 in Jerome's *Commentary* was based on his Latin and therefore slightly varies from the Jewish Publication Society translation cited here.

[4]   A further link between Dan 1 and Isa 39 concerns the treasures taken by King Sennacherib from King Hezekiah. See Ginzberg, *Legends,* 4, 276; 2, 125-6; and 5, 361, n. 338.

In Sanhedrin 93b we find two traditions regarding the interpretation of "eunuchs" cited in the above verse. The interpretation of Rab (Abba Arika, Babylonian *amora,* d. 247 C.E.) is literal while Rab Ḥanina (Palestinian *amora,* d. *c.* 250 C.E.) gives a figurative view: idol worship was sterilized and became impotent in their days.[5] According to the second view, Daniel and his three associates were perfect in body as well as intellect. Rabbi Ḥama ben Ḥanina (Palestinian *amora* of the third century C.E.) substantiates this view by citing Dan 1:4, "in whom was no blemish" and remarking: "They did not even bear the scar made by bleeding."[6]

Jerome also cites this verse as opposed to the interpretation that Daniel and his associates were eunuchs.[7] He might possibly have been aware of this second tradition as well, although he does not mention it wherever else he quotes the "eunuch tradition." Nor does any other Church Father who is of the opinion that Daniel, H, M, and A were eunuchs mention this second view.

In the Jerusalem Talmud[8] we find a compromise view. After quoting Dan 3:25, "and there is no hurt in them,"[9] the Talmud states: "This teaches us that they [H, M, and A] had been eunuchs, but were healed" by passage through the fiery furnace. This would pertain only to H, M, and A since only they, and not Daniel, went through the furnace. It is interesting to note that while we have no rabbinic traditions that Daniel had any children, we do have a tradition that after emerging from the furnace, H, M, and A "went up to the Land of Israel, married and begat sons and daughters."[10] This could very well be an extension of the view in the Jerusalem Talmud which also involved H, M, and A only.

There is no doubt, however, that the dominant tradition in rabbinic

---

[5] The figurative interpretation can be better understood when compared with several midrashic statements in Song of Songs Rabbah, according to which the deliverance of H, M, and A from the fiery furnace (Dan 3:26-30) had a great effect upon the heathens. In Song of Songs Rabbah 7:8, we find, according to the Rabbis, that through them the evil impulse in man to worship idols was uprooted. A long account of their heroism is given there. In Song of Songs Rabbah 7:9 we find that on this occasion the heathens "took their idols and broke them, and made them into bells." Song of Songs Rabbah 1:15, and 4:1, its parallel, credits them with influencing many heathens to convert on this occasion.

[6] Sanhedrin 93b.

[7] Among the classical Hebrew commentators, only Abraham ibn Ezra (d. 1167) in his commentary on Dan 1:3 opposes the view that Daniel, H, M, and A were eunuchs, since "there is no blemish worse than castration" and Dan 1:4 explicitly states that they had "no blemish."

[8] Shabbat, ch. 6, halacha 9, end = Krotoshin, 8d.

[9] This verse is also quoted in Sanhedrin 93b with a more literal explanation given, namely, that they had not been hurt by the fire.

[10] Sanhedrin 93a, with parallels in Yalḳuṭ, Zechariah, 570, and Yalḳuṭ, Daniel, 1060.

literature is that Daniel and his associates were literally eunuchs.[11] Sanhedrin 93b[12] identifies the "eunuchs who observe my Sabbaths" in Isa 56:4-5 with Daniel,[13] H, M, and A. Although the Talmud tries to interpret the verse according to both the literal and figurative traditions cited above, the literal interpretation is less forced. Indeed Pirké de Rabbi Eliezer,[14] after citing Isa 39:7 states: "These were H, M and A, who were made eunuchs in the palace of the king of Babylon, and they did not beget children. Concerning them the Scripture says, 'For thus saith the Lord to the eunuchs, etc.'" (Isa 56:4, 5).[15]

Another tradition which indicates that Daniel was a eunuch is to be found in the Targum to Esth 4:5 where the eunuch Hathach is identified with Daniel. Midrash Megillah,[16] after identifying Hathach with Daniel, gives the following as one explanation why he was called Hathach:[17]

---

[11] We wish here to take issue with S. Krauss in his article "The Jews in the Works of the Church Fathers," 156, where he cited Rab's view in Sanhedrin 93b "from which we see that this [eunuch] tradition did not survive in the popular consciousness, it is stated as simply an individual opinion." It is difficult to understand this deduction. Both views, the literal and figurative ones, are stated in Sanhedrin 93b as the individual opinions of Rab and Rab Ḥanina. Certainly the literal one is much more frequent in rabbinic literature. Cf. nn. 12, 13, 14.

[12] So does Seder Eliyahu Rabba, ed. Friedmann, ch. 26, p. 131. Daniel's name does not appear here. This is in apparent agreement with the Jerusalem Talmud (above n. 8), according to which only H, M, and A were eunuchs.

[13] Furthermore, the "everlasting memorial" which God promises to these faithful eunuchs is interpreted in Sanhedrin 93b as the Book of Daniel, named after its hero.

[14] Translated and annotated by Gerald Friedlander, ch. 52, end, 426-427.

[15] Note that the manuscript which Friedlander used, claiming it to be more reliable than the *editio princeps,* did not list the name "Daniel" among the eunuchs, although it was inserted in the first editions (Friedlander, ibid., 427, n. 1). "Daniel" is also missing in MS. Casan, published by Higger in *Horeb* 10 (1948) 250.

[16] Published from a tenth century manuscript by M. Gaster in *Semitic Studies in Memory of Alexander Kohut* (ed., G. A. Kohut; Berlin: S. Calvary & Co., 1897) 176. Reprinted by J. D. Eisenstein in *Ozar Midrashim* 1 (New York, 1915) 60. Gaster claims (p. 169) that his text is "probably the oldest form of the Midrash to Esther following upon the close of the Talmud, and based . . . exclusively on it."

[17] All explanations of the name Hathach in rabbinic literature derive from חתך, to cut off or decide. In Midrash Megillah we find three explanations: the first, cited above, has no parallel in other midrashim; the second, that all the affairs of state were "decided" by his word; the third, that through his word decrees were "decided" against the — [lacuna in Gaster's manuscript]. We find two parallels to this in Talmud: Megillah 15a and Baba Bathra 4a. Each gives the same two explanations for the name: the first, identical to the second above (affairs of state "decided"); the second, because he was "cut off" by Ahasuerus from the important position he had held under the former king. In another parallel, the Targum to Esth 4:5, we find the explanation that he "decided" the affairs of the state. In Esther Rabbah 8:4 we find two explanations: the first, that he was "cut off" from the position; the second, that he "decided" the affairs of the state.

He cut out his masculinity in the time of the evil Nebuchadnezzar, he and his friends H, M, and A, at the time when the enemies of Israel informed upon them and told Nebuchadnezzar: "those Jews which you brought are committing fornication with the maidservants of the king and the wives of the princes." As soon as Daniel and his friends H, M, and A heard this, they cut out their masculinity, as it is written: "Thus saith the Lord to the eunuchs, etc." (Isa 56:4).

This is the only source in rabbinic literature which refers to Daniel and his friends castrating themselves. This tradition could very well be related to the Jewish interpretation of "the side of the king" (מצד מלכותא) in Dan 6:5, quoted in Jerome's *Commentary on Daniel* 6:4:[18]

And in this passage the Hebrews suspect some such [meaning] as this: "the 'side of the king' is the queen or his concubines and the other wives who slept at his side. Therefore, they were seeking a pretext in things of this sort, to see whether they could accuse Daniel in his speech or touch or nodding [of his head] or sense-organ. But, they say, they could find no cause for suspicion, since he was a eunuch and they could not even accuse him on the score of lewdness."[19]

This Jewish interpretation cited by Jerome cannot be found in extant rabbinic literature. However, the above citation from Midrash Megillah, wherein Daniel and his friends subjected *themselves* to castration in order to remove suspicions of immorality, could have a common origin with Jerome's tradition.

In Josephus (*Antiquities* 10.186-187) we find a clear paraphrasing of the biblical account in the opening verses of Daniel. Speaking of the Jewish youths whom Nebuchadnezzar took with him, Josephus states: "making *some* of them eunuchs"[20] (italics mine). Note that Josephus never states clearly that Daniel and his friends were among those who were eunuchs, although he certainly had his opportunity to mention this specifically. His statement that some were made eunuchs has no direct basis in Jewish tradition,[21] and does not make it certain that Daniel and H, M, and A were

---

[18] *PL* 25:658=*CCSL* 75A, 830, 1. 256; 831, 1. 262. The tradition cited by Jerome is certainly closer than any of the "remote . . . but by no means similar" parallels cited by Gaster, 169: Sanhedrin 93b, Pirḳé de Rabbi Eliezer 52, end (see n. 14), and Yalḳuṭ Machiri *ad loc.,* p. 213.

[19] For a further discussion of this comment, see Chapter 8.

[20] Translation by Ralph Marcus, 261. The Niese edition of Josephus shows no textual variants at this point.

[21] In Sanhedrin 93b there is a parallel of which Josephus could perhaps have been aware. An anonymous interpretation is there given that among those who were exiled to Babylonia, *some* were actually castrated ("literal eunuchs") and *others* lived to see idolatry rendered impotent ("figurative eunuchs").

among those who were made eunuchs. Nor does it contradict the tradition that they castrated themselves, but by providing another explanation for the eunuchs it makes that story unnecessary.

The earliest record of this tradition in patristic literature[22] is found in Origen's writings.[23] In his *Commentary on Matthew* 15:5[24] we find:

> [Concerning] Daniel also, and the three boys with him, H, A, and M, the sons of the Hebrews hand down a tradition that they had been castrated in Babylon. That prophecy having been completed from Isaiah to Hezekiah "And of thy sons . . . shall they take away and they shall be eunuchs in the palace of the king of Babylon" (Isa 39:7). And it was concerning them that Isaiah prophesied, asserting "Neither let the alien, etc." (Isa 56:3), and the rest, up to this point: "better than sons and daughters" (Isa 56:5).

Origen therefore was not only aware of the tradition itself, but also of the connections with Isa 39:7, and of Isa 56:3-5, as cited in Pirḳé de Rabbi Eliezer.

Origen again refers to this tradition in *Catena Regia in Prophetas* to Ezek 14:16,[25] "For he [Daniel] did not have sons of the flesh since he was a eunuch, as they say, and it is manifest from this: because he was handed over to the leader of the eunuchs." Here Origen does not mention the Hebrews as the source. He also omits the exegetically coupled texts of Isa 39:7 and 56:4,5. Instead he offers another "proof" for Daniel being a eunuch: He was handed over to Ashpenaz, the chief eunuch, for his education at the court.[26] This point is not found in rabbinic traditions and seems to be original with Origen.

Origen mentions the tradition once more in his *Homily 4 on Ezekiel.*[27] He identifies the Daniel mentioned together with Job and Noah in Ezek 14:14ff. as identical with the famous Daniel.

> Daniel who was handed over to the leader of the eunuchs with H, A, and M, was a eunuch, and he was spoken of in the present passage: "They will not liberate the sons and daughters of Noah, Daniel and Job, etc." (Ezek 14:16).

---

[22] The first extant patristic commentator on Daniel, Hippolytus of Rome, who wrote his commentary *c.* 202, is silent concerning this tradition.

[23] Eusebius (*Historia Ecclesiastica* 6, 8) notes that Origen, in his youth (*c.* 202), took literally the words ". . . some have made themsevles eunuchs for the sake of the kingdom of heaven. . . ." (Mt 19:12) and emasculated himself. This should be kept in mind while analyzing his references to the tradition that Daniel was a eunuch.

[24] *PG* 13:1263-5.

[25] *PG* 13:808.

[26] Dan 1:3.

[27] *PG* 13:700-701. This is one of a group of homilies by Origen lost in the original Greek but preserved in Latin translation by Jerome.

Indeed let us imagine that Noah had sons, how will sons of Daniel be explained, who, according to Jewish tradition, was a eunuch? But . . . his spirit was fertile and holy and he procreated many children with prophetic and divine sermons.

Origen here expresses a problem to which parallels can not be found in rabbinic literature, although the identification of the Daniel in Ezek 14:14 with the famous Daniel is discussed there, as will soon be shown. His answer that Daniel "procreated many children with prophetic and divine sermons" reminds us of a statement in Sanhedrin 93b. After citing the verse referring to God's promise to the "eunuchs who keep my Sabbaths": "I will give in My house . . . a monument . . . better than sons and daughters; I will give them an everlasting memorial that shall not be cut off" (Isa 56:5), the Talmud then states: "This alludes to the Book of Daniel which was named after him."

Near the end of this same homily[28] Origen reports another Hebrew tradition regarding Noah, Daniel, and Job in Ezek 14:14 which is worth citing in full in order to compare it with similar rabbinic statements.

I once heard from a certain Hebrew expounding and declaring this passage that these [Noah, Daniel, and Job] were named for this reason: because each one of them saw three periods, a happy, a sad, and again a happy one. See Noah before the flood, consider the whole world; and the same one, Noah, afterwards in the shipwreck of the whole universe when he alone was saved with his sons and the animals in the Ark, consider how he went out after the flood and planted a vineyard, how again he became the creator of a second world. Such is the just man; he saw the world before the flood, that is before the consummation; he saw the world in the flood, in corruption and in the destruction of sinners which will come about on the day of judgment. Again he will see the world in the resurrection of all sinners.

Someone says to me: I grant you about Noah that he saw three times: what will you answer to me about Daniel? And he flourished before the captivity in the nobility of his fatherland, and then having been carried away to Babylon, he was made a eunuch as it is clearly able to be understood from his own book; he saw also the return to Jerusalem. Now, in order that it may be proved that he was before the captivity in Jerusalem, and after the captivity was made a eunuch, let us cite this, which was said to Hezekiah: "They shall take of thy sons and make them eunuchs in the house of the king" (Isa 39:7). Then after seventy years, he is found praying to God so that, the time of captivity having been completed now, he may enter Jerusalem.[29] We have his speech written in

---

[28] *Homily 4 on Ezekiel, PG* 13:703-4. Note that although Ginzberg cites this homily (vol. 5, p. 384, n. 14) he omits the passage cited above and does not draw any parallels from it to rabbinic literature.

[29] Dan 9:3-19.

his own volume; nevertheless we are not able to find where he died. Therefore he saw three times, before the captivity, in the captivity, and after the captivity. Such is the just man.

Now, let us see whether Job also had three times. Indeed, he was rich: indeed, he had seven thousand sheep, three thousand camels, five hundred yoke of oxen and very much furniture, seven sons, three daughters. Then the devil received power against him. See the changed times. The father, rich in children, suddenly is made childless; the master, rich in property, is reduced to the greatest poverty. Behold two times. After this the Lord appears to him, and speaks to him from a cloud, and Job himself replied those things which have been written in his book.

Therefore, in the first [period of] time, he is extolled by the praises of God; in the second, he is handed over to a trial, and, having been smitten by a very cruel sore, he endures sad and hard things from his feet up to his head. At the end his sheep have become fourteen thousand, the camels six thousand, the yoke of oxen a thousand, the pasturing she-asses a thousand, and there are born to him seven sons and daughters. And thus also in Job we discover the three times which we find in just men.

In reading this lengthy exegetical homily, we are first confronted with a basic question: how much of it is the exposition of the Hebrew, and how much is Origen's?[30] The statement preceding the explanation of Daniel's three periods, "Someone says to me: I grant you about Noah etc.," does not necessarily mean that this is a real quotation, for it may be only rhetorical substitution of the first person. A second question which confronts us is even more difficult to answer: how much of the *Jew's* explanation represented tradition, and how much was his personal exegesis? Analysis of extant parallel rabbinic texts will not yield a definitive answer, for the full exposition of the Jew may be a tradition of which we presently have no written record. With these questions and limitations in mind, let us present all relevant Jewish midrashic material.

The rabbis asked why Noah, Daniel, and Job were mentioned together in Ezek 14:14.[31] In one source we find a striking resemblance to Origen's

---

[30] There is no doubt that the last sentence of the homily, which immediately follows the long passage cited above, is Origen's own conclusion: "Just men see three times: the present, and a time of change, when God is going to judge, and the future after the resurrection of the dead, that is, the everlastingness of heavenly life in Jesus Christ, to whom is the glory and the empire forever and ever. Amen."

[31] They also assumed that the Daniel there was identical with the famous one, despite a slight difference in the spelling and vocalization of the name: דָּנִאֵל in Ezekiel; דָּנִיֵּאל in Daniel. We do find a contact between Daniel and Ezekiel in midrashic tradition. In Song of Songs Rabbah 7:8 (referred to previously in note 5), H, M, and A, upon being ordered by Nebuchadnezzar to worship the idol which he had constructed (Dan 3), asked Daniel for advice whether to bow down to it, or refuse and subject themselves to martyrdom. Daniel referred

homily cited above. After citing Ezek 14:14 the midrash[32] continues:

Why are these three mentioned out of all the prophets?[33] Because each one of them saw three worlds. Noah saw an established world, a destroyed one, and an established one. Job saw his house built, torn down and built. Daniel saw the [First] Temple established, desolate, and [the Second Temple] established. Therefore these names were mentioned in one verse.[34]

We are now prepared to compare Origen's homily with the above Jewish

---

them to Ezekiel, saying: "Here is the prophet within reach, go and consult him." (This in accordance with the view in Sanhedrin 94a and Megillan 3a that Daniel was not a prophet.) Ezekiel could thus have been aware of Daniel's wisdom. He cited Daniel's name again speaking to the prince of Tyre: "Behold, thou art wiser than Daniel" (Ezek 28:3). Modern exegesis does not identify the "Daniel" of the Book of Ezekiel with our Daniel, but rather with a Daniel, father of Aqhat, the hero of a Ugaritic legend. A bibliography of modern archeological findings on this point may be found in Robert de Langhe, *Les textes de Ras Shamra — Ugarit* 1, 165. For a thorough discussion and evaluation of modern research concerning this point see Shalom Spiegel, "Noah, Daniel and Job."

[32] *Midrash Version to the Pentateuch* found in the MS belonging to the Jewish Theological Seminary, edited by Jacob Mann in *The Bible as Read and Preached in the Old Synagogue,* Hebrew part, 151.

[33] Note that this midrash considers Daniel a prophet, as do other Palestinian sources, tannaitic as well as amoraic, cited in Ginzberg, *Legends,* 6, 413, n. 76. Cf. Chapter 3, n. 73. It should be noted, however, that in the Hebrew scriptural canon, Daniel is not found among the Prophets but in the Hagiographa. In the Christian canon, the opposite is the case. Josephus refers to Daniel not only as a prophet (*Antiquities* 10.249) but an unusual one in various respects (*Antiquities* 10.266-269). In Mt 24:15 he is referred to as "Daniel the prophet." The Dead Sea Scroll text 4Q174, after referring to "The book of Isaiah the prophet," and "The book of Ezekiel the prophet," later notes "as it is written in the book of Daniel the prophet" and quotes from Dan 12:10 and 11:32 (J. Allegro, ed., *Discoveries in the Judean Desert of Jordan* 5, Qumran Cave 4, I [Oxford, 1968] 54, col. 2, 1.3). According to J. Strugnell, "Notes en marge du volume 5 des *Discoveries in the Judean Desert of Jordan," RQ* 7 (1970) 177, 220, this manuscript is pre-Christian.

[34] There are many parallels to the above in midrashic tradition, but none are identical to it in structure. The main differences concern the starting point of the homily. Some begin with the exegetical problem why the name "Noah" is mentioned three times in Gen 6:9, and then go on to show that Noah was one of three who saw three worlds: Noah, Daniel, and Job (Tanḥuma Noah, 5; Yalḳut, Noah 50; Excerpts from Midrash Avkir [ed. Buber; Vienna, 1887] 4, no. 8.; Midrash Hagadol on Genesis [ed. Margolioth; Jerusalem, 1947] 152). The Yelammedenu passage no. 29 excerpted by Mann, *The Bible,* Hebrew part, 282, from Yalḳut Talmud Torah by Jacob Sikili, begins with the same problem, but answers it more logically than the above sources by stating that Noah *himself* experienced three stages of the world; likewise have Daniel and Job. Another group of parallels are less similar to the one cited in the text above, although they clearly show us the Noah-Daniel-Job tradition upon a changed but wider background. Rabbi Levi states that all those in connection with whom the text used the verb "was" lived to see a new world; Rabbi Samuel ben Naḥman pointed out that there are five such: Noah, Joseph, Moses, Job, and Mordecai (Genesis Rabbah 30:8; Esther Rabbah 6:3; Tanḥuma [ed. Buber], *Noah,* 180).Note the absence of Daniel's name in this list.

sources and its parallels. Certainly the basic point of the "three periods" or "three worlds" is identical. With regard to the exact three worlds that each one saw we have variations within Jewish tradition as well as between Jewish tradition and Origen. Origen points out that Noah's three periods were before, during, and after the flood. Such is the explanation in all rabbinic sources. Origen explains Daniel's three periods as before the captivity,[35] during the captivity when he was made a eunuch, and after the seventy years when he "saw the return to Jerusalem" although "we are not able to find where he died." Three rabbinic sources[36] refer to his three worlds as the era of the First Temple, its destruction, and the establishment of the Second Temple. A fourth source refers to "the settlement of Jerusalem, its destruction, and its [re] settlement."[37] Origen explains Job's three periods as when he was rich, had children, and was extolled by the praises of God; then when he became childless, poor and was tested through bodily affliction; and then when he became rich again and blessed with children. Four rabbinic sources[38] refer to his three worlds as when his house was built, destroyed and rebuilt. A fifth[39] refers to when "he was perfect, he was tried through trials, and afterwards he was healed."

It seems therefore, that on the basis of available rabbinic sources, Origen closely followed the outlines of the Noah — Job — Daniel rabbinic tradition in his lengthy homily, but filled in these outlines with his own extended explanations suitable for didactic homiletics. It is interesting to note that even in these extended explanations Origen makes use of other related Jewish traditions. In explaining the period of captivity in Daniel's life, he is in accord with the rabbinic tradition that he was made a eunuch and, like the rabbis, gives the supporting text of Isaiah 39:7. Regarding Daniel's third period after the captivity, Origen correctly states that in the Book of Daniel "we are not able to find where he died." A few lines earlier, however, Origen writes that "he saw also the return to Jerusalem." The rabbinic parallels on this point refer either to the establishment of the Second Temple[40] or the resettlement of Jerusalem.[41] Here again it seems that in the

---

[35] Origen, as a Christian, would tend to downgrade the importance of the physical Temple and thus depart from the description of the "three worlds" that we find in the three rabbinic sources cited below. It is also possible that Origen based his remarks on the fourth tradition found in Midrash Hagadol (cf. n. 37).

[36] *Midrash Version to the Pentateuch,* cited in the text above; Tanḥuma Noah and Yelammedenu passage no. 29 excerpted by Mann, both cited in n. 34.

[37] Midrash Hagadol, Genesis, 152.

[38] Cited in nn. 36 and 37.

[39] Tanḥuma (ed. Buber, Noah, 180.

[40] See n. 36.

[41] See n. 37.

absence of biblical statement[42] Origen relies on rabbinic tradition. In Song of Songs Rabbah 5:5 we find "Daniel and his associates and his company went up [to Judea] at that time" [when Cyrus issued his declaration to the Jews granting them permission to return from Exile] (Ezra 1:1ff.). Probably the tradition that Daniel returned and was present when the Second Temple was built is based upon his identification with Sheshbazzar[43] (= Zerubbabel)[44] who led the Jewish exiles back to Judea,[45] was appointed governor by Cyrus,[46] and indeed laid the foundations of the Second Temple as stated in Ezra 5:16.[47] Thus the "eunuch tradition" as seen in the works of Origen is involved with other traditions concerning Daniel that are basically Jewish.

The next Church Father who refers to this tradition is Jerome himself. In addition to his *Commentary on Daniel* 1:3 quoted above, Jerome in several other works mentions that Daniel and his associates were eunuchs. In analyzing his statements we must bear in mind that he was acquainted with Jewish traditions from three possible sources: his Jewish teachers and certain Hebrew manuscripts; Josephus' writings;[48] and the writings of other Church Fathers who preceded him, especially Origen.[49]

The first time that Jerome mentioned this tradition was in 381,[50] when he translated fourteen homilies of Origen on *Ezekiel* including No. 4, which contains the lengthy reference to Daniel quoted above.

[42] The only verse in the Book of Daniel which intimates that he may have returned to Jerusalem is Dan 1:21: "And Daniel continued even unto the first year of King Cyrus." This certainly was not the year of Daniel's death, since we have a vision of his, recorded in Dan 10:1ff., which took place in Cyrus' third year. Therefore, it might be implied from Dan 1:21 that Daniel returned to Judea with his fellow Jews after Cyrus' declaration (Ezra 1:1ff.). It must be admitted, however, that none of the extant rabbinic traditions concerning Daniel's return to Judea cite Dan 1:21.

[43] Pesiḳta Rabbati, ch. 6, sec. 3 (ed. Friedmann; Vienna, 1880; 23b) with a parallel in Yalḳuṭ, Ezra, 1068.

[44] Ezra 2:2. See comment of Ibn Ezra to Ezra 1:8 where he identifies Sheshbazzar with Zerubabel.

[45] Ezra 1:8, 11.

[46] Ezra 5:14.

[47] This hypothesis is strengthened by the assumption made in Sanhedrin 93b that Daniel was a governor of Judea prior to Nehemiah, since the Talmud claims that Neh 5:15 ("But the former governors that were before me laid burdens upon the people, etc.") refers, among others, to Daniel.

[48] Philo, who usually must be carefully studied when analyzing Jewish traditions found in the Church Fathers, does not refer to the Book of Daniel.

[49] In the case at hand, excepting Origen, other Church Fathers before Jerome whose works are extant today are silent on this matter.

[50] Berthold Altaner, *Patrology,* 469.

Next we find mention of this in *Adversus Jovinianum* 1.25[51] written in 393:[52]

It is superfluous, however, to speak about Daniel since the Hebrews, up to the present day, declare that both he and the three boys were eunuchs, drawing the proof from that sentence of God which Isaiah speaks to Hezekiah, "And of your sons that shall issue from you shall they take away and they shall make them eunuchs in the house of the king" (Isa 39:7). And again we read in Daniel, "And the king spoke unto Ashpenaz, the chief of the eunuchs, that he should bring in certain of the children of the captivity of Israel . . . knowing wisdom" (Dan 1:3,4). And they argue that if Daniel and the three boys were chosen from the royal seed (Dan 1:3) and if Scripture predicted that there would be eunuchs from the royal seed (Isa 39:7), these men were those who were made eunuchs. If indeed one would oppose [the view that Daniel was a eunuch with] that which is said in Ezekiel (14:14ff.) [that] Noah, Daniel, and Job in a sinning land were not able to liberate sons and daughters, it must be answered that it was stated according to a hypothesis. For Noah and Job were not in existence at that time; we know that they lived many generations before. And this is the sense: If such and such men would have lived in a sinning land, they would not be able to liberate their own sons and daughters; because the righteousness of the father will not liberate the son; nor will the sin of one be imputed to the other. "For the soul which will have sinned, it itself will die" (Ezek 18:4). But this too must be stated, that Daniel, according to the history of his book, was captured with King Joachim[53] at that time when Ezekiel also

---

[51] *PL* 23:244-245.

[52] Altaner, 470.

[53] Dan 1:1 has Johoiakim. Jerome is guilty here of falling into a trap which he himself later clearly warned against in his *Commentary on Daniel* 1:1 "Joacim [= Jehoiakim = יהויקים, 2 Kgs 23:34, 2 Chr 36:5] son of Josia [Josiah] . . . reigned over the tribes of Judah and Jerusalem eleven years. His son Joiachin [= Jehoiachin = יהויכין, 2 Kgs 24:6 and 2 Chr 36:8. Migne's text has the obvious misprint 'Joachim' which is corrected in *CCSL* 75A, 776, 1.7 as 'Joiachin'] surnamed Jechonias [= Jechoniah of Esth 2:6], followed him in the kingship. . . . Let no one therefore imagine that the Joacim [= Jehoiakim] in the beginning of Daniel is the same person as the one who is spelled Joiachin [= Jehoiachin] in the commencement of *Ezekiel*. For the latter has 'chin' as its final syllable, whereas the former has 'cim.'" In the above passage from *Adversus Jovinianum* (written fourteen years before his *Commentary on Daniel*) Jerome made just that mistake! He assumed that Ezekiel was led into captivity with Daniel, together with King Joachim (= Jehoiakim), and quotes Ezek 8:1 as referring to this same "Joachim," when it clearly refers to the exile of Jehoiachin, as do all the dates of the prophecies in Ezekiel, beginning with 1:2, the superscription of the entire book. The mistake here is definitely not due to an error in the text of *Adversus Jovinianum* since the whole argument that Daniel was still a boy when Ezekiel referred to him is based on this assumption, that they were exiled under the same Judean king. Why then did Jerome make this mistake in *Adversus Jovinianum* (written in 393) and what prompted him to correct it in *Commentary on Daniel* (written in 407)? See above in Chapter 3 the circumstances which led to the production of the Vulgate. It is evident that when he wrote *Adversus Jovinianum*, Jerome had not yet

was led into captivity.[54] How, therefore, was he able to have sons, who was

---

composed a reliable text of Ezekiel, and so whatever text he did use was undoubtedly based on the LXX. "The Christian tradition following the unfortunate identification by the LXX of the names Jehoiakim and Jehoiachin as *Ioakeim* (2 Kgs 23:36-24:1) blundered through the royal succession of this age [2 Kgs 24:6, where the names of *both* these kings occur, has the identical name for both kings, although the death of one and the accession of the other, his son, is clearly indicated. This is indeed the most striking example of this confusion]. Mt 1:10ff. identifies the two under *Iechonias* despite Jerome's argument against Porphyry that two kings are required here (*Commentary on Daniel* 1:1)." Cf. Montgomery, *Daniel,* 115. A few lines later we find regarding Jerome's *Commentary on Daniel* 1:1: "Jerome gives to both kings the one and the same name Ioacim, but is obscure as to his deductions." It is hard to understand how Montgomery concluded thus, as Jerome seems very clear on this point, unless confusion arose because of the misprint discussed above. Hippolytus, the first patristic commentator on Daniel, in his *Commentary on Daniel* 1:2 also confuses Jehoiakim with Jehoiachin. And so, it was not until Jerome established his Vulgate Latin text, which was certainly completed by 407, the year the *Commentary on Daniel* was written, that he detected this gross error and warned others about it.

[54] It should here be noted that although there is no specific verse in Ezekiel that states he was exiled with King Jehoiachin, internal evidence from the book overwhelmingly leads us to this conclusion: the superscription of the book 1:2, specifically states "the fifth year of king Jehoiachin's captivity," and the prophecies which are dated, although not mentioning Jehoiachin, assume his captivity. After giving two dates in 33:21 and 40:1, Ezekiel refers to "our exile," thus certainly identifying himself with Jehoiachin. The only ancient source that stands in opposition to this conclusion is Josephus, *Antiquities* 10:98, where he states that Ezekiel was included in the exile of Jehoiakim. It is interesting to note that in Niese's edition of Josephus 2, p. 351, l. 9, two variants are noted as follows: in the margin of manuscript L we find *Iechonia* and manuscript V has *Iechonias*. However, the Latin Josephus has *Ioachim*. [Ginzberg, *Legends* 6, 380, n. 132 cites two rabbinic sources which, contrary to the majority of Jewish sources, consider the "exile of the scholars" to have taken place during the reign of Jehoiakim, but these do not mention Ezekiel, as does Josephus.] To add to the problem Josephus fails to mention Daniel and his associates in *Antiquities* 10.98 who, we know from Dan 1:1, were definitely in this exile. Moreover, in *Antiquities* 10.186 ff., where Josephus discusses the history of Daniel, no reference to the period of his exile is given at all — only the ambiguous "Nebuchadnezzar, the Babylonian king, took the Jewish youths of noblest birth and the relatives of their king Sacchias [= Zedekiah]. . . ." In fact, if we follow the chronological order of Josephus' chapters, this deportation occurred after the fall of Jerusalem, well after the exiles of Jehoiakim, Jehoiachin, and Zedekiah. Even if one may argue that Josephus is not chronological in this respect and could very well assume that Daniel was taken captive in an earlier exile under King Jehoiakim, why then does Josephus refer to Zedekiah as "their king"? He was certainly not king during the exile of Jehoiakim, being appointed by Nebuchadnezzar after the exile of Jehoiachin. If Josephus assumed the deportation of Daniel to have taken place together with Jehoiachin, he would have certainly mentioned *this* king's name as "their king." Thus it seems that Josephus believes Daniel's exile to have taken place at the end of the reign of Zedekiah. This may be the reason that Josephus, alone again among all ancient sources, mentions the young deportees as relatives of Zedekiah. (See n. 74.) But it can be clearly shown that Jerome could not have accepted the tradition of Josephus, for if he had, then his subsequent proof from Ezek 8:1, which refers definitely to King Jehoiachin would contradict his earlier point.

still a boy? And when three years had been completed he was led in to serve the king. And lest anyone think that Ezekiel mentioned Daniel when the latter was already a man and not a boy, "it took place," he says, "in the sixth year," that is, of King Joachim, "in the sixth month, on the fifth of the month." And, "I was sitting in my house, and the old men of Judah were sitting in my presence" (Ezek 8:1). And on the same day it was said to him, "if Noah and Daniel and Job will have been [etc.]" (Ezek 14:14). Therefore Daniel was still a boy, and known to the people either because of his interpretation of the dreams of the king, or because of the freeing of Susanna and the slaying of the elders.[55] And it is clearly proved that at that time when these things were being said about Noah and Daniel and Job, Daniel was still a boy, and could not have had sons and daughters whom he might liberate by his righteousness. Thus far concerning the Law.

In this passage Jerome quotes Isa 39:7 and links it to Dan 1:3, a connection found both in rabbinic sources and in Origen. The problem he raises concerning the "sons and daughters" of Daniel in Ezek 14:16 is indeed raised by Origen in *Homily 4 on Ezekiel,*[56] but Jerome gives a different solution: instead of interpreting the "children" figuratively, as does Origen, Jerome takes a practical historical approach[57] to show that when Ezekiel prophesied concerning Noah, Daniel, and Job, "Daniel was still a boy and could not have had sons and daughters." The reference in Ezek 14:16 to sons and daughters "was stated according to a hypothesis," i.e., if each had children at that time, they could not have liberated them from the desolation of the land.

The next time Jerome mentioned the "eunuch tradition" was in his *Commentary on Daniel* 1:3 (written in 407) quoted at the head of this Chapter. The link, Isa 39:7, is there given. In 408-410 Jerome wrote his *Commentary on Isaiah* and there we find in 11.39 on Isa 39:7, after citing

---

[55] According to the apocryphal Book of Susannah which has no parallel in rabbinic sources. See Ginzberg, *Legends* 6, 415, n. 79. See also n. 31 for contact between Daniel and Ezekiel in midrashic tradition.

[56] Quoted above, cf. n. 27. This problem is not found in rabbinic literature.

[57] It is interesting to note that 393, the same year that Jerome wrote *Adversus Jovinianum,* marks the beginning of his involvement in the "so-called 'first Origenist Controversy' which led to the ugly quarrel with Bishop John of Jerusalem and especially with Rufinus, the friend of his youth" (Altaner, *Patrology,* 464). "It is sometimes asserted that, on account of this controversy, the year 393 forms an important turning point in Jerome's attitude toward the great Alexandrian theologian. It is true that his ardent admiration for Origen's exegetical writings did cool off considerably during this period of his life. No doubt the anti-Origenist controversy had something to do with this. But this point can be easily exaggerated" (Louis F. Hartmann, "St. Jerome as an Exegete," 46). It would probably be an exaggeration to conjecture that this controversy was connected with the departure from Origen's exegesis cited above.

the verse: "From which the Hebrews wish to say that Daniel, Hananiah, Mishael, and Azariah, who were of the royal seed, were made eunuchs, who, there is no doubt, were in the service of King Nabuchodonosor."[58] These exhaust the references to this tradition from Jerome. One should note that not once did he refer to the other text of Isa 56:3,4, linked to this tradition in rabbinic sources, and cited in Origen's *Commentary on Matthew* 15:5.

Next in patristic sources we find mention of this tradition, including the connection with Isa 39:7, in the *Commentary on Daniel* of Theodoret (393-457):[59]

And nevertheless here [in Dan 1:3] the prophecy of Isaiah which he foretold to King Hezekiah, is fulfilled: "Thus Isaiah said to Hezekiah '. . . and they shall be made eunuchs in the house of the king of Babylonians' " [Isa 39:7].

Later patristic traditions puts stress on Daniel's chastity rather than accept the rabbinic tradition that he was a eunuch. Pseudo-Epiphanius writes: "And he was a temperate man so that it seemed to the Jews that he was a eunuch."[60] The *Chronicum Alexandrinum*[61] cites this verbatim. And lastly St. John Damascene (*c.* 657-749) writes: "And what about the three children [H, M, and A]? Was it not by practising virginity that they became stronger than the fire, because by virginity their bodies had become impregnable to fire? Was there not a Daniel whose body the teeth of the wild beasts could not penetrate, because it had been hardened by virginity?"[62]

The Genealogy of Daniel, Hananiah, Mishael and Azariah

It seems evident from Dan 1:6, "Now among these [captive children] were, of the children of Judah, Daniel, Hananiah, Mishael, and Azariah," that Daniel and his friends were of the tribe of Judah. There are various

---

[58] *PL* 24 (1845):399 (paragraph 479).

[59] *PG* 81 (1864):1274 (paragraph 1068-9).

[60] *De Vitis Prophetarum* 10; cf. Theodor Schermann in *Prophetarum Vitae Fabulosae,* 14. Concerning this work, Johannes Quasten, *Patrology 3,* 396, says: "The legends of prophets go back to a Jewish source with various additions by Christians of the third and fourth century." Schermann gives four recensions of the work in his text. The one cited above is from the earliest recension; the other three are identical. Cf. C.C. Torrey, *The Lives of the Prophets* JBL MS 1; 1946) 24. Torrey claims that his emended text, based on "text Q," is "very near to the text of the original Greek translation (p. 12)."

[61] Author unknown. Printed in *Maxima Bibliotheca Veterum Patrum* 12 (1677) 912.

[62] St. John of Damascus, *The Orthodox Faith,* ch. 24, in *Writings* tr. by Chase, 395. Note that the views concerning H, M, and A are the very opposite of the view in the Jerusalem Talmud, Shabbat 8d, cited in n. 8.

midrashic traditions to this effect as well.[63] Beginning with the sources of his earliest ancestry, we find Daniel, listed after Judah and David, as one of three descendants of the matriarch Leah.[64] Then we find another clear midrashic tradition with many parallels that Daniel and his three associates descended from Judah.[65] Again we find a direct statement that Daniel stemmed from Judah, who was compared to a lion in Jacob's blessing (Gen 49:9); it is thus fitting that through Daniel's hands, Babylonia, the kingdom of the lion (Dan 7:4), fell.[66] None of the above sources refer to Dan 1:6, but simply state the genealogy of Daniel, H, M, and A. There is, however, one opinion in Sanhedrin 93b that although Daniel was from Judah, H, M, and A were of other tribes.[67] We find no parallel to this view in the rest of rabbinic literature.[68]

The midrash further points out that Daniel, H, M, and A were of royal blood.[69] Combining Dan 1:3 and Isa 39:7, Jewish tradition further specifies

[63] Perhaps the midrash saw fit to stress the genealogy of Daniel from the tribe of Judah to differentiate him from Daniel the priest mentioned in Neh 10:7 and Ezra 8:2. See below.

[64] Genesis Rabbah 71:5, with parallels and variants in Tanḥuma Vayetze, 6; Yalḳuṭ, Genesis, 126 and Job 920; Leḳah Tob. Genesis (ed. Buber, 1884) 29:35, p. 150; Midrash Samuel (ed. Buber; Krakow, 1893) ch. 28, p. 130; Midrash Hagadol, Genesis, p. 525.

[65] Genesis Rabbah 99:8 with parallels in Tanḥuma, Vayechi, 10; Leḳah Tob, Genesis (ed. Buber) ch. 49, p. 234; Yalḳuṭ, Genesis, 159; Midrash Birchat Yaaḳob in *Bet Hamidrash* (ed. Jellinek 2; Leipsig, 1853-1877) 75; Shochar Tob on Samuel, ch. 9; Midrash Samuel (ed. Buber) 9:6, p. 75; Agadat Bereshit, ch. 27:82 (only H, M, and A mentioned in this last reference, the very opposite of the passage in Sanhedrin 93b).

[66] Genesis Rabbah 99:2 with parallels in Tanḥuma, Vayechi, 14; Tanḥuma (ed. Buber; Lemberg, 1885) Vayechi, p. 219 (where Daniel's name is obviously missing from H, M, and A); Midrash Birchat Yaaḳob (Jellinek 2) 80.

[67] This view is probably based on a strictly literal rendering of the first Hebrew word in the verse (the singular) as: "And *he* was," excluding H, M, and A.

[68] In fact, although H, M, and A are usually listed with Daniel as stemming from the tribe of Judah, we find in Midrash Birchat Yaaḳob (Jellinek 2) 76, a reference that H, M, and A came from Judah, unusual in that Daniel is not mentioned together with them at this place, although he is earlier (p. 75).

[69] Sanhedrin 93b states that they descended, together with David and the Messiah, from Ruth and Boaz. Parallels are found in Targum to Ru 3:15; Leḳah Tob to Ru 3:15 (ed. Bamberger; Mainz, 1887); Midrash Zuta to Ruth (ed. Buber; Berlin, 1894) 53; Yemenite manuscript to the book of Ruth in Berlin Royal Library, ms. or fol. 1203, p. 167b, quoted in Hartmann, *Das Buch Ruth in der Midrasch-Litteratur*, 72, n. 2. In Ruth Rabbah 7:2 we find a somewhat inexact parallel in that H, M, and A are counted as one person, and Josiah and Hezekiah are added to complete the six descendants of Ruth and Boaz. There are other midrashic traditions giving the royal genealogy of Daniel, H, M, and A. In Numbers Rabbah 13:11, with a parallel in Yalḳut, Genesis, 159, Daniel, H, M, A and David and the Messiah are listed as descendants of Nahshon, the son of Amminadab, prince of the tribe of Judah. In Midrash Birchat Yaaḳob (Jellinek 2) 77, we find a parallel where six persons are initially mentioned, but in subsequent enumeration we find: David, H, M, and A (grouped), Hezekiah, Daniel, and the Messiah — a total of only five. A parellel to the above, where again only five are enumerated, is found in

that Daniel, H, M, and A were descendants of King Hezekiah of Judah.[70]

Josephus again is our first extra-rabbinic source in this matter. In his paraphrasing of the biblical account in the opening verses of Daniel[71] we find another deliberate insertion which is lacking in the biblical text: "Nebuchadnezzar, the Babylonian king, took the Jewish youths of noblest birth and the relatives of their king Sacchias [= Zedekiah] who were remarkable for the vigor of their bodies, etc."[72] Dan 1:3 has only "children of Israel and of royal seed, and of the nobles." This insertion appears again a few lines later:[73] ". . . among them were four of the family of Sacchias [= Zedekiah], the first of whom was named Daniel, etc." This is a paraphrase of Dan 1:6 which says that they were "of the sons of Judah." Apparently Josephus had a definite tradition that they were of Zedekiah's family, or else why would he deliberately insert this name twice in his paraphrase?[74] In comparing Josephus with rabbinic tradition, we find that although he does not cite Isa 39:7 in connection with Daniel and his associates, since he calls them relatives of Zedekiah they would also be descendants of King Hezekiah, because Zedekiah was a great grandson of Hezekiah.

We do not find any reference to Daniel's genealogy in patristic sources. Origen, who quotes Isa 39:7 twice[75] in connection with Daniel and the

---

Yalkut, Genesis, 159. Another tradition is seen in Midrash Abba Gorion on Esther printed in *Sifré d'Agadata* (ed. S. Buber; Vilna, 1886) 3 (reprinted in Jellinek 1, 2). Six descendants of David are listed: Solomon, Josiah, Daniel, H, M, and A. We find an obvious parallel to this in *Dmut Kisseh shel Shlomo Hamelech* (Jellinek 2) 83, except that the six are listed as Hezekiah, Josiah, Daniel, H, M, and A. Buber, *Sifré,* 3 n. 42 claims that the latter source copies from the ms. which was the basis of his edition.

[70] Sanhedrin 93b, according to the views of both Rab and Rabbi Ḥanina; Pirḳé de Rabbi Eliezer (ed. and tr. Friedlander) ch. 52, end, 426-427; Pseudo-Saadia, *Commentary on Daniel* 1:6. Also see n. 69, where Hezekiah is mentioned in several sources with Daniel, H, M, and A. Among the medieval commentators, only the Karaite, Jephet ibn Ali in his *Commentary on Daniel* (ed. and tr. Margoliouth) 3 on Dan 1:6 rejects the rabbinic tradition that the four men were of royal blood: "Among them [the captive children] were some of the seed-royal, whom the Scripture does not mention. Had these four been of it, he would have said [in 1:6] 'there were among them of the seed-royal,' mentioning their rank. This disproves the view that Isaiah 39:2 [*sic:* read 7] refers to these."

[71] *Antiquities* 10. 186ff. See n. 20 above.

[72] Ibid., 186.

[73] Ibid., 188.

[74] See n. 54 for another reason why Josephus may have mentioned Zedekiah. Since Josephus in *Antiquities* 10.131-185, had just completed the history of the fall of Jerusalem, Zedekiah's imprisonment in Babylonia, and the end of the community in Judea, Josephus may have interpreted "royal-seed" to mean "relatives of their king Zedekiah," despite the fact that he did not have a definite tradition to this effect.

[75] In his *Commentary on Matthew* 15:5, *PG* 13:1263-5, and *Homily 4 on Ezekiel, PG* 13:704.

eunuch tradition, assumed that he was a descendant of King Hezekiah, but says no more. Epiphanius,[76] a Greek Father who was an older contemporary of Jerome, mentions in one place[77] that the father[78] of Daniel, according to tradition, was Sabaa.[79] Pseudo-Epiphanius adds little more than the biblical account:[80] "He was of the tribe of Judah of the race of the eminent men of the royal service."[81]

Jerome not only quotes Isa 39:7 each time that he mentions the eunuch tradition,[82] but in his *Commentary on Daniel* 1:3 he adds: "If, moreover, they were of seed-royal there is no doubt but that they were of the line of David." At first this statement seems quite perplexing since it is obvious that if they were descendants of King Hezekiah,[83] they were *ipso facto* "of the line of David." What seems to be bothering Jerome is a point which he stresses both in the prologue to his *Commentary* and in his comment on 2:25 as well. In the prologue[84] we read:

> Just as we find in the title of that same story of Bel, according to the Septuagint:[85] "There was a certain priest named Daniel the son of Abda,[86] a table-companion of the King of Babylon," though Holy Scripture testifies that Daniel and the three [Hebrew] children were of the tribe of Judah.

---

[76] He was known as Epiphanius Constantiensis of Salamis, born *c.* 315, died 403. Jerome cites him in *Adversus Rufinus* 2.22, 3.6 as understanding Greek, Syriac, Hebrew, Egyptian, and also some Latin.

[77] *Adversus Haereses* 2.1.55:3 = *PG* 41:976.

[78] The only other mention of Daniel's father in any source is found in the Septuagint version of Bel 1:2, where Daniel is reported to have been a priest, the son of Abal. See nn. 85, 86.

[79] The original reading may have been "Abaa," serving as the base for "Sabaa," "Abda," and "Abal."

[80] Cf. Dan 1:3,6.

[81] *De Vitis Prophetarum* 10; cf. Schermann, 14.

[82] *Adversus Jovinianum* 1.25, *PL* 23:244; *Commentary on Daniel* 1:3, *PL* 25:496; and *Commentary on Isaiah* 11.39 on Isa 39:7, *PL* 24:399.

[83] Jerome had just quoted Isa 39:7 prior to this statement.

[84] *PL* 25:492 = *CCSL* 75A, 773, 1. 55; 774, 1. 58.

[85] This indeed is found in Bel 1:2 according to the LXX. It is not found in the Theodotion version of Bel. This is unusual, for whenever Jerome mentions the LXX or vulgate in his *Commentary on Daniel,* unless otherwise clearly indicated, he refers to Theodotion's version. See Chapter 2, n. 61. And as is the case with the book of Daniel according to the Hebrew canon, so it is with regard to the portions of Daniel for which no Semitic original exists; he consistently quotes the Theodotion version. Cf. Chapter 3, n. 75, 84. The problem remains, therefore, why Jerome does not make special mention that here he was actually quoting the LXX and *not* the Theodotion version of Bel.

[86] Ziegler's text of Bel (LXX version) has "Abal," supported by two manuscripts. Cf. Joseph Ziegler, *Susanna, etc.,* 215. See Epiphanius' reference to "Sabaa" above.

In his *Commentary* on 2:25 we find: "And note that Daniel is of the sons of Judah, rather than being a priest as the story of Bel contains at the end."[87] This statement that Daniel was a priest may be based on identifying him with the priest named Daniel in Neh 10:7.[88] This name also appears in Ezra 8:2 as a member of the priestly family of Ithamar. It is interesting to note that the names Mishael, Azariah, and Hananiah appear in Neh 8:4, 10:3,24[89] respectively as contemporaries of this priest Daniel. In any event, Jerome is clearly against the possibility that Daniel was a priest.

Theodoret[90] quotes Isa 39:7 in connection with the "eunuch tradition" but says nothing else about Daniel's genealogy.

There remains one more tradition found in two medieval sources to cite. In the beginning of *Ma'aseh Daniel*[91] we find Daniel mentioned as the son of King Jechoniah (= Jehoiachin). Gregorious Abulfarag Bar Hebraeus, the thirteenth century Jacobite Syrian historian, also mentions this tradition, in more detail and with much confusion. In his most famous work, *Chronicon Syriacum,*[92] we find four sons of King Josiah listed: Jechoniah, Jehoiakim, Jehoahaz, and Zedekiah. Jechoniah was the father of Daniel, and Jehoiakim was the father of Hananiah, Mishael, and Azariah. (Thus Daniel and H, M, and A were cousins.) The following chart graphically shows this:

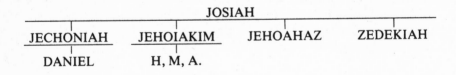

JOSIAH

JECHONIAH	JEHOIAKIM	JEHOAHAZ	ZEDEKIAH
DANIEL	H, M, A.		

[87] *PL* 25:501. Since the father of Daniel is mentioned at the beginning of Bel, in the passage quoted above from Jerome's prologue, the phrase "as the story of Bel contains at the end" most probably refers to the end of the Book of Daniel since that is where the story of Bel is appended.

[88] Ginzberg, *Legends* 6, 448, n. 56 middle.

[89] These verses may well be the basis for Rabbi Joḥanan's statement in Sanhedrin 93a that after emerging from the furnace, H, M, and A "went up to the Land of Israel, married and begat sons and daughters." See n. 10.

[90] *Commentary on Daniel PG* 81 (1864):1274 (paragraph 1068-9), quoted above, cf. n. 59.

[91] This is a Persian manuscript which was translated into Hebrew in Jellinek, *Beth Hamidrash* 5, 117-130. Jellinek explains (ibid., xxxvi-xxxvii) that internal evidence seems to refer to events until 1160, but he gives no definite opinion as to when it was written. Nor can we establish whether it might have influenced Bar Hebraeus cited below.

[92] Written in Syriac, translated into English by Budge as *The Chronography of Gregory . . . Bar Hebraeus,* p. 25.

Neither the Bible nor tradition know of Jechoniah, a son of Josiah.[93] The only Jechonia (= Jehoiachin) mentioned in the Bible is the *son* of Jehoiakim (2 Kgs 24:6 and 2 Chr 36:8), not his brother. Bar Hebraeus could not have confused his Jechoniah son of Josiah with the Jechoniah of the Bible, because he himself is aware of Jechoniah of the Bible: "After Jehoiakim, his son Jehoiachin, who is called in the gospel of Matthew 'Jechoniah'[94] and who is also called by his father's name Jehoiakim, [reigned] three months."[95] Where, then did Jechoniah the son of Josiah come from? To confuse matters even more, in his *Scholia on Daniel,*[96] Bar Hebraeus presents Daniel as the son of Jechoniah who was the son of Jehoiakim; H, M, and A are given as the sons of Jehoiakim. (This would make them his uncles.)

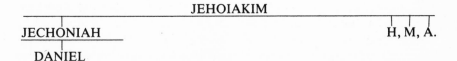

JEHOIAKIM

JECHONIAH   H, M, A.

DANIEL

Note that in both sources Bar Hebraeus maintains that Daniel was the son of Jechoniah and that H, M, and A were the sons of Jehoiakim. The entire confusion is based on who is the father of this Jechoniah. The father of Jechoniah in his *Scholion* agrees with the biblical account. Making Daniel and his friends the sons of Jechoniah and Jehoiakim respectively would fulfill the Jewish tradition regarding Isa 39:7, since both the above kings were direct descendants of King Hezekiah. Neither *Maʿaseh Daniel* nor Bar Hebraeus mentions this verse, however.

[93] 1 Chr 3:15 lists four sons of Josiah; Johanan, Jehoiakim, Zedekiah, and Shallum (= Jehoahaz of 2 Kgs 23:30 and 2 Chr 36:1).

[94] See n. 53, end, for the confusion caused by this name in Mt 1:10.

[95] Budge, *Chronography,* 26.

[96] Freimann, ed. and trans., *Scholien zum Buche Daniel,* 4. The original is in Syriac and the translation in German.

CHAPTER 5

JEROME'S *COMMENTARY ON DANIEL* 2:1

ובשנת שתים למלכות נבכדנצר חלם נבכדנצר חלם נבכדנצר חלמות ותתפעם רוחו ושנתו
נהיתה עליו. (דניאל ב':א')

And in the second year of the reign of Nebuchadnezzar Nebuchadnezzar
dreamed dreams; and his spirit was troubled, and his sleep broke from him
(Dan 2:1).

In Jerome's *Commentary on Daniel* 2:1 we find:

If the lads had entered in his sight at the end of three years as he himself had
commanded, how is it that he is now said to have seen the dream in the second
year of his reign? The Hebrews solve [the difficulty] in this way, that the
second year refers here to his reign over all the barbarian nations, not only
Judea and the Chaldeans, but also the Assyrians and the Egyptians and the
Moabites and the rest of the nations which by the permission of God he had
conquered.[1] For this reason Josephus also writes in the tenth book of the
Antiquities: "After the second year from the devastation of Egypt
Nebuchadnezzar beheld a marvelous dream."[2]

Jerome, as well as his Hebrew source and Josephus, were bothered by an
apparent chronological contradiction between the first and second chapters
of Daniel. According to Dan 1:5 the young Israelites of noble birth (including Daniel and his companions) whom Nebuchadnezzar had taken to
Babylon were to be educated for three years in the literature and wisdom of
the Chaldeans. In Dan 1:18 we find explicitly stated that at the end of the
period designated by the king (i.e., three years), the chief of the eunuchs
presented them to the king. But according to Dan 2:1, Nebuchadnezzar had
his dream in the *second* year of his reign, and Daniel and his companions
were already ranked among the wise men of Babylon (Dan 2:13)!

Both Jerome's Hebrew source as well as Josephus[3] give the same essential
answer, which Jerome adopts, offering no alternatives: the "second year"
of Nebuchadnezzar's reign does not refer to his reign over Judea alone;

---

[1]   This seems to be a reference to Jer 27:3,6 where the nations of Edom, Moab, Ammon,
Tyre, and Sidon are told that they will be subject to Nebuchadnezzar.

[2]   *PL* 25:498 = *CCSL* 75A, 783, 11. 139-148.

[3]   We clearly see here that although Jerome cites a Hebrew tradition he does not include
Josephus under the designation, but cites him independently although his interpretation is
similar.

72

instead it refers to the time he subsequently enlarged his empire by conquering other nations. In Josephus, *Antiquities* 10:195[4] we do find: "Two years after the sacking of Egypt, King Nebuchadnezzar had a wonderful dream. . . ." The Hebrew source of Jerome, however, is more difficult to trace. There seems to be no exact parallel to it in extant rabbinic literature. In Seder Olam Rabbah[5] we do find an attempt to solve the same problem. After citing the verse Dan 2:1 this source states:

> Is it possible to say so [that Nebuchadnezzar dreamt his dream in the second year of his reign]? However, the verse reckons two [years after] the destruction of the Temple.[6]

Admittedly, the *terminus a quo* found in Seder Olam Rabbah, the destruction of the Temple, is earlier than the establishment of Nebuchadnezzar's world empire in Jerome's Hebrew tradition. We may safely assume, however, that the author of Seder Olam Rabbah was bothered by the same chronological problem as was the author of Jerome's Hebrew source.

Rashi cites Seder Olam in his commentary to Dan 2:1. However, the eleventh century Karaite commentator Jepheth ibn Ali comments as follows:

> Just as we said of the "third year of the reign of Jehoiakim" that the phrase did not refer to his reign literally, so this again does not refer to Nebuchad-nezzar's *reign,* as Daniel is the person who interpreted the dream. Plainly it must refer to something else. . . . Others have referred it to the *fall of Jerusalem,* imagining that he did not consider himself king till he had subdued Israel; which is not unprobable. To my mind what is most probable is that it means [the second year] *after he had become king of the entire world (infra* 2:38). Now it is well known that he took Jerusalem before he took Tyre: and Tyre before he took Egypt. It is most probable that he took Egypt in the thirtieth year of his reign. . . . Now Egypt was the last of his conquests, as no other king stood before him save Pharaoh; so that the words "in the second year" will refer to the thirty-second year of his reign, thirteen years after the destruction of the Temple.[7]

---

[4] Translation by Marcus, 267.

[5] This is a Hebrew chronicle extending from Adam until the revolt of Bar Kochba generally ascribed by Jewish authorities to Rabbi Jose ben Ḥalafta, a Palestinian *tanna* of the fourth generation (second century C.E.). B. Ratner in his *Introduction to Seder Olam Rabbah* (Vilna, 1894) concludes that R. Joḥanan (third century Palestinian scholar) was its author although R. Jose was its principal authority.

[6] This is the translation of B. Ratner's text. *Seder Olam Rabbah* (Vilna: Romm Brothers, 1897) ch. 28, 124. A parallel is found in Yalḳuṭ, Daniel 1059. Ratner brings several variant readings in n. 2 *ad loc.*

[7] Jepheth ibn Ali, *Commentary on the Book of Daniel,* 5-6.

Jepheth ibn Ali thus rejects the interpretation of Seder Olam Rabbah. His preference is equivalent to a synthesis of Jerome's Hebrew tradition and Josephus' remark: the conquering of Egypt by Nebuchadnezzar made his dominion complete.

Abraham ibn Ezra (1092-1167) also seems to follow the Hebrew tradition of Jerome: ". . . [the interpretation which is] correct to me is: [in the second year] of his reign over all the nations which Jeremiah mentioned that he would capture [cf. Jer 27:3,6]."[8]

Isaac Abrabanel (1437-1508) clearly presents the chronological problem and offers two solutions: the first is the citation from Seder Olam Rabbah and the second is essentially the Hebrew tradition of Jerome. Interestingly enough, he ascribes the latter interpretation to "the Christian commentators":

> . . . the Christian commentators have already explained it [the apparent chronological contradiction] well by saying that Nebuchadnezzar was originally only the king of Babylon and he ascended against Jerusalem three times and after he destroyed it he conquered Egypt and Ammon and Moab and the Land of Philistines and all the twenty-one nations which Jeremiah mentioned and he ruled them with force, and to this large general kingdom which existed after the destruction of Jerusalem and which they call a monarchy the verse referred when it stated "in the second year [of the reign] of Nebuchadnezzar."[9]

Abrabanel thus clearly distinguishes between the interpretation of Seder Olam Rabbah and the one he ascribes to Christian commentators, but which we have seen cited by Jerome as a Hebrew tradition.

The early patristic commentators on Daniel are generally mute concerning the above chronological problem. Hippolytus, Ephraem Syrus, and Theodoret concern themselves with other exegetical problems. John Chrysostom (347-407), however, is definitely concerned with a chronological problem, though it is not identical with our specific problem. In his commentary on Dan 2:1, he states:

> And this is the twelfth year, for if there were three years after the city was captured, and it was captured in the ninth year, this is the twelfth year. Some say that both this [2] and that [12] number are expressed among the Hebrews by the same symbol.[10] And either it is a scribal slip or the children stood before

---

[8] Ibn Ezra's commentary on Dan 2:1.

[9] Abrabanel's commentary on Dan 2:1, *The Wellsprings of Salvation* (Hebrew), part 6, section 1 (ed. Jerusalem: Abrabanel Publishing House, 1960) 305.

[10] Certainly not the same symbol. However שתים עשרה (12) can be mistaken as שתים (2) by the omission of עשרה.

him in the second year. But it would not make sense.[11]

Chrysostom thus offers us two exegetical alternatives. The first is that there was a scribal error in the text of Dan 2:1 and instead of reading "in the second year" it should be "in the twelfth year." To substantiate this point, Chrysostom refers to the fact that Jerusalem was captured in the ninth year of King Nebuchadnezzar's reign. It seems quite obvious that Chrysostom based this assumption on 2 Kgs 25:1 which states "And it came to pass in the ninth year of his reign . . . that Nebuchadnezzar, King of Babylon came, he and all his army against Jerusalem. . . ." Chrysostom obviously interpreted the phrase "in his reign" as referring to "Nebuchadnezzar." However, in Jer 39:1, we find an obvious parallel to this verse, where it is explicitly stated: "In the ninth year of Zedekiah King of Judah." The verse in Jeremiah notwithstanding, Chrysostom probably forgot Jer 39:11, misinterpreted 2 Kgs 25:1, and thus established the fall of Jerusalem in the ninth year of King Nebuchadnezzar. Add to this the three years referred to in Dan 1:5 and 1:18, and we arrive at the conclusion that Dan 2:1 took place in the twelfth year of King Nebuchadnezzar.

There is yet another difficulty in Chrysostom's chronology. Assuming that 2 Kgs 25:1 refers to Nebuchadnezzar's ninth year, it is quite obvious from the next verse as well as from the preceding verses at the end of chapter 24 that this siege of Jerusalem took place during the reign of King Zedekiah. Yet we are explicitly informed in Dan 1:1 that Daniel and his friends were taken to Babylonia during Nebuchadnezzar's siege which (the author believed) took place in the third year of King Jehoiakim (at the latest 605 B.C.E.), well before the reign of Zedekiah which ended with the destruction of Jerusalem in 587 B.C.E.[12]

The second alternative of Chrysostom's hypothesis is that the children indeed stood before Nebuchadnezzar in the second year, as found in the present text. He adds: "But it would not make sense." The obvious meaning of Chrysostom's words is that it would hardly be possible for the children to stand before Nebuchadnezzar in the second year, if they were not captured and brought to him until his ninth year.

Polychronius (first half of fifth century), on the other hand, follows Josephus and Jerome: "After Nabouchodonosor had conquered Judea and Egypt, he decided to count himself king from that, judging that to be a true reign, to which nothing stood in opposition."[13] Curiously, however,

---

[11] *PG* 56:193.

[12] According to the accepted calculation of biblical chronology, the last three kings of Judea and the years of their reigns are as follows: Jehoiakim (609? 608?-597), Jehoiachin (in 597, for three months), and Zedekiah (597-587).

[13] *Commentary on Daniel* (fragments), in *Scriptorum Veterum Nova Collectio* 1, part 3, 2.

Polychronius does not resort to this interpretation because of the chronological difficulty that bothered all of the commentators cited previously. He asserts that Nebuchadnezzar called upon Daniel to interpret the dream before his three-year period of education was over.[14]

> For he did not concede that three years' time should pass in which indeed the children were arranged to be educated, but when scarcely a year had passed by, he shows the dream.[15]

---

[14] This apparently contradicts Dan 1:18.
[15] Polychronius, ibid.

CHAPTER 6

JEROME'S *COMMENTARY ON DANIEL* 2:12-13

כל קבל דנה מלכא בנס וקצף שניא ואמר להובדה לכל חכימי בבל. ודתא
נפקת וחכימיא מתקטלין ובעו דניאל וחברוהי להתקטלה. (דניאל ב':יב'-יג')

For this cause the king was angry and very furious, and commanded to destroy
all the wise men of Babylon. So the decree went forth, and the wise men were
to be slain; and they sought Daniel and his companions to be slain (Dan 2:12-
13).

In Jerome's *Commentary on Daniel* 2:12-13 we find:

> The Hebrews question why Daniel and the three lads did not enter before the
> king along with other wise men, and why they were ordered to be slain with the
> rest when the decree was issued. They have explained [the difficulty] in this
> way, that at that time, when the king was promising rewards and gifts and the
> greatest honor, they were unwilling [to go before him] lest they should appear
> to be shamelessly grasping after the wealth and honor of the Chaldeans. Or, at
> any rate,[1] the Chaldeans themselves, being envious of their [i.e. the Jews']
> glory and knowledge, entered alone [before the king], as if they intended to
> obtain the rewards by themselves, and afterwards were willing to have those
> whom they had denied hope of glory to share in the peril.[2]

The above Jewish interpretation cited by Jerome cannot be found in
extant rabbinic literature nor in the medieval Jewish commentaries. Only
Jepheth ibn Ali makes the point that Daniel and his friends were not present
with the Chaldean wise men in their audience before the king. His answer is
based on Daniel's modesty, somewhat similar to the first answer brought by
Jerome:

> The words "and they sought Daniel and his comrades" point to the fact that
> they had not been present with them during the colloquy which passed between

---

[1] It is not clear whether this second solution is also a Jewish interpretation or if it is
Jerome's own opinion. It seems that Jerome preferred this second interpretation, since he
comments on Dan 2:15: "Knowing that Daniel and the three youths possessed a knowledge
and intelligence tenfold as great as that of all the soothsayers of Chaldea put together [cf. Dan
1:20], the Chaldeans concealed from them the king's inquiry, lest they should receive
preference over them in the matter of interpreting the dream" (*PL* 25:499-500 = *CCSL* 75A,
786, 1. 214ff).

[2] *PL* 25:499 = *CCSL* 75A, 786, 1.203-211.

77

the Chaldees and the king; and this was because they had never professed that they understood mysteries as these [the Chaldeans] had professed.[3]

Hippolytus, Ephraem Syrus, Aphraates, John Chrysostom, Theodoret, and Polychronius, the early patristic commentators on Daniel, are also silent on this matter.

---

[3] *Commentary on the Book of Daniel,* 8.

CHAPTER 7

JEROME'S *COMMENTARY ON DANIEL* 5:2

בלשאצר אמר בטעם חמרא להיתיה למאני דהבא וכספא די הנפק נבוכדנצר
אבוהי מן היכלא די בירושלם וישתון בהון מלכא ורברבנוהי שגלתה ולחנתה.
(דניאל ה':ב')

Belshazzar, while he tasted the wine, commanded to bring the golden and silver vessels which Nebuchadnezzar his father had taken out of the temple which was in Jerusalem; that the king and his lords, his consorts and his concubines, might drink therein (Dan 5:2).

In Jerome's *Commentary on Daniel* 5:2 we find:

The Hebrews hand down a story of this sort[1]: Belshazzar, thinking that God's promise had remained without effect until the seventieth year, by which Jeremiah had said that the captivity of the Jewish people would have to be ended (cf. Jer 25:12, 20:10ff.)—a matter of which Zechariah also speaks in the first part of his book (Zech 1:12ff.)—and turning the occasion of the failed promise into a celebration, gave a great banquet, by way of scoffing at the expectation of the Jews and at the vessels of the Temple of God.[2]

The prophet Jeremiah promised Israel that the destruction of their land and their exile would be temporary. After seventy years, they would return to their land and previous glory while Babylon, their oppressor, would be destroyed. This is mentioned in Jer 25:12 and 29:10ff. It is also mentioned in Zech 1:12ff. and Dan 9:2. The basic chronological problem is: which year begins the seventy-year period indicated by Jeremiah. In Megillah 11b Raba[3] explains that Belshazzar began his count with the first year of Nebuchadnezzar's reign (605 B.C.E.):

He reckoned forty-five years of Nebuchadnezzar, and twenty-three years of

---

[1] Jerome may mean by this phrase, "huiuscemodi fabulam," either that this is not the exact version or that there is more than one version. Indeed Jerome does not make it clear in his presentation of the tradition that Belshazzar waited until the seventy years had expired according to his computation before scoffing at God's promise and arranging his banquet. The rabbinic sources make this clear.

[2] *PL* 25:519 = *CCSL* 75A, 821, 11. 30-36.

[3] Babylonian *amora* of the fourth generation, born *c.* 280, died 352.

79

Evil-merodach, and two of his own, making seventy in all. He then brought out the vessels of the Temple and used them.[4]

Thus, according to Belshazzar's calculation, the seventy-year period of Jeremiah had ended with the second year of Belshazzar's reign. Seeing that there was no sign of the redemption of Israel, he deemed the prophecy to be invalid, and in the third year of his reign, made a feast using the Temple vessels in derision of Israel.[5] This is indeed the same tradition that is cited by Jerome above.

The Talmudic source in Megillah 11b-12a explicitly states that Belshazzar erred in his calculation,[6] a point not mentioned but implied by Jerome. The source of his error as substantiated by the citation in Megillah 12a, taken from Seder Olam Rabbah,[7] was that the seventy-year computation should not have begun with Nebuchadnezzar's first year, but rather his second year (605/4), when he subjugated Jehoiakim (2 Kgs 24:1). Thus, another year after Belshazzar's feast was needed to complete the seventy-year period, and this took place with the one-year reign of Darius the Mede. He was succeeded by his son-in-law, Cyrus, who combined the Persian, Median, and Babylonian Empires and issued a proclamation that the Jews of Babylonia were free to return to Israel[8] (Ezra 1:2ff.). This therefore constituted the fulfillment of Jeremiah's seventy-year prophecy.

Hippolytus, Ephraem Syrus, Aphraates, John Chrysostom, Theodoret, and Polychronius, the early patristic commentators on Daniel, do not connect the banquet of Belshazzar with Jeremiah's prophecy of seventy years.

---

[4]   The Talmudic text continues to explain in detail the biblical basis for arriving at Nebuchadnezzar's reign of forty-five years. Evil-merodach's reign of twenty-three years is ascribed to tradition. In Seder Olam Rabbah, ch. 28, we find explicitly stated "Nebuchadnezzar reigned forty-five years, Evil-merodach his son, twenty-three and Belshazzar his son, three." No basis for the above calculation is given.

[5]   Chapter five in Daniel, wherein the feast is described, makes no mention of the year of Belshazzar's reign when the feast took place. Seder Olam Rabbah explicitly states that it was in the third year, obviously based on tradition; see Ratner's edition, 126, n. 18. The only other two events of Belshazzar's reign dated in Daniel are found in 7:1 (Daniel's dream which took place in Belshazzar's first year) and 8:1 (Daniel's vision which took place in Belshazzar's third year). Applying the principle that there is not necessarily chronological order in the Bible, we understand that Belshazzar's feast could not have taken place before the third year of his reign.

[6]   It is interesting to note that in Seder Olam Rabbah, no mention is made that Belshazzar erred in calculating the seventy years of Jeremiah, although reference is made to the seventy year period.

[7]   Chapter 28, with a parallel in Yalḳuṭ, Daniel, 1066.

[8]   According to currently accepted chronology, Cyrus issued his declaration in 539/8 B.C.E., which is actually several years earlier than the termination of either of the seventy-year periods proposed above.

CHAPTER 8

JEROME'S *COMMENTARY ON DANIEL* 6:4

אדין סרכיא ואחשדרפניא הוו בעין עלה להשכחה לדניאל מצד מלכותא וכל
עלה ושחיתה לא יכלין להשכחה כל קבל די מהימן הוא וכל שלו ושחיתה לא
השתכחת עלוהי. (דניאל ו':ה')

> Then the presidents and the satraps sought to find occasion against Daniel as
> touching the kingdom; but they could find no occasion nor fault; forasmuch as
> he was faithful, neither was there any error or fault found in him (Dan 6:5).

In Jerome's *Commentary on Daniel* 6:4 (Vulgate = 6:5 Masoretic text) we
find:

> And in this passage the Hebrews suspect some such [deduction] as this: the
> "side of the king" is the queen or his concubines and the other wives who slept
> at his side. Therefore, they were seeking a pretext in things of this sort, to see
> whether they could accuse Daniel in his speech or touch or nodding [of his
> head] or sense-organ. But, they say they could find no cause for suspicion,
> since he was a eunuch and they could not even accuse him on the score of
> lewdness. This [interpretation] was made by those [Jews] who make a practice
> of weaving long tales on the pretext of a single word. We would interpret it in a
> simple fashion, that they found no pretext against him in any matter in which
> he had been harmful to the king, "for the reason that he was a faithful man
> and no suspicion of blame was discoverable in him."[1]

The tradition that Daniel and his associates Hananiah, Mishael, and
Azariah were eunuchs is well known both in rabbinic and patristic
literature, as we have seen in Chapter 4. Jerome himself cited this tradition
in his *Commentary on Daniel* 1:3 as well as in several other works.
However, the source for the above Jewish interpretation cited by Jerome in
his *Commentary on Daniel* 6:4 could not be located in extant rabbinic
records or in the commentaries of the medieval Jewish exegetes. There is
one source from the medieval compilation Midrash Megillah[2] which could
very well have a common origin with Jerome's tradition. It relates that
Daniel and his friends subjected *themselves* to castration in order to remove
suspicions of immorality:

---

[1] *PL* 25:658 = *CCSL* 75A, 830, 1. 256-831, 1. 267.
[2] See Chapter 4, n. 16.

He [Daniel] cut out his masculinity in the time of the evil Nebuchadnezzar, he and his friends Hananiah, Mishael, and Azariah, at the time when the enemies of Israel informed upon them and told Nebuchadnezzar: "those Jews which you brought are committing fornication with the maidservants of the king and the wives of the princes." As soon as Daniel and his friends Hananiah, Mishael, and Azariah heard this, they cut out their masculinity, as it is written: "Thus saith the Lord to the eunuchs etc." (Isa 56:4).

In comparing this citation with the Hebrew tradition in Jerome, one should note the following differences. In the former, the king involved was Nebuchadnezzar; in the latter, Darius. In the former the queen and concubines are mentioned, in the latter, the maidservants and the wives of the princes. In the former, Daniel and his friends castrated themselves to remove suspicion of immorality; in the latter, only Daniel is mentioned, and he seems to have already been a eunuch prior to the attempted accusations.

It is interesting to note that Jerome departs from the literal translation of the Aramaic phrase מצד מלכותא = from the side of the *kingdom,* and renders it as "ex latere regis" = from the side of the king.[3] We would assume that this translation reflects the Jewish tradition except that Jerome severely criticizes this tradition and substitutes his own interpretation, also based on the word "king" rather than "kingdom."

Jerome's criticism that the Jews practice "weaving long tales on the pretext of a single word" is certainly not unusual for Jerome.[4] However, in this case, the Hebrew interpretation is quite plausible, assuming the tradition that Daniel was a eunuch. Perhaps Jerome was not convinced that Daniel was a eunuch, as he remarked at the end of his *Commentary on Daniel* 1:3: "But perhaps the following words are opposed to this [eunuch] interpretation: '. . . lads or youths, who were free from all blemish . . . '" [Dan 1:4].

In Josephus, *Antiquities* 10.251, we find the following amplification of

---

[3]   Although Ziegler's text of Daniel has this phrase entirely missing, some manuscripts of the Theodotion recension read "from the sides of the kingdom." The LXX reads "accused to the king." Cf. *Susanna, etc.,* on Dan 6:4. The most dependable edition of Jerome's Vulgate translation, *Biblia Sacra: Iuxta Vulgatam Versionem,* ed. R. Osb (Stuttgart, 1969) 2, 1536, has "ex latere regni," although there are several manuscripts which have "ex latere regis."

[4]   Indeed in light of Jerome's harsh satire of those fellow Christians with whom he disagreed in biblical exegesis, he could hardly be silent against the Jews, in spite of his self-admitted intellectual debt to them. On the contrary, it is remarkable that in his entire *Commentary on Daniel,* the above statement is his harshest invective against Jewish biblical interpretation. The comparative docility of this criticism is readily apparent when we compare his phrases elsewhere describing Jewish learning as "belching and nausea" (*Praef. in librum de nom. heb., PL* 23:816A) and Jewish Scriptural interpretations as "foolish tales, inept inventions and anile fables" (*PL* 25:356C and 1411B). Cf. Wiesen, *St. Jerome as a Satirist,* 188-195, and above, Chapter 1, *passim.*

JEROME'S *COMMENTARY ON DANIEL* 6:4

Dan 6:5-6 as to the nature of the attempted slander of Daniel:

> He never gave them a single cause, for, being superior to considerations of
> money and scorning any kind of gain and thinking it most disgraceful to
> accept anything even if it were given for a proper cause, he did not let those
> who were envious of him find a single ground for complaint.[5]

Josephus clearly does not reflect our tradition; his interpretation stresses
Daniel's honesty rather than his chastity.

Among the early patristic commentators on Daniel, John Chrysostom[6]
mentions, concerning this matter, that Daniel was well-disposed to the king
and he trusted God. Theodoret[7], on the other hand, explains that his
enemies tried to charge Daniel with the crime of *laesa maiestas,* action
contrary to the interest of the ruler of the state. Polychronius echoes
Josephus in praising the honesty of Daniel:

> Neither bartering justice for bribes, nor taking away the claims of justice for
> the sake of base gain, that is, by no means of withdrawing from justice and
> truth.[8]

[5]   Marcus, 297.
[6]   *PG* 56:225.
[7]   *PG* 81:1312.
[8]   *Commentary on Daniel* in *Scriptorum Veterum Nova Collectio* 1, part 3, 9.

CHAPTER 9

JEROME'S *COMMENTARY ON DANIEL* 7:5

וארו חיוה אחרי תנינה דמיה לדב ולשטר חד הקמת ותלת עלעין בפמה בין
שניה ובן אמרין לה קומי אכלי בשר שגיא. (דניאל ז':ה')

And behold another beast, a second, like to a bear, and it raised up itself on one side, and it had three ribs in its mouth between its teeth; and it was said thus unto it: "Arise, devour much flesh" (Dan 7:5).

In Jerome's *Commentary on Daniel* 7:5 we find:

And what is said [about the bear], that "it stood up on one side," the Hebrews interpret thus, that they [the Persians] perpetrated nothing cruel against Israel. Hence they are also described in the prophet Zechariah as "white horses" [Zech 1:8, 6:3,6].[1]

The Hebrew interpretation of the bear "standing on one side" cited by Jerome points out that the Persians stood aloof from perpetrating cruelty against Israel. It is clear that he refers to the Persian Empire established by Cyrus in 550 B.C.E. since Jerome specifically refers to Cyrus in his *Commentary on Daniel* 7:5. The empire of Cyrus included Media and Babylonia. This Achaemenid Empire was brought to an end by Alexander the Great, who invaded it in 334 B.C.E. Subsequent to him, the Seleucids ruled for more than seventy years until the Parthians gained supremacy. They governed Persia for nearly five centuries (240 B.C.E.-226 C.E.). The first Parthian ruler was named Arsaces; hence the designation Arsaces for all Parthian rulers of the Arsacid dynasty. During their rule, the Jews generally had religious freedom, and were certainly never persecuted. In 226, Ardashir I established a new dynasty over Persia, the Sassanids. They were strict adherents of the Zoroastrian faith called Mazdaism, and their priests, the Magi or Guebers,[2] were often intolerant of the Jews and other religious minorities.[3]

---

[1] *PL* 25:529 = *CCSL* 75A, 840, 11. 499-502.

[2] In the Talmud a Gueber is referred to as *ḥabbār* because the original home of the Sassanids was Ḥaber near Shiraz, S. Persia. For Talmudic sources on the differences before and after the Guebers came to Babylon and the persecution they brought in their wake, see Yebamoth 63b, Sanhedrin 74b, Gittin 17a, Kiddushin 72a, and Samuel Krauss, *Persia and Rome in the Talmud and Midrashim* (Heb.; Israel, 1948) 156-157.

[3] For a detailed description of the above historical periods, see Neusner, *A History of the Jews in Babylonia.*

When we examine the Jewish attitude in rabbinic literature toward the Persians, we are confronted with several problems of historical identification. Samuel Krauss[4] points out that in the Talmud most remarks concerning the Persians refer to the Sassanid dynasty. The matter is complicated by the fact that sometimes "Persia" was substituted for "Rome" because of problems with the censors. Sometimes, however, it is possible to identify "Persia" with the Empire of Cyrus, either when Media is mentioned with it, or when it is mentioned after Babylonia and before Greece and Rome in the list of the four world empires.[5] Indeed, Media is often mentioned alone, with Persia. And to make matters even more difficult, the Parthians are almost never[6] referred to in Rabbinic literature by their proper name (פרת). In several sources we find the word "Persians" (פרס) where clear reference is made to the Parthians,[7] especially when they are contrasted with the Guebers[8] or the Romans,[9] as contemporaries, the latter being characterized as the destroyers of the Temple while the Parthians are called their protectors.

Louis Ginzberg points out the different opinions that the Palestinian and Babylonian authorities had toward Cyrus and the Persians.

The Roman yoke which weighed heavily upon the Palestinian Jews made them

---

[4] *Persia and Rome*, 27.

[5] For example, see Jerusalem Targum on Lev 26:44.

[6] One exception to this generalization is the Targum to Lam 4:21, 22 which mentions the Parthians by name (פרתואי) and is cited by S. Krauss in his *Monumenta Talmudica*, 5, 52, paragraph 95.

[7] For example, Jerusalem Talmud Berakhoth 7:2 and Nazir 5:3 tell of a Parthian embassy which came to Alexander Jannaeus (reigned 103-76 B.C.E.) in Judea. Both texts however, use the term מלכותא דפרס = the Persian kingdom. For the historical foundation for this story, see Neusner, *History of the Jews in Babylonia* I, 25-26.

[8] A good example of this is found in Kiddushin 72a where Rabbi asks Levi [b. Sisi], who had just returned from a visit to Babylonia around the turn of the third century C.E., to compare the Parthians with the new Persians: " 'Show me the Persians.' — 'They are like the armies of the House of David,' he replied. 'Show me the Guebers.' — 'They are like the destroying angels.' "

[9] For example, in Yoma 10a, we find: "R. Joshua b. Levi in the name of Rabbi said: 'Rome is designed to fall into the hands of Persia' [= Parthia]. . . . Rabbah b. Bar Ḥana in the name of R. Joḥanan, on the authority of R. Judah b. Ilaʿi said: 'Rome is designed to fall into the hands of Persia, that may be concluded by inference *a minori ad majus:* If in the case of the first Sanctuary, which the sons of Shem [Solomon] built and the Chaldeans destroyed, the Chaldeans fell into the hands of the Persians [Belshazzar into the hands of Darius, cf. Dan 5], then how much more should this be so with the second Sanctuary, which the Persians built and the Romans destroyed that the Romans should fall into the hands of the Persians [Parthians].' " Also see Berakoth 56a, where R. Joshua b. R. Ḥananyah tells the Emperor of Rome [probably Trajan] that in a dream he will see "Persians" [= Parthians] making him do forced labor.

look at the Persians as friends of the Jews. Their favorable opinion of Cyrus expresses their sympathy for the Persians. The Babylonian Jews, on the other hand, suffered terribly at the hands of the Mazdic[10] priests who were very powerful in the Sassanid empire, and they considered the Romans as "the lesser evil," and the "destroyers of the Temple" were preferred to "the builders of the Temple" [= the Persians under Cyrus], so that Cyrus and the Persians came in for a great deal of blame.[11]

Thus it would be most likely that Jerome heard favorable traditions concerning the Persians from his Jewish contacts, since he spent the last thirty-five years of his life, 386-420, in Bethlehem. With all of the above limitations in mind, let us present all relevant rabbinic sources.

The identification of Persia with a bear is well known in rabbinic literature. Most famous is the bitter invective of Rabbi Joseph.[12] He identifies the bear in Dan 7:5 with the Persians "who eat and drink like bears, and are coated with flesh like bears and are hairy like bears and can never keep still[13] like bears."[14] Rabbi Ammi,[15] upon seeing a Persian riding, would say: "there is a wandering bear."[16] R. Huna and R. Hama in the name of R. Hanina[17] identify Media with a bear on the basis of Am 5:19.[18] This reference is clearly to the Medo-Persian Empire since it is mentioned after Babylonia and before Greece and Edom (Rome). We also find the guardian angel of Persia referred to as "Dubiel"[19] [literally, 'bear-god'].

There is, however another tradition identifying Media with a wolf, based on the same verse cited above, Dan 7:5.

[10] Ginzberg is referring to the Mazdean priests. For a more detailed account of the preference of the Babylonian Jews for the rule of Rome rather than that of the Magi, see Neusner, *History of the Jews in Babylonia* 2, 35-38.

[11] *Legends* 6, 433, n. 7.

[12] A third-generation Babylonian *amora* who experienced persecution under Shapur II at the beginning of the fourth century. It is quite probable, therefore, that he referred to the Persians (i.e., Sassanids) of his time.

[13] L. Lewysohn, *Die Zoologie des Talmuds* (Frankfurt, 1858) 99, explains that the bear gulps its food, is covered with a thick layer of fat so it can hibernate through the winter with little food, its skin is wooly and thick, and it is constantly rolling about.

[14] Megillah 11a with parallels in Kiddushin 72a; Abodah Zarah 2b (parallel to Yalkut, Isaiah, 452); Lekah Tob to Esther (ed. Buber) 44a; Yalkut, Proverbs, 962; Yalkut, Daniel 1064.

[15] This is most probably the Babylonian Ammi who was a contemporary of Rabbi Joseph.

[16] Kiddushin 72a.

[17] Palestinian *amora* of first generation (first half of third century).

[18] Proem to Esther Rabbah, 5 with parallels in Midrash Tehillim 18:11; Yalkut, Amos, 545; Yalkut, Esther, 1045.

[19] Yoma 77a.

[Jacob blessed] Benjamin in allusion to the empire of Media; the former being likened to a wolf [Gen 49:27] and the latter being likened to a wolf [Dan 7:5]. . . . Rabbi Johanan[20] said: "The word is written רלב[21] [instead of ולדב] and דב was its name.''[22] That is Rabbi Johanan's view, for Rabbi Johanan said: '''Wherefore a lion out of the forest doth slay them' [Jer 5:6] alludes to Babylon; 'a wolf of the deserts doth spoil them' [ibid.], to Media.''[23]

The reference to Media here is also clearly to the Medo-Persian Empire since it is mentioned after Babylonia and before Greece and Edom (Rome). Rabbi Berekiah[24] identifies the "wolf" in Dan 7:5 with the kings of Media and Persia, while he adds: "In Babylon, [referring to the tradition cited by Rabbi Joseph, above] however, they say: 'This refers to the kings of Media and Persia who eat like a bear, etc!''[25] It is interesting to note that Jerome lived in Palestine approximately fifty years after Rabbi Berekiah and yet quotes the "Babylonian" tradition that Persia = bear. Evidently this was not a tradition limited to Babylon in the fourth century, just as Rabbi Hanina in Palestine, 150 years before Jerome, identified Media with a bear.

Both the identifications of bear and wolf are certainly pejoratives and the opposite of the tradition brought by Jerome. In addition to his comparison of Persia to a bear as cited above, Rabbi Joseph refers negatively to "the manner of the Persians who perform their conjugal duties in their clothes,''[26] and refers Isa 13:3 to the Persians "who are consecrated and destined for Gehinnom.''[27] Rabbi Joseph, however, seems to be opposing (in reference to the Sassanids of his day) other rabbinic statements in praise of the Medo-Persians or Parthians. In Berakoth 8b we find: "Rabbi Gamliel[28] says, 'For three things do I like the Persians: they are temperate in their eating, modest in the privy and chaste in other [i.e., sexual] matters.'''" His son, Rabbi Simeon ben Gamliel[29] is credited with the following similar statement:

[20] Theodore, Albeck, *Genesis Rabbah* 3 (2nd ed.; Jerusalem: Wahrmann Books, 1965) 1273, n. 10, emends so according to the Vatican manuscript and various parallels.

[21] Albeck, ibid., explains that Rabbi Johanan interpreted דב according to the Aramaic and Syrian דיבא = wolf.

[22] Albeck, ibid., explains that this refers to the fact that it was not only compared to a wolf, but it was called by that name as well, as seen in Jer 5:6.

[23] Genesis Rabbah 99:2; with parallels in Leviticus Rabbah 13:5; Proem to Esther Rabbah, 5; Tanhuma, Vayehi, 14; Tanhuma (ed. Buber), Vayehi, 13; Yalkut, Leviticus, 536.

[24] A Palestinian *amora* of the fourth generation (first half of the fourth century).

[25] Esther Rabbah 10:13.

[26] Ketuboth 48a.

[27] Berakoth 8b.

[28] A second generation *tanna* who lived in Palestine in the last half of the first century C.E.

[29] A fourth generation *tanna* who lived in Palestine the middle of the second century C.E.

For three things I like the Medians: they do not tear [meat with their teeth] and eat, but cut it and eat; they kiss not on the mouth, but on the hand; and they take counsel only in a field [to prevent eavesdropping].[30]

Rabbi Ḥiyah b. Abba[31] is credited with the following very laudatory statement: "The kings of Media were faultless and God has nothing against them except the idolatry which they received from their forefathers."[32] And we even find one statement in praise of the Persians from the Babylonian Exilarch contemporary with Rabbi Joseph! "Said the Exilarch to R. Shesheth:[33] Although you are venerable Rabbis, yet the Persians are better versed then you in the etiquette of a meal."[34]

We cannot find, however, any positive rabbinic statements concerning the Persians specifically derived from the phrase "standing on one side" in Dan 7:5, or referring to the Persians' never perpetrating any cruelty against Israel, as does Jerome's Hebrew tradition. It seems quite plausible, however, that such a tradition could have been prevalent in Jerome's time in Palestine, during the end of the fourth and beginning of the fifth centuries.

After mentioning the Hebrew interpretation concerning the Persians in his *Commentary on Daniel* 7:5, Jerome adds: "Hence they [the Persians] are described in the prophecy of Zechariah as white horses" [Zech 1:8, 6:3,6]. It is difficult to determine whether this is part of the Hebrew tradition or an *addendum* of Jerome's. We do find one reference in rabbinic tradition[35] identifying the red, black, white, and grizzled bay horses in Zech

---

[30] Genesis Rabbah 74:2, with parallels, all with slight variants, in Tanḥuma (ed. Buber), Ḥukath, 11; Yalḳut, Genesis, 130 (instead of "Medians," we find "sons of the Medians"); Pesiḳta de Rab Kahana (ed. Mandelbaum), Parah, 3, p. 60 = ed. Buber, 33b-34a ("sons of the east"); Tanḥuma, Ḥukath, 6 ("sons of the East"); Tanḥuma (ed. Buber), Vayetze, 24 ("sons of the East"); Numbers Rabbah 19:3 (only a cryptic reference: "Rabbi Simeon b. Gamliel, for three things, etc."); Ecclesiastes Rabbah 7:23 (sons of the East"); Yalḳut, Kings, 177 ("sons of the East"); Sekel Tob (ed. Buber), Vayetze, 4 ("sons of the East"); Leḳaḥ Tob (ed. Buber), Vayetze, 4 ("sons of the East"). In the latter two sources, Resh Laḳish is the author of this statement. S. Buber in Sekel Tob *ad loc.* (p. 157, n. 14) suggests the possible confusion of רשב"ג with רשב"ל. The above statement of Rabbi Simeon b. Gamliel is almost identical with one attributed to Rabbi Akiba in Berakoth 8b: "For three things I like the Medes: When they cut meat, they cut it only on the table; when they kiss, they kiss only the hand; and when they hold counsel, they do so only in the field." This has a parallel in Sekel Tob (ed. Buber), Vayetze, 4.

[31] A third generation *amora* in Palestine (end of third century).

[32] Pesiḳta de Rab Kahana (ed. Mandelbaum), Parah, 9, p. 75 = ed. Buber, 40b with parallels in Pesiḳta Rabbati, 14 (ed. Freedman) p. 75a; Tanḥuma 27 (ed. Buber) p. 60a; Yalḳut Ḥukath, 759.

[33] A Babylonian *amora* of the third generation (end of third century); an older contemporary of Rabbi Joseph.

[34] Berakoth 46b.

[35] Yalḳut, Zechariah, 574.

6:1-3 with the four world empires of Babylonia, Medo-Persia, Greece, and Rome respectively. The *black* horses, however, are identified as Medo-Persia, with the added reference to Dan 7:5 and the remark that "they [the Medo-Persians] blackened the faces of Israel with the edict of Haman."[36]

The early patristic commentators on Daniel do not interpret "the bear standing on one side" in any way similar to Jerome's tradition. Theodoret,[37] in fact, stresses the opposite:

And he [Daniel] says that it [Persia] was similar to a bear because of the savageness and cruelty of their punishments. For of all the barbarians the Persians are more savage with regard to their punishments, employing the stripping off [of skin] and devising long punishments by the cutting of the limbs into parts, and punishing with a bitter death those who were punished [by them].

[36] Ibid. Rashi, the famous medieval Jewish commentator (1040-1105), in his comments on Zech 6:3, 6 associates the white horses with the Persians, the builders of the Temple (under Cyrus). Prof. S. Lieberman pointed out to the author that Rashi most probably quoted another version of the Pesiḳta (not extant in our editions) cited by Yalḳuṭ, Zechariah, 574.

[37] *PG* 81:1416-17.

CHAPTER 10

JEROME'S *COMMENTARY ON DANIEL* 7:7

באתר דנה חזה הוית בחזוי ליליא וארו חיוה רביעיא דחילה ואימתני ותקיפא
יתירה ושנין די פרזל לה רברבן אכלה ומדקה ושארא ברגליה רפסה והיא
משניה מן כל חיותא די קדמיה וקרנין עשר לה. (דניאל ז׳:ז׳)

After this I saw in the night visions, and behold a fourth beast, dreadful and terrible, and strong exceedingly; and it had great iron teeth; it devoured and broke in pieces, and stamped the residue with its feet; and it was diverse from all the beasts that were before it; and it had ten horns (Dan 7:7).

In Jerome's *Commentary on Daniel* 7:7 we find:

The fourth empire is the Roman Empire, which now occupies the world. . . . The Hebrews think that what is here silent [i.e., the fact that no *specific* beast is mentioned as the fourth beast in Dan 7:7] has been mentioned in the Psalms: "A boar from the forest laid her waste, and a strange wild animal consumed her" (instead of this the Hebrew [text] reads "all the beasts have torn her apart")[1] [Ps 79:14 LXX and Vulgate = 80:14 Hebrew Masoretic text].[2]

Rabbinic literature indeed links the four beasts mentioned in Dan 7:3ff. with Ps 80:14.

. . . "and four great beasts came up from the sea" [Dan 7:3]: if you [Israel] will so merit it [the animal] will come up out of the sea, but if not, from the forest. An animal coming up from the sea is timid, whereas if it comes from the forest, it is not timid.[3] Similar is [the interpretation of] "The boar of the wood [יער] doth ravage it" (Ps 80:14). The letter ע is suspended [i.e. raised above the level of the other letters, indicating that it might also be read as יאור = river, meaning]: If you will prove worthy, it [i.e., the boar] will come from the river; if you will not prove worthy, from the wood; an animal coming from a river is timid, one coming from a forest is not timid.[4]

---

[1] The Masoretic text reads *weẑîz śāday yirʿennâ,* which is translated by the Jewish Publication Society, "that which moveth in the field feedeth on it."

[2] *PL* 25:530 = *CCSL* 75A, 842, 1. 550.

[3] The parallel text in Midrash Psalms 80:6 explains that "creatures of the sea die as soon as they come upon dry land."

[4] Leviticus Rabbah 13:5 (tr. J. Israelstam; London: Soncino Press, 1939), 2, 171, with slight changes. Parallels, with variants, of this citation are found in Song of Songs Rabbah 3:4, Midrash Psalms 80:6, Abot de Rabbi Natan A, 34 and Yalḳuṭ 1, 536.

In the above citation, and all of its parallels except one, no specific mention is made linking the *fourth* beast in Dan 7:7 with Ps 80:14. One parallel passage continues, and does make this link:

> R. Phinehas and R. Hilkiah taught in the name of R. Simon: Why did not the prophet Daniel give the name of the beast which stands for the fourth kingdom? Because Moses and Asaph had already done so. For Moses, in saying "And the boar, because he parteth the hoof . . ." (Lev 11:7). . . . And likewise Asaph named the fourth beast in saying: "The boar out of the woods doth ravage it."[5]

Jerome begins his *Commentary on Daniel* 7:7 with the identification of the fourth beast as Rome. In the rabbinic passages cited above, no mention is made of Rome as the fourth beast. There are, however, numerous other citations which independently identify the beasts in Dan 7:7 and Ps 80:14 with Rome.

One method of the midrash is to link Dan 7:7 with Abraham's vision in Gen 15:12. The midrash interprets the last five words of this verse as referring to the four world empires[6] which subjugated the Jewish people: Babylon—Chaldea, Media—Persia, Macedonia—Greece, and Edom (=Rome).

> "And lo a dread, even a great darkness, fell upon him" (Gen 15:12). . . . "Dread" alludes to Edom, as it is written "After this I saw . . . a fourth beast, dreadful and terrible" (Dan 7:7).[7]

There are also many other sources which identify the beast in Dan 7:7 with Edom (=Rome), independently of Gen 15:12.[8] We find, as well, a midrashic tradition which links with Rome the fourth beast, described in Dan 7:23 as "a fourth kingdom upon earth which shall be diverse from all the kingdoms, and shall devour the whole earth, and shall tread it down and

---

[5] *The Midrash on Psalms* 80:6 (Braude 2, 51). Parallels in Genesis Rabbah 65:1; Leviticus Rabbah 13:5; Sekel Tob, Toldot, 26:33; Yalkut 1, 112; Yalkut, Psalms 830. It is interesting to note that in all the above parallels (except Midrash Psalms 80:6) no specific mention is made of the fourth beast in Dan 7:7, nor of Daniel at all. They deal only with the fact that Moses and Asaph were the only ones to specifically mention the pig or boar, and cite the appropriate two verses.

[6] For further sources on the four world-kingdoms see Krauss, *Monumenta Talmudica* 5, 14-26; Ginzberg, *Legends* 5, 223, n. 82.

[7] Genesis Rabbah 44:17 (2nd interpretation) with parallels in Leviticus Rabbah 13:5 (2nd interpretation); Mekilta, Jethro, 9; Pirké de Rabbi Eliezer, 28; Yalkut 1, 76-77.

[8] Exodus Rabbah 15:6, 25:8; Tanhuma, Tazria, 8; Tanhuma (Buber), Tazria, 10; Pesikta de Rab Kahana, ed. Mandelbaum, Vatomer Zion, 4 (v. 1, p. 285)=ed. Buber, 131b; Yalkut 1, Vayelek, 941; Yalkut 2, 562, 1064.

break it in pieces." "Rabbi Joḥanan says that this refers to Rome, whose power is known to the whole world."[9]

In most of the above citations, reference is made specifically to Edom. The use of *Edom* and its cognates *Seir* and *Esau* to designate Rome is an ancient one in rabbinic tradition.[10] Epstein[11] gives us an interesting reason for this association. In addition to the fact that both of these nations were similar in their antipathy towards Israel, each worshipped a deity associated with the planet Mars. The philological association of Edom, which means "red" in Hebrew, with Mars, the "red planet" is quite clear.[12] On the other hand, the myth that Romulus and Remus were sons of Mars is well known. Indeed the Romans named their first month, March, after this god. As we will soon point out, both Edom and Rome were further linked, since both were compared with and identified as pigs, boars, and swine.

While there is only one citation in rabbinic literature which specifically links Ps 80:14 with the fourth beast in Dan 7:7,[13] there are many references which identify the boar in Ps 80:14 with Rome. First we refer to the parallels cited in note 5 above. In Pesaḥim 118b[14] "the beast that dwells among the reeds" in Ps 68:31 is identified with Rome by citing Ps 80:14. Rabbi Ḥiyya bar Abba gives another interpretation why Rome is considered "the beast that dwells among the reeds": "all of its actions may be recorded with the same pen." The above statement is rendered more intelligible when it is compared with its parallel in Midrash Psalms 68:15: "all of its writings are done with [one] reed, imposing religious persecution on Israel and commanding them to worship idols." Another connection between Rome and reeds is given in Sanhedrin 21b and its parallels[15] through the statement of

[9]   Abodah Zarah 2b, with parallels in Shebuoth 6b, Yalḳuṭ 2, 192, 452.

[10]   For rabbinic references which use "Edom" in place of "Rome," see Ginzberg, *Legends* 5, 272-3, n. 19. Add to his citations: Targum Jerushalmi 1 (Pseudo-Jonathan) London MS to Gen 15:12 (ed. M. Ginsburger, *Pseudo-Jonathan* [Berlin: S. Calvary & Co., 1903] 25) and Targums Jerushalmi 1 and 2 (Fragmentary) to Lev 26:44, and Genesis Rabbah 44:15 and 83:3. Even in the earliest mention of *Edom* as the "fourth kingdom," in *TJ*1 and *TJ*2 to Gen 15:12 and *TJ*1 to Lev 26:44, *Rome* is meant, since Edom is mentioned after Babylonia, Media, and Greece. A medieval Jewish legend further links Edom to Rome by identifying Zepho, the son of Eliphaz, the son of Esau (=Edom) with the first king of Italy. Cf. Ginzberg, *Legends* 5, 372, n. 425.

[11]   A. Epstein, "The Beasts of the Four Kingdoms," in *Bet Talmud* 4 (1885) 173-177, and *Mikadmoniot Hayehudim* (Jerusalem: Mossad Harav Kook, 1957) 33.

[12]   In Tanḥuma, Terumah, 7 and Tanḥuma (Buber), Terumah, 6 we find a clear reference to the "redness" of Rome. Four materials of the Tabernacle are associated with the four kingdoms, with the red ram's skins equivalent to Rome.

[13]   Cf. note 5.

[14]   Parallels in Exodus Rabbah 35:5 and Yalḳuṭ 2, 800.

[15]   Shabbat 56b and Song of Songs Rabbah 1, 6:4.

Rabbi Isaac that the site of Rome was a thicket of reeds. In Abot de Rabbi Natan A, 34 the boar in Ps 80:14 is identified with Rome; in Yalkut 2, 830 it is identified with Romulus; in Midrash Ps 120:6[16] it is identified with "the evil Esau."

There are interesting midrashic traditions which give reasons why both Esau (or Edom) and Rome were compared with a boar or swine.

> . . . When the swine is lying down, it puts out its hooves, as if to say, "I am clean" [cf. Lev 11:7]; as does this wicked state [Rome] rob and oppress, yet pretend to be executing justice, so for forty . . . years Esau used to ensnare married women and violate them, yet when he attained forty years, he compared himself to his father . . .[17]

In addition to the above, on the basis of homiletic exegesis, Edom (= Rome) is compared to a swine because it reviles and blasphemes God;[18] it slays righteous men;[19] it will one day restore the sovereignty of the world to its rightful owner (God);[20] one day God will return to judge them with justice.[21] Perhaps the most elementary reason for associating the boar with Rome is found in Abot de Rabbi Natan A, 34; "the boar of the forest kills people, injures and smites men," so do the enemies of Israel, represented by the Roman Empire.

Epstein[22] again gives us further insights regarding the symbolism of Rome as swine. Mars was depicted in ancient times as a swine, and as we previously pointed out, both Edom and Rome worshipped deities associated with Mars. In addition, it is well known that the Romans sacrificed the pig — Porca Praesentanea — on their holidays, when they consummated a treaty, and when they buried their dead. The pig was especially effective as a sacrifice since they believed that its blood would atone for their sins in a greater degree than that of any other animal. Despite the obvious pejorative association of Rome with swine, Ginzberg points out that "originally it was

---

[16] With parallels in Midrash Samuel 16 and Yalḳuṭ 2, 829.

[17] Genesis Rabbah 65:1. Parallels with variants are found in Leviticus Rabbah 13:5 (no mention is made of Esau here); Midrash on Ps 80:6 (here the analogy is made directly from the pig to "wicked Esau [who] displays himself so openly on the seats of justice that the legal tricks whereby he robs, steals and plunders appear to be just proceedings."); Sekel Tob, Toldot, 6:33 ("so does the wicked state rob and oppress and pretend to dispense loving-kindness"); Yalḳuṭ 1, 112; Yalḳuṭ, Psalms, 830.

[18] Leviticus Rabbah 13:5, with parallels Yalḳuṭ Makiri 73:22, Yalḳuṭ 1, 536.

[19] Leviticus Rabbah 13:5 and Yalḳuṭ 1, 536.

[20] Leviticus Rabbah 13:5 and its parallels Ecclesiastes Rabbah 1:9 (here we find "owners," i.e., Israel); Pirké de Rabbi Eliezer 11 (in the first editions we find "owner," in the later editions, "owners"), Yalḳuṭ 1, 536.

[21] Tanḥuma (Buber), Shmini, 14.

[22] See n. 11.

not intended as an expression of contempt, but was coined with reference to the standard of the Roman legion stationed in Palestine which had as its emblem a boar, a wild swine. . . ."[23] Krauss adds that

> there is reason to believe that this [symbolization of Rome as a pig in rabbinic literature] came into prominence only since the time of Hadrian and the fall of Betar (135 c.e.) since, in order to insult the Jews, the image of a pig was attached on the South gate of Jerusalem which had been transformed into the Roman colony, Aelia Capitolina.[24]

Hippolytus, Ephraem Syrus, Aphraates, John Chrysostom, Theodoret, and Polychronius do not link the fourth beast in Dan 7:7 with the boar in Ps 80:14. On the basis of available patristic writings it seems that Jerome was the only Church father aware of this midrashic tradition.

[23] *Legends* 5, 294, n. 162.
[24] *Monumenta Talmudica* 5, 15.

CHAPTER 11

JEROME'S *COMMENTARY ON DANIEL* 8:16

ואשמע קול אדם בין אולי ויקרא ויאמר גבריאל הבן להלז את המראה. (דניאל
ח׳:טז׳)

And I heard the voice of a man between the banks of Ulai, who called, and
said: "Gabriel, make this man to understand the vision" (Dan 8:16).

In Jerome's *Commentary on Daniel* 8:16 we find:

The Jews assert that this man who directed Gabriel to make Daniel understand
the vision was Michael. Quite appropriately it was Gabriel, who has been put
in charge of battles, to whom this duty was assigned, inasmuch as the vision
was concerning battles and contests between kings and even succession of
kingdoms. For "Gabriel" is translated into our language as "the strength of,"
or "the mighty one of, God."[1]

We do not find, in extant rabbinic literature, any tradition which links the
anonymous "voice of a man" in Dan 8:16 with the angel Michael. In fact,
the only rabbinic tradition concerning this phrase identifies the voice as
God's, whom the prophets many times describe in human terms.[2] However,
several verses above, in Dan 8:13 we find: "Then I heard a holy one
speaking; and another holy one said to the first one who spoke. . . ."
According to the one midrashic tradition the first "holy one" who spoke
was Michael.[3] Michael is referred to by name as "one of the chief princes"
in Dan 10:13. Thus, Gabriel, in Dan 8:16 and 9:21, together with Michael,
in Dan 10:13, 21, are the only two angels personally identified in the
Hebrew Scriptures.[4] It is thus understandable that Michael and Gabriel are
the most popular angels in rabbinic literature.[5] Based on Dan 10:13 a

---

[1]   *PL* 25:538 = *CCSL* 75A, 857, 11. 918-923.
[2]   Genesis Rabbah 27:1 with parallels in Ecclesiastes Rabbah 2:21 and 8:1; Pesiķta de Rab
Kahana, Parah, 36; Pesiķta Rabbah, Parah, 14:10; Tanḥuma Ḥuḳath 6; and Numbers Rabbah
19:4.
[3]   Tanḥuma (Buber), Genesis, 23 with a parallel in Yalķuṭ 2, 1066.
[4]   Likewise, Michael and Gabriel are the only two angels mentioned by name in the New
Testament.
[5]   See Ginzberg, *Legends* 5, 4, n. 8 and 7 (Index), 172-174, *s.v.* Gabriel and 311-312 *s.v.*
Michael; Dov Neuman (Noy), *Motif-Index of Talmudic-Midrashic Literature*, 783, 788, 789,
792, 800, 802, 806, 817. See the new edition of M. R. James, *The Biblical Antiquities of Philo*,
Introduction, section 10a. In this work, the angel mentioned in each case is Gabriel. Cf. *The*

95

tradition developed that Michael was the prince of angels.[6] Thus, although there is no extant rabbinic tradition that the "voice of a man" in Dan 8:16 refers to Michael, Jerome's Hebrew identification of Michael is certainly in keeping with the above traditon.

Jerome's characterization of Gabriel as the angel of war[7] is borne out by rabbinic tradition which ascribes to this angel the annihilation of Sennacherib's camp, the destruction of Sodom, and the burning of the Temple in Jerusalem.[8] Origen in *De Principiis* 1.8.1 also ascribes to Gabriel "the conduct of wars."

Neither Hippolytus, Ephraem Syrus, Aphraates, John Chrysostom, nor Polychronius identify the "voice of a man" in Dan 8:16. Theodoret comments: "it is possible from the things that were said to conjecture that the one who ordered was the Lord."[9] This coincides with the only extant rabbinic tradition identifying the "voice of a man."

War of the Children of Light against the Children of Darkness 9:16, where the first human tower is Michael and the second is Gabriel.

[6] Hullin 40a; Berakot 4b with parallels in Yalḳuṭ 2, 407, 1066. Ginzberg, *Legends* 5, 4, n. 8 and 71 n. 13, points out that an alternate tradition developed, especially among Babylonian Jews, giving Gabriel superior, or at least equal prestige in the angelic hierarchy. Cf. Genesis Rabbah 78:1 where Michael and Gabriel, alone among the angels, are given the distinction of permanence, and do not vanish.

[7] The basis of the association is the similarity of "Gabriel" with the Hebrew word *gibbôr* = mighty warrior.

[8] Ginzberg, *Legends* 5, 71, n. 13.

[9] *Commentary on Daniel* 8:16, *PG* 81:1448.

CHAPTER 12

JEROME'S *COMMENTARY ON DANIEL* 9:2

בשנת אחת למלכו אני דניאל בינתי בספרים מספר השנים אשר היה דבר
יהוה אל ירמיה הנביא למלאות לחרבות ירושלם שבעים שנה. (דניאל ט':ב')

In the first year of his reign I Daniel meditated in the books, over the number of the years, whereof the word of the Lord came to Jeremiah the prophet, that He would accomplish for the desolations of Jerusalem seventy years (Dan 9:2).

In Jerome's *Commentary on Daniel* 9:2 we find:

Jeremiah had predicted seventy years for the desolation of the Temple, after which the people again would return to Judea and the Temple and Jerusalem would be rebuilt. This fact does not make Daniel negligent but it provokes him more to make his request [of God] so that what God had promised through His clemency He should fulfill through their [Daniel's and others'] prayers, in order that negligence and haughtiness should not beget offense. Finally, we read in Genesis [6:3] that one hundred and twenty years of penitence had been decided upon before the flood; since, in so much time, that is, one hundred years, they were unwilling to do penitence, He did not wait for the other twenty years to be completed but brought on the flood earlier which He had threatened for later. And it is said to Jeremiah because of the hardness of the heart of the Jewish people: "Do not pray for this people, for I will not hearken unto thee" [Jer 7:16]. Samuel also is told: "How long will you mourn over Saul? I also have rejected him" [1 Sam 16:1]. Therefore in ashes and in sackcloth he [Daniel] asks that which God had promised to be fulfilled, not because he was incredulous of the future but in order that unconcern and negligence not beget offense.[1]

Jerome's basic exegetical problem is: Why did Daniel pray to God to restore Jerusalem and its Temple (Dan 9:3-19, especially 9:17,18) when God had already promised, through his prophet Jeremiah (Jer 25:12 and 29:10ff.) that after seventy years Israel would be restored to the place whence it had been previously carried away into captivity. Jerome's answer stresses that God's promise of restoration was not automatic but was dependent upon the proper attitude of those to be redeemed. This answer is supported by Jer 29:12 which required Israel to "call upon me, and go, and pray unto me, and I will hearken unto you," even though two verses earlier

---

[1] *PL* 25:539 = *CCSL* 75A, 860, 1. 16-861,1. 32.

97

Israel was specifically promised "I will remember you, and perform my good word toward you, in causing you to return to this place" (Jer 29:10).[2]

We have already pointed out in the analysis of Jerome's comment on Dan 5:2 that there were two historical events with which one may begin to calculate Jeremiah's seventy-year period: The beginning of Nebuchadnezzar's reign, or his second year, when he subjugated Jehoiakim. The citation in Megilla 12a prefers that the reckoning begin with Nebuchadnezzar's second year, and end with the declaration of Cyrus (Ezra 1:2ff.)[3] Dan 9:2, however, substitutes the phrase "for the desolations of Jerusalem seventy years" in interpreting Jeremiah's prophecy. This means that Daniel calculated the seventy-year period beginning with the destruction of Jerusalem and the Temple (587 B.C.E.) in the eleventh year of King Zedekiah's reign (2 Kgs 25:2), eighteen years after the subjugation of Jehoiakim. Thus, the termination of the seventy-year period was approximately the time of the building of the Second Temple[4] begun in the second year of Darius (Ezra 4:24 and Hag 1:15).

No extant rabbinic source discusses why Daniel prayed concerning the fulfillment of the seventy-years prophecy of Jeremiah.[5] In truth, Jerome himself does not specifically mention any Hebrew tradition in his lengthy comment on Dan 9:2. However, his reference to Genesis "that one hundred and twenty years of penitence had been decided upon before the flood" is well known in rabbinic literature, although it is not there connected to the text of Dan 9:2.

Although Jerome does not specifically cite a verse in Genesis as the basis for his statement "one hundred and twenty years of penitence had been decided upon before the flood," it is obvious that he is referring to Gen 6:3: "And the Lord said 'My spirit shall not abide in man for ever, for that he is also flesh; therefore shall his days be a hundred and twenty years.'" In

---

[2]   This is not the unanimous opinion presented in the Talmud. In Sanhedrin 97b we find: "Rab said: all the predestined dates [for redemption] have passed, and the matter [now] depends only on repentance and good deeds. But Samuel maintained it is sufficient for a mourner to keep his period of mourning" [i.e., Israel's suffering in the Diaspora sufficiently warrants their redemption even without their repentance]. The Talmud then establishes that this controversy is based on an earlier tannaitic controversy.

[3]   This would not be exactly seventy years according to current chronology.

[4]   Modern chronology places this at 520 B.C.E.

[5]   In Megillah 12a we do find, after a discussion of the calculation errors of Belshazzar and Ahasuerus, "Daniel also made a mistake in this calculation" (Parallel in Yalḳuṭ 2, 1066). No details are given. However, the difficulty in arriving at the exact date of the termination of Jeremiah's prophecy is quite evident from the context. Perhaps, in keeping with extant rabbinic sources, Daniel prayed for understanding Jeremiah's prophecy, or for forgiveness of his original error in computation.

Jerome's *Quaestiones Hebraicae in Genesim* he rejects a literal interpretation of this verse on the following grounds:

> Furthermore, lest He [God] may seem to be cruel in this, that He had not given to sinners a place for repentance, he added, "But their days will be 120 years," that is, they will have 120 years to do repentance. It is not, therefore, that human life, as many wrongly assert, was contracted to 120 years, but that 120 years were given to that generation for repentance, since, indeed, we find that after the flood Abraham lived 175 years and others more than 200 and 300 years. Since, indeed, they despised to do repentance, God was unwilling for his decree to await its time, but, cutting off the space of 20 years, he brought on the flood in the one hundredth year that had been destined for doing repentance.[6]

Rabbinic exegesis likewise shunned a literal interpretation of this verse[7] which seems to limit man's life span to one hundred and twenty years. Both rabbinic and patristic commentaries interpret this verse as an example of God's leniency:[8] He gave the generation of the flood a maximum of one

---

[6] *PL* 23:997 = *CCSL* 72, 9-10 (Lagarde 12.9-19).

[7] The one rabbinic source which advocates a literal interpretation of Gen 6:3 is Ecclesiastes Rabbah 1:15. "From the time the Holy One, blessed be He, reduced their [the generation of the Flood's] years, as it is said 'therefore shall his days be a hundred and twenty years' (Gen 6:3) — they [the years of man's life span] have never been restored to their original number." It is interesting to note that Philo in *Quaestiones,* Gen. 1:91; Josephus in *Antiquities* 1.75 and Lactantius, *Institutiones* 2.14-15 adopt a literal interpretation of Gen 6:3. It should be noted that Jerome was against this literal interpretation.

[8] Jerome even interprets the *first part* of this verse as an example of God's leniency. Referring to the Hebrew original, in *Quaestiones Hebraicae in Genesim* 6:3, he translates it as follows: "My spirit shall not judge these men for *or* to eternity, because they are flesh." Jerome continues: "that is, because man's nature and condition is full of fraility, I will not reserve them to eternal torments, but I will, in this world, render them their deserts. So that thus this judicial visitation of God affords us an instance of his leniency, and not of that severity expressed in our copies." [The LXX reads: "My spirit shall certainly not remain among these men forever" which is obviously a strict judgment.] It is interesting to note that Jerome does not mention in *Quaestiones in Geneism* (written *c.* 390) the interpretation concerning the shortening of the one hundred and twenty year period of repentance into one hundred years, as found in his *Commentary on Daniel* 9:2 (written in 407).
In rabbinic tradition, the Generation of the Flood does not have a share in the world to come (i.e., will not be granted Eternal Life). Cf. Mishna Sanhedrin 10:3; Tosefta Sanhedrin 13:6; Tosefta Sotah 10; Talmud Babli, Sanhedrin 108a; Talmud Yerushalmi, Sanhedrin 10:3; Seder Olam Rabbah 4; Genesis Rabbah 26:6 (with a parallel in Yalḳuṭ 1, 44); Genesis Rabbah 28:8; Genesis Rabbah 32:1; Leviticus Rabbah 4:1; Tanḥuma (Buber), Genesis, 40, Abot de Rabbi Natan A, 32; Pirḳé de Rabbi Eliezer, 34. Several of these sources follow the view added in Mishna Sandedrin 10:3 that the Generation of the Flood will also not stand judgment in the world to come since they had already been judged in the flood itself. This view is based on this same verse, Gen 6:3. (In Pirḳé de Rabbi Eliezer 34, the verse Isa 26:14 is cited.) No indication is given in rabbinic sources that this results from God's mercy or leniency as Jerome claims.

hundred and twenty years in which to repent their evil ways.[9]

According to the above interpretation, there is an apparent chronological difficulty in arriving at the one hundred and twenty year period from the decree of God in Gen 6:3 concerning the length of man's days until the year the Flood began. In Gen 5:32 we find that Noah was five hundred years old after the birth of Shem, Ham, and Japheth. In Gen 7:6 we find that Noah was six hundred years old when the Flood began. Assuming that the decree in Gen 6:3 took place after the birth of Shem, Ham, and Japheth mentioned previously in Gen 5:32, we could not account for a period of one hundred and twenty years; at best, one hundred years. Seder Olam Rabbah, at the end of chapter 28, solves this difficulty by placing the decree twenty years previous to Gen 5:32 (i.e., when Noah was four hundred and eighty years old).[10] Jerome's comment in his *Commentary on Daniel* 9:2 cited above solves — *without specifically mentioning* — this chronological difficulty.

> Finally, we read in Genesis [6:3] that one hundred and twenty years of penitence had been decided upon before the Flood; since, in so much time, that is, one hundred years, they were unwilling to do penitence, he did not wait for the other twenty years to be completed but brought on the Flood earlier which he had threatened for later.[11]

[9]   Ginzberg, *Legends* 5, 174, n. 19, gives us the basic rabbinic sources that one hundred and twenty years were given prior to the Flood to enable that generation to repent. (Correct his citation "Sifré, Numbers, 43, end" to "Sifré, Deuteronomy, 43, end".) Add the following sources: Abot de Rabbi Natan A, 32, Leḳah Tob 7:4; Yalḳuṭ 1, 47. The first two sources mention an additional seven days which were given for repentance after the one hundred and twenty year period. Add the following parallel to Mekilta, Shirah, 5, 38b: Yalḳuṭ 1, 246. There are two curious variants of the one hundred and twenty year tradition. In Pirḳé de Rabbi Eliezer, 23, Noah spent 52 years constructing the ark and preaching repentance. In *Sefer Hayashar,* Noah, 14a-14b, five years are mentioned. In patristic tradition, in addition to Jerome's *Quaestiones in Genesim* 6:3 cited above, the following sources mention the one hundred and twenty year period of repentance prior to the Flood: Aphraates (the earliest Syrian Church Father, who lived during the first half of the fourth century), Homily 2:8 (in *Text und Untersuchungen* III, ed. Gebhardt and Harnack [Leipsig, 1888] 3.26); Ephraem the Syrian (born c. 306 died 373) on Gen 6:3 in the edition of Benedictus and Assemanus (Rome, 1737-1743), translated in *Select Works of S. Ephrem the Syrian* (tr. J. B. Morris; Oxford, 1847) 263, n. a; Cyril of Jerusalem (d. 386), *De Cathech.* 2:8 (*PG* 33:391B).

[10]   In Numbers Rabbah 14:12 we find that the decree heralding the Flood was issued to Noah twenty years before he had children. This seems to follow the tradition in Seder Olam Rabbah. Rashi, in his commentary on Gen 6:3 refers to Seder Olam Rabbah and gives the exegetical basis for its interpretation: there is not necessarily a chronological order in the verses of the Torah.

[11]   *PL* 25:539 = *CCSL* 75A, 860, 1. 22-861, 1. 26. This interpretation that 120 years were shortened to 100 years has no parallel in extant rabbinic literature. In fact, on Gen 7:4 "For yet seven days, and I will cause it to rain upon the earth forty days and forty nights," the Targum of Pseudo-Jonathan adds the following: "For, behold, I give you a space of seven days; if they [the generation of the Flood] will be converted. . . ." Thus, a seven-day extension of the one

Thus Jerome implies that God shortened the period of repentance from one hundred and twenty years to one hundred years in punishment for man's unwillingness to repent.

More than a century prior to Jerome the tradition that it took one hundred years to build the ark was already mentioned by the Church Fathers. Origen mentions it in passing in *Contra Celsum* 4.41. Julius Africanus is more specific and points out that although Gen 6:3 limits man's years to one hundred and twenty (the literal interpretation), this refers only to the generation of the Flood. The oldest members of this *particular* generation were twenty years old[12] when God issued his decree of one hundred and twenty years.[13] Thus, when the Flood came one hundred years later, the oldest victims of this generation were one hundred and twenty years old.

God decreed to destroy the whole race of the living by a Flood, having threatened that men should not survive beyond one hundred and twenty years. Nor let it be deemed a matter of difficulty because some lived afterwards a longer period than that. For the space of time meant was one hundred years up to the Flood in the case of the sinners of that time; for they were twenty years old.[14]

Although the biblical text of Genesis does not even hint at Noah's role as a preacher of repentance to his generation, this tradition is well known in Josephus, rabbinic, and pseudepigraphic literature.[15] In 2 Pet 2:5 Noah is called "the preacher of righteousness." The following citation from the *Apocalypse of Paul,* a New Testament apocryphal work first attested to in the beginning of the fifth century, is quite vivid. Paul meets Noah in Paradise. Noah says:

I spent a hundred years making the ark when I did not take off the shirt I wore nor cut the hair of my head. Moreover I strove after continence, not coming near my wife; and in those hundred years the hair of my head did not grow in

---

hundred and twenty year period of repentance was given to them. Ginzberg, *Legends* 5, 175-176, nn. 19-20, gives ample rabbinic sources to prove that the above view was accepted.

[12] The age of majority in biblical times.

[13] Africanus thus presents an alternate solution to the chronological difficulty presented above. Gen 5:32 and Gen 7:6 are one hundred years apart, and only one hundred years were given, *ab initio,* to the sinners to repent. This interpretation has no parallel in extant rabbinic literature.

[14] *PG* 10:68. *Chronography of Julius Africanus,* tr. S. D. F. Salmond (*Ante-Nicene Christian Library* 9; Edinburgh: Clark and Co., 1869) 173.

[15] Cf. Josephus, *Antiquities* 1.74; Genesis Rabbah 30:7; Ecclesiastes Rabbah 9:15.1; Babylonian Talmud Sanhedrin 108 a-b; Tanḥuma, Noah 5; Pirḳé de Rabbi Eliezer, 22; Ecclesiastes Zuta, 125; Aggadat Bereshit, 1; Sibylline Oracles 11.177-233.

length, nor were my clothes dirty. And I implored the men of that time saying: "Repent, for a flood of water will come upon you." But they ridiculed me and mocked my words.[16]

Noah is also depicted as a preacher in many patristic references.[17]

Thus the tradition that one hundred and twenty years were given to the generation of the Flood for repentance affords a good example comparing extant rabbinic and patristic interpretations.

---

[16] Edgar Hennecke, *New Testament Apocrypha* II, (ed. Wilhelm Schneemelcher, tr. R. McL. Wilson; Phila: Westminster Press, 1964) 794.

[17] Pseudo-Tertullian, *Apol. I adv. Marc.* 3.3 (*PL* 2:1127) and Augustine *in Civ. Dei* 15:27 (*CSEL* 40:2,120) and in *De Catech.* 19.32 (*PL* 40:334) note that Noah preached repentance for one hundred years. Theophilus, *ad Autol.* 3:19; Methodius, *Conv. decem. virg.* 10:3, and Hippolytus, *Arabic Fragment to Pentateuch* Gen 6:18 mention Noah as a preacher, without noting the hundred-year period. John Chrysostom, *In Genes. Homil.* 25 (*PG* 53:218-219) notes that Noah tried to influence his generation to repent during the first 500 years of his life, but to no avail. Therefore, God granted an additional 120 years for repentence, during which time Noah carefully built the Ark. Chrysostom does not comment on the chronological problem of 120 *vs.* 100 years.

CHAPTER 13

JEROME'S *COMMENTARY ON DANIEL* 9:24-27

כד'. שבעים שבעים נחתך על עמך ועל עיר קדשך לכלא הפשע ולחתם חטאות ולכפר עון ולהביא צדק עלמים ולחתם חזון ונביא ולמשח קדש קדשים . כה'. ותדע ותשכל מן מצא דבר להשיב ולבנות ירושלם עד משיח נגיד שבעים שבעה ושבעים ששים ושנים תשוב ונבנתה רחוב וחרוץ ובצוק העתים. כו'. ואחרי השבעים ששים ושנים יכרת משיח ואין לו והעיר והקדש ישחית עם נגיד הבא וקצו בשטף ועד קץ מלחמה נחרצת שממות. כז'. והגביר ברית לרבים שבוע אחד וחצי השבוע ישבית זבח ומנחה ועל כנף שקוצים משומם ועד כלה ונחרצה תתך על שומם. (דניאל ט':כד'-כז')

24. Seventy weeks are decreed upon thy people and upon thy holy city, to finish the transgression, and to make an end of sin, and to forgive iniquity, and to bring in everlasting righteousness, and to seal vision and prophet, and to anoint the most holy place.

25. Know therefore and discern, that from the going forth of the word to restore and to build Jerusalem unto one anointed, a prince, shall be seven weeks; and for threescore and two weeks, it shall be built again, with broad place and moat, but in troublous times.

26. And after the threescore and two weeks shall an anointed one be cut off, and be no more; and the people of a prince that shall come shall destroy the city and the sanctuary; but his end shall be with a flood; and unto the end of the war desolations are determined.

27. And he shall make a firm covenant with many for one week; and for half of the week he shall cause the sacrifice and the offering to cease; and upon the wing of detestable things shall be that which causeth appalment; and that until the extermination wholly determined be poured out upon that which causeth appalment (Dan 9:24-27).

In Jerome's *Commentary on Daniel* 9:24-27 we find:

As for the view which the Hebrews hold concerning this passage, I have touched upon it leaving the credibility of their assertions to those who asserted them. And so let me put it in the form of a paraphrase, in order to bring out the sense more clearly. "O Daniel, know that from this day on which I now speak to you—now that was the first year of Darius, who slew Belshazzar and transferred the Chaldean Empire to the Persians and Medes—unto the seventieth week of years, that is, four hundred and ninety years, the following events shall befall your people, step by step. First of all, God, whom you now beseech greatly, shall be appeased by you, and sin shall be destroyed and transgression shall come to an end. For now, although the city is deserted and the

Temple lies destroyed to its very foundations so that the nation is plunged into mourning, yet within no great time it shall be restored. And not only shall it come to pass within these seventy weeks that the city shall be built and the Temple restored, but the Christ, that is, eternal righteousness, shall be born. And the vision and the prophecy shall be sealed, so that there shall be no more any prophet to be found in Israel, and the Saint of saints shall be anointed. We read concerning Him in the Psalter: 'Moreover, because God, even your God, has anointed you with oil of gladness above your fellows' [Ps 45:8]. And in another passage he says of himself: 'Be you holy, for I am holy' [Lev 19:12]. Know therefore that from this day on which I speak to you and make you the promise by the speech of the Lord that the people shall return and Jerusalem shall be restored, there shall be sixty-two weeks numbered unto the time of Christ the prince and of the perpetual desolation of the Temple; and that there shall also be seven other weeks in which the two events shall take place, according to their order, which I have already mentioned before, namely that the people shall return and the courtyard shall be rebuilt by Nehemiah and Ezra. Therefore, at the end of the weeks the decree of God shall be accomplished in distressing times, when the Temple shall again be destroyed, and the city taken captive. For 'after the sixty-two weeks the Christ shall be slain, and the people which is going to reject him shall go out of existence' [Dan 9:26-27] (or, as they [the Jews] put it, 'the kingdom, which he thought he would retain, will not be his')." And why do I speak of the slaying of Christ, and of the utter forfeiture of God's help by the people, since the Roman people, were going to demolish the city and sanctuary under Vespasian, the leader who was to come; upon his death the seven weeks, that is, forty-nine years, were complete, and Aelius Hadrian, by whom afterwards the city of Aelia was established upon the ruins of Jerusalem, vanquished the revolting Jews in their conflict with the general Tinus Rufus. It was at that time that the sacrificial offering ceased and "the desolation will endure even unto the consummation and end of the world" [Dan 9:27]. "We are not," say the Jews, "impressed by the fact that the seven weeks are mentioned first, and afterwards the sixty-two, and again a single week which is divided into two parts. For this is the idiomatic usage of the Hebrew language, as well as of Latin, the speech of the ancients, that in quoting a figure, the small number is given first and then the larger. For example, we do not, according to good usage in our language, say 'Abraham lived a hundred and seventy-five years'; on the contrary, they [the Hebrews] say, 'Abraham lived five and seventy and one hundred years.'[1] And so the

---

[1]   Jerome's point is well taken, but his biblical proof text is not valid. Gen 25:7 states "And these are the days of the years of Abraham's life which he lived, a hundred years and seventy years and five years." This order is found thus in both the LXX and Vulgate. In Josephus, *Antiquities* 1.256 the paraphrase of this verse has "seventy-five in addition to one hundred years." Perhaps Jerome confused Josephus' paraphrase with the Bible. In Gen 12:4 we find, however, ". . . and Abram was five and seventy years when he departed out of Haran." Another possibility might be that Jerome had *this* text in mind and simply erred. It does seem unusual, however, that a careful scholar such as Jerome did not check his source in this case.

fulfillment is not to follow the [literal order of the] words, but it has been accomplished in terms of the whole sum, taken together." I am also well aware that some of them [i.e., the Jews] assert that as for the single week about which it has been written, "He has established a covenant with many for one week" [Dan 9:27], the division is [between the reigns] of Vespasian and Hadrian. According to the history of Josephus, Vespasian and Titus concluded peace with the Jews for three years and six months. And the [other] three years and six months are accounted for under Hadrian, when Jerusalem was completely destroyed and the Jewish nation was massacred in crowds at a time, with the result that they were even expelled from the borders of Judea. This is what the Hebrews say, paying little attention to the fact that from the first year of Darius, King of the Persians, until the final overthrow of Jerusalem which befell them under Hadrian, the period involved is a hundred and seventy-four Olympiads, that is, six hundred ninety-six years,[2] which total up to ninety-nine Hebrew weeks and three years, [that being the time] when Cochebas, the leader of the Jews, was crushed and Jerusalem was demolished to the very ground.[3]

Our first task is to attempt to clarify this most complex and confusing chronological Hebrew tradition found in Jerome's *Commentary on Daniel* 9:24-27. Jerome points out that from the day Darius slew Belshazzar until the end of the 490 year period, the following events will occur: 1) Within a short time (seven "weeks" or 49 years) the nation shall return, the city rebuilt by Nehemiah and Ezra, and the Temple restored. These seven weeks seem to be part of the first 62 week period, although Jerome never explicitly mentions this. 2) Before the end of the 62 week period, Christ will be born, marking the end of prophets and prophecy. 3) After the sixty-two weeks (Jerome is not explicit how much later), Christ shall be slain, the Temple will again be destroyed, Jerusalem taken captive and Vespasian killed. Since the first Jewish tradition cited by Jerome does not account for one week, perhaps we may assume that Christ will be slain one week after the sixty-two week period. 4) The phrase "upon his [Vespasian's] death the seven weeks or forty-nine years were complete" is most ambiguous. Judging from the continuation of the above phrase, the *terminus ad quem* of the entire seventy-week period is the establishment of Aelia upon the ruins of Jerusalem and the crushing of the Jewish revolt by Hadrian and his general, Tinus Rufus. Since we have already accounted for sixty-three weeks, there must be a seven-week or forty-nine year period from the death of Vespasian

---

[2]   According to currently accepted chronology, this period involved six hundred and *fifty* six years, from 521 B.C.E. until 135 C.E.

[3]   *PL* 25:694 = *CCSL* 75A, 886, 1. 551-889, 1. 617.

to the Hadrianic persecutions.[4] This hypothesis is indeed supported by the point Jerome subsequently makes in the name of the Jews that "the fulfillment is not to follow the literal order of the words"; i.e., despite the fact that in Dan 9:25-27 we first read of a seven-week period, then a sixty-two week period, then a one-week period, in actual fulfillment, there first came a sixty-two week period (then a one-week period?) and then the seven-week period described above. Thus the phrase "upon his [Vespasian's] death the seven weeks or forty-nine years were complete" is most difficult to understand. It seems most plausible to assume that the final forty-nine year period *began* with Vespasian's death.

Jerome states an alternate Jewish tradition concerning the single week (Dan 9:27): Vespasian and Titus concluded peace with the Jews for three years and six months, and so did Hadrian. The chronological difficulty with this interpretation is that the two halves of the single week were not successive, as the verse states, but rather interrupted by approximately sixty-five years.[5]

The Hebrew tradition cited by Jerome in his *Commentary on Daniel* 9:24-27 is the longest one in this book, and one of the longest in all his works. Unfortunately it can not be found, *in toto,* in extant rabbinic literature. Several parts of it, however, are quite well known, as will soon be demonstrated.

Jerome prefaces his presentation of the Hebrew interpretation of Dan 9:24-27 with the words "paraphrase, in order to bring out the sense more clearly." This is the only time in his *Commentary on Daniel* when Jerome admits that he is paraphrasing the Jewish interpretation. It seems clear that the one aspect of the Jewish interpretation of Dan 9:24-27 which needed paraphrasing for Christian consumption was the reference to the Messiah. Krauss[6] has clearly pointed out

> that the Messiah was called in Judaeo-Hellenic circles *Ēleimmenos,* the 'anointed,' an exact equivalent of the Hebrew משיח, but that this term must

---

[4] This hypothesis is substantiated by modern chronology. Vespasian died in 79 C.E. Hadrian succeeded Trajan in 118 and provoked the Bar Kochba rebellion in 132. Thus, forty-nine years after 79 C.E., or 128 C.E., did approximately mark the era of Hadrianic persecutions. (Cf. Baron, *Social and Religious History of the Jews* 2, 97.)

[5] Vespasian's peace would have ended in 66 C.E. with the war which led to the destruction of the Second Temple (Baron, *Social and Religious History* 2, 90); Hadrian's peace would have ended in 132 C.E. with the beginning of the Bar Kochba Revolt. Admittedly, there is a further difficulty regarding this hypothesis, in that Jerome speaks of a peace concluded by Vespasian and *Titus,* while in fact Titus was not involved in Judea in 66.

[6] "The Jews in the Works of the Church Fathers," 243-244. See n. 3 on p. 244 for specific examples from the works of Jerome.

be distinguished from *Christos,* by which the Christians denominated their Messiah. The name Christ was not pleasant to the Jews, since it had become the watchword of their bitterest enemies, and therefore they preferred to connote the same idea by the expression 'the anointed.' . . . In Jerome's time the word had obtained wide currency among the Jews, and he cannot hide his chagrin at the fact.

Thus it is evident that Jerome's frequent use of the word "Christus" in this passage shows that it is a Christian paraphrase.

In at least one place Jerome oversteps the bounds of paraphrase and gives an indigenous Christian interpretation of ואין לו which is quite forced: "For after the sixty-two weeks the Christ shall be slain, and the nation who shall reject him shall go out of existence," a definite reference to the perfidious Jews. Jerome then continues: "or, as they [the Jews] put it, 'the kingdom, which he thought he would retain, will not be his,' " the converse.

The first time Jerome mentions "Christ the Prince" he places him chronologically at the same time as the "perpetual desolation of the Temple." The various dates which have been advanced for the crucifixion of Jesus, ranging from 29-35 C.E. are not very close to 70 C.E., the date of the destruction of the Second Temple, but Jerome was willing to overlook this. In rabbinic literature, however, we find the destruction of the Temple linked with the *birth* of the Messiah. Louis Ginzberg in his *Legends* 6, 406, n. 53 cites the parallels of this legend.[7] Its basic content is that an Arab advises a Jew that on the same day that the Temple was destroyed, the Messiah was born. No indication is given in the various parallel sources whether the First or Second Temple is meant, except in Aggadat Bereshit 67, 133, where the First Temple is definitely indicated.

The oldest source in rabbinic literature which gives the chronology of the "seventy-weeks" in Daniel is found in Seder Olam Rabbah ch. 28. Most other rabbinic sources and medieval Jewish commentators follow this account.[8] Near the end of this chapter we find the following anonymous chronological interpretation of Dan 9:24-27:

---

[7] Yerushalmi Berakot 2, 5a; Lamentations Rabbah 1, 89-90; Lamentations Zuta, 133; Panim Aherim, 78; Aggadat Bereshit 67, 133; an excerpt from an unknown Midrash quoted by Grünhut in his edition of Makiri on Proverbs, p. 103b.

[8] The most notable Jewish commentators are: Saadiah Gaon, in his *Book of Beliefs and Opinions,* Treatise 8, ch. 9 (tr. Samuel Rosenblatt; New Haven: Yale U. Press, 1948) 320ff.; Rashi, in his *Commentary on Daniel* 9:24ff.; Pseudo-Saadia, in his commentary *ad loc.;* Nachmanides, *The Book of Redemption,* Section 3 (Dov Chavel, ed.; *The Writings of Nachmanides* 1 [Hebrew, Jerusalem: Mossad Harav Kook, 1963] 281ff.); Isaac Abrabanel, in his commentary to Daniel *The Wellsprings of Salvation* 370ff.

"Seven weeks" (9:25), these refer to the years which they spent in exile, and then returned [to Israel].

"Sixty-two weeks" (9:26), these refer to the years they spent in the land [of Israel].

"One week" (9:27), was partially spent in the land [of Israel], and partially in exile.

Immediately following this anonymous view, we find the statement of Rabbi Jose, the author of Seder Olam Rabbah. He is most interested in establishing the exact *terminus a quo* ("from the destruction of the first Temple") and *terminus ad quem* ("to the destruction of the second Temple").[9] He disregards the 7-62-1 sequence of the verses in Daniel, and instead substitutes "seventy years of its [the First Temple's] destruction, and 420 years[10] of its [the Second Temple's] existence." Rabbi Jose does concern himself with the exegetical problem of the "seventy-weeks" beginning retroactive to Daniel's vision in the first year of Darius. He brings other biblical instances of retroactive decrees to show that this phenomenon occurs elsewhere.

The chronology found in Seder Olam Rabbah ch. 28 has little in common with Jerome's Hebrew tradition. It does interpret the seventy-weeks as equivalent to 490 years. This period begins, however, according to Rabbi Jose, with the destruction of the First Temple, approximately 51 years before the year that Darius slew Belshazzar, the *terminus a quo* of Jerome's Hebrew tradition. It ends with the destruction of the Second Temple, approximately 65 years before Jerome's *terminus ad quem,* the fall of Betar.

Another major difference between the anonymous account in Seder Olam Rabbah and Jerome's account is that the former follows the obvious chronological sequence in Dan 9:25-27, i.e., the seven-week period

---

[9]   In Nazir 32b, Abaye assumes that the destruction of the Second Temple occurred at the end of the "seventy-weeks."

[10]   In Seder Olam Rabbah, ch. 30, Rabbi Jose itemizes the kingdoms which rule over Judea during the 420 year period in which the Second Temple stood. A parallel to this is found in Avodah Zarah 8b-9a. In Yoma 9a and Arakin 12b we also find explicit mention that the Second Temple stood 420 years. This is obviously not in agreement with modern chronology which calculates that the Second Temple stood from 516 B.C.E. until 70 C.E., a period of approximately 586 years. Loeb points out in *Revue des études juives* 19 (1919) 202-205, that the tradition that the Second Temple stood 420 years began with Rabbi Jose, the author of Seder Olam Rabbah, who forced this chronology to agree with Dan 9:24-27, i.e., that 490 years would elapse from the destruction of the First Temple until the destruction of the Second. Since the Babylonian Exile after the destruction of the First Temple was assumed to last 70 years, in accordance with Jer 25:12 and 29:10ff., this left 420 years for the duration of the Second Temple. Josephus, *Antiquities* 10.147 mentions that "the [second] temple was burned four hundred and seventy years, six months and ten days after it was built."

preceding the sixty-two weeks. The seven-week period = 49 years, to which we add 3 years, to bring us to the proclamation of Cyrus and return to Judea, which, according to rabbinic chronology, took place 52 years after the destruction of the First Temple.[11] Although the chronology of Rabbi Jose disregards the 7-62-1 sequence of the verses in Daniel, no indication whatsoever is given in Seder Olam Rabbah, or in any other source in extant rabbinic tradition, that the seven-week period was to *follow* the 62 weeks as Jerome's Hebrew tradition indicated. In light of Jerome's remarks, citing the Jews on biblical Hebrew style, giving the smaller number before the larger, it seems quite plausible that in Jerome's time a Hebrew tradition did indeed exist placing the 62 weeks prior to the seven weeks. Unfortunately it has not been preserved in other sources.

Josephus is unusually evasive in giving no direct reference or interpretation to the Seventy-Weeks prophecy in Dan 9:24-27. Although Josephus devotes more attention to Daniel than to any other prophet (*Antiquities* 10.186-281), giving us a detailed picture of his life together with clear references to verses or events in Daniel 1—6 and 8, he omits any reference to the celebrated prophecy in Daniel 9. At best, there is only one oblique reference found in *Antiquities* 10.276 where, after referring to the vision found in Daniel 8, we find: "In the same manner Daniel also wrote about the empire of the Romans and that Jerusalem would be taken by them and the Temple laid waste."[12] Evidently, he is referring to Dan 9:24-27 or perhaps to Dan 11:30ff. Marcus points out that the phrase "Jerusalem . . . laid waste" is an addition from the excerpt in Chrysostom.[13] He also cites the opinion that the entire phrase is an interpolation. Marcus cannot see why Josephus hesitates to mention the Roman conquest of Judea and the destruction of Jerusalem. Perhaps we can shed light on Josephus' hesitation by the following.

Antiquities 10.276 without Chrysostom's addition is not at all clear, and

---

[11] Although the text in Seder Olam Rabbah ch. 28 does not mention the addition of these 3 years, we do find in ch. 29, "for fifty-two years after the destruction of the [First] Temple Israel remained in the Chaldean Empire, and were remembered and went up [to Judea]." Also in ch. 27, in the name of Rabbi Jose we find that Judea remained desolate for 52 years, obviously referring to the period from the destruction of the Temple until the proclamation of Cyrus. Parallels to the above text are found in Shabbat 145b and Yoma 54a. Cf. Rashi's comment in Yoma 54a which clarifies the statement in light of Megillah 11a. There is an even more explicit source, stating that from the destruction of the Temple until the downfall of the Chaldean kingdom fifty-two years elapsed (Cf. Song of Songs Rabbah 2:13, with parallels in Pesikta Rabbati 15, 74b; Pesikta de Rab Kahana 5, 50b-51a).

[12] Josephus, *Antiquities* 9-11 (Marcus, 311).

[13] Ibid., 310-311, n. "c." This excerpt is found in Chrysostom's *Adv. Judaeos* 5.8. The Latin translation of Josephus omits this entire phrase. Cf. Niese's edition of Josephus.

may be translated alternately, as does Montgomery,[14] as follows: "In the same manner Daniel also wrote about the empire of the Romans and that it [ambiguous] would be desolated by them [ambiguous]." Even a cursory glance at Dan 9:26 shows that the "people of a prince" [i.e., Rome] who "shall destroy the city" [i.e., Jerusalem] and the "sanctuary" [i.e., the Temple] will afterwards, in turn, be "destroyed by a flood." Thus, Josephus could very well have written the above cryptic sentence intending an oblique reference to the destruction of Rome = "it," by the Jews = "them."[15] However, only one familiar with Dan 9:26 would catch this double entendre purposely constructed by Josephus. The alien [i.e., Roman] eye would interpret it simply as the destruction of Jerusalem and the Temple by the Romans. It is quite clear that Josephus could not dare to be more explicit about the eventual triumph of Israel because of his Roman patrons who were very sensitive to any spark of Jewish rebellion.

This interpretation of Josephus' double entendre is substantiated by his interpretation of Nebuchadnezzar's dream in Dan 2:36ff. found in *Antiquities* 10.210ff. The text of Daniel is quite explicit that a stone cut out without hands smote the image upon its feet of iron and clay, broke them into pieces [Dan 2:34, 45], and "became a great mountain and filled the whole earth" [Dan 2:35]. The ultimate supremacy of this "stone" is made quite clear by the text in Daniel. Curiously enough, Josephus writes as follows:

> And Daniel also revealed to the king the meaning of the stone, but I have not thought it proper to relate this, since I am expected to write of what is past and done and not what is to be; if, however, there is anyone who has so keen a desire for exact information that he will not stop short of enquiring more closely but wishes to learn about the hidden things that are to come, let him take the trouble to read the Book of Daniel, which he will find among the sacred writings.[16]

Marcus' notes on this passage are self-evident:

> a) Josephus has omitted the scriptural detail about the division of the fourth kingdom and its composition of iron and clay, probably because, like the rabbis, he identified it with Rome and did not wish to offend Roman readers.
> c) Josephus' evasiveness about the meaning of the stone which destroyed the kingdom of iron (vss. 44ff.) is due to the fact that the Jewish interpretation of

---

[14] *Commentary on the Book of Daniel,* 396-397.

[15] Chrysostom may have added the phrase "Jerusalem . . . laid waste" to remove the ambiguity.

[16] *Antiquities* 9-11 (Marcus, 275).

it current in his day took it as a symbol of the Messiah or Messianic kingdom which would make an end of the Roman empire.[17]

Evidently, Josephus was confident that his Roman audience would not check his source by snooping in the Book of Daniel itself. With this precedent in mind, the double entendre of Josephus' later passage in *Antiquities* 10.276 is better understood. In both cases, he was writing for two different audiences, telling each one what it wanted to hear.

Rabbinic literature is well aware of Hadrian's general, Tinus Rufus, whom Jerome credits with vanquishing the revolting Jews. In Taꜥanit, chapter 4, mishna 4 (26b), we find a chronological list of five tragic events which befell the people of Israel on the ninth day of Ab. The last one enumerated is: "the city [Jerusalem] was plowed under." From the subsequent discussion in the Talmud, Taꜥanit 29a, it is quite evident that "Turnus Rufus," as he is there called, was responsible for this act.[18] Since the list of five is definitely chronological, and the fourth event is the capture of Betar, this final plowing of Jerusalem must have taken place subsequently.

Jerome's final note "It was at that time that the sacrifice and offering ceased"[19] is thus a *coda* to the list of tragedies associated with the ninth day of Ab in rabbinic literature. According to the same rabbinic source cited above[20] the cessation of the daily sacrifice occurred on the seventeenth of Tammuz, prior to the destruction of the Second Temple, almost fifty years before the rule of Hadrian (118-138 C.E.). Josephus in his *Jewish War* 6.93 specifically mentions that this occurred because of lack of lambs[21] during the seige of Titus. There is no extant reference in rabbinic literature to a cessation of sacrifices during the time of Hadrian.

Near the end of his lengthy comment on Dan 9:24-27, Jerome cites Josephus that "Vespasian and Titus concluded peace with the Jews for three years and six months." I could not find this reference in the extant works of Josephus. In *The Jewish War* 6.333 ff., Josephus credits Titus with a long speech delineating his humanitarian nature and repeating, time

---

[17] Ibid., 274-275.

[18] Maimonides, in his *Mishneh Torah,* Laws of Fasts, ch. 5, law 2, specifically attributes this act to Tinus Rufus, in fulfillment of the verse Mic 3:12 cited in Jer 26:18: "Zion shall be plowed as a field."

[19] The prophecy concerning the cessation of daily sacrifice is repeated often in Daniel. Cf. 8:11ff; 9:27; 11:31; 12:11.

[20] Cf. also Pierre Bogaert, *Apocalypse de Baruch* 1 (Paris: Editions du Cerf, 1969) 255-257, regarding the date of the seventeenth of Tammuz in Josephus, rabbinic, and patristic literature.

[21] Cf. the corrected text brought by Thackeray, in his edition of Josephus, *The Jewish War* IV-VII *LCL* 403, n. d.

and again, how he and his father Vespasian invited the Jews to accept peace. There is no mention however, that any peace was concluded.[22]

Next in Jerome's comment on Dan 9:24-27 we find: "and the [other] three years and six months are accounted for in Hadrian's reign, when Jerusalem was completely destroyed and the Jewish nation was massacred in large groups at a time, with the result that they were even expelled from the borders of Judea." Jerome is obviously referring to the Bar Kochba revolt.[23] It is not clear whether Jerome is here referring to Josephus, as in his previous citation, or to another Hebrew tradition. In Seder Olam Rabbah, ch. 30, we find: "The war of Ben - Koziba[24] [lasted] two and one - half years." The Talmudic texts Sanhedrin 93b and 97b also mention two and a half years. Azariah de Rossi in *Me^cor ^Enayim*[25] gives the reading in Seder Olam Rabbah as three and a half years. This variant is corroborated by several manuscripts of Seder Olam.[26] It is also substantiated by Jerusalem Talmud Ta^canit 4, 68d and Lamentations Rabbah 2,5.[27]

The other early patristic commentators on the book of Daniel do not cite interpretations concerning Dan 9:24-27 which shed light on Jerome's Hebrew tradition.

---

[22] It is interesting to note that Abraham ibn Ezra, in his *Commentary on Daniel* 9:24 corroborates Jerome's citation of Josephus: " 'And he shall make a firm covenant with many for one week' (Dan 9:27): It was known that Titus made a covenant with Israel for seven years, and [during this period] after three and one-half years, the daily sacrifice was nullified in the Second Temple before its destruction; thus is it written in the book of Joseph, son of Gurion [Josephus]." Abrabanel, in his *The Wellsprings of Salvation,* 374 gives an interpretation very similar to Josephus'. He adds, however, the connection to the "last week" in 9:26 which Josephus does not mention, but Jerome does. There is no mention, however, of an actual period of peace as we find in Jerome's reference to Josephus.

[23] The rebellion of Bar Kochba is generally accepted as having occurred between 132-135 C.E. Cf. Baron, *Social and Religious History of The Jews* 2, 97.

[24] Bar Kochba's original name was Bar/Ben Koseba. When his revolt failed, his name may have been given a derogatory twist, Bar Koziba, alluding to the Hebrew *kazav*, "a lie". Cf. Jerusalem Talmud Ta^canit 4:8 (= 68d Krotoshin).

[25] (Warsaw ed., 1899) pt. 1, 198.

[26] Cf. Ratner's ed., 145, n. 82.

[27] S. Lieberman in *Shkiin* (Hebrew; Jerusalem: Wahrmann Books, 1939) 78 cites Raymund Martini's text of Sanhedrin 93b in *Pugio Fidei* as "three and one-half years." Cf. Midrash Mishlé (ed. Buber) 48 n. 105 concerning the frequent occurrence of "three and one-half years" in rabbinic literature, not necessarily reflecting chronological accuracy.

CHAPTER 14

JEROME'S *COMMENTARY ON DANIEL* 11:20

ועמד על כנו מעביר נוגש הדר מלכות ובימים אחדים ישבר ולא באפים ולא
במלחמה. (דניאל יא':כ')

Then shall stand up in his place one that shall cause an exactor to pass through
the glory of the kingdom; but within few days he shall be destroyed, neither in
anger, nor in battle (Dan 11:20).

In Jerome's *Commentary on Daniel* 11:20 we find:

The Hebrews claim that by the "one most vile and unworthy of kingly honor"
[Dan 11:20] Trypho is meant, for as the guardian of the boy [Antiochus VI] he
seized the throne [for himself].[1]

The above commentary is obviously based on Jerome's text of Dan 11:20,
which is identical with the Vulgate:

And there shall stand up in his place one most vile and unworthy of kingly
honor, and in a few days he shall be destroyed, not in rage nor in battle.

In the Masoretic Hebrew text the phrase "one most vile and unworthy of
kingly honor" is missing; instead we find "one that shall cause an exactor
to pass through the glory of the kingdom."[2] Curiously, the LXX and its
versions also lack the Masoretic Hebrew phrasing of this passage.[3]
We do not find, in extant rabbinic literature, any identification of the
figure in Dan 11:20 with Trypho. The first detailed account of Trypho is
found in 1 Mac 12:39ff. In 1 Mac 13:31-32 we find:

Now Trypho dealt treacherously with King Antiochus the younger [VI] and
killed him, and became king in his place and assumed the diadem of Asia, and
brought great calamity upon the country.

Previous to this, Demetrius II had been crowned king of Syria in 145 B.C.E.[4]
In *Antiquities* 13:131ff. Josephus follows the account of Trypho found in 1

---

[1] *PL* 25:565 = *CCSL* 75A, 913, 11. 1168-1170.
[2] It seems that Jerome based his reading of "one most vile and unworthy of kingly honor"
on the LXX version of Daniel 11:21, which he adapted.
[3] The LXX has "a man smiting the glory of the king."
[4] Tcherikover, *Hellenistic Civilization and the Jews* 236.

113

Mac 12:39ff. According to current scholarly opinion, Trypho's reign is to be dated from 142 or 141 B.C.E.[5]

Among the medieval Jewish commentaries only two place the chronology of Dan 11:20 at the approximate time of Trypho. Rashi in his commentary on this verse identifies the "one who shall cause an exactor to pass through the glory of the kingdom" with the famous Mattathias who "repelled the Greek oppressor from Israel." Mattathias died in 166 B.C.E.,[6] approximately 24 years prior to Trypho's reign.

Gersonides places the chronology even earlier. He identifies the "one who shall cause an exactor" with Seleucus IV, son of Antiochus the Great (III), who reigned from 187-175 B.C.E., and who, relates Gersonides, planned to force Israel to abandon the Torah by oppressive means. He was followed by his son Demetrius I, alluded to in Dan 9:21.

Among the extant early patristic commentators on Daniel, Polychronius comes closest to the Jewish tradition presented by Jerome. He places chapter 11 within the framework of Maccabean history, and from verse 5 following, he sees the victory of Alexander Balas, son of Antiochus Epiphanes, over Demetrius I (150 B.C.E.) and his subsequent marriage with Ptolemy Philometor's daughter.[7] Polychronius then continues the subsequent historical exegesis of the chapter with the wars of Trypho against the Jews.

---

[5]   Schürer, *Geschichte des jüdischen Volkes im Zeitalter Jesu Christi*, 172.
[6]   S. Krauss, *Revue des études juives* 30 (1895) 215.
[7]   *Commentary on Daniel*, part 3, 55.

CHAPTER 15

JEROME'S *COMMENTARY ON DANIEL* 11:31

ל'. ובאו בו ציים כתים ונכאה ושב וזעם על ברית קודש ועשה ושב ויבן על
עזבי ברית קדש.
לא'. וזרעים ממנו יעמדו וחללו המקדש המעוז והסירו התמיד ונתנו השקוץ
משמם. (דניאל יא':ל'-לא')

For ships of Kittim shall come against him, and he shall be cowed, and he shall
return, and have indignation against the holy covenant, and shall do his
pleasure; and he shall return, and have regard unto them that forsake the holy
covenant. And arms shall stand up on his part, and they shall profane the
sanctuary, even the stronghold, and shall take away the continual burnt-
offering, and they shall set up the detestable thing that causeth appalment
(Dan 11:30-31).

In Jerome's *Commentary on Daniel* 11:31 we find:

The Jews,[1] however, would have us understand this as referring not to Antiochus Epiphanes or the Antichrist but to the Romans, of whom it was earlier
stated: "And triremes (or Italians) and Romans shall come, and he shall be
humbled." "Considerably later," it [the Jewish tradition] says, "a king,
Vespasian, shall emerge from the Romans themselves, who had come to
Ptolemy's assistance and threatened Antiochus. It is his arms and descendants
who will rise up, namely his son Titus, who with his army will defile the
sanctuary and remove the continual sacrifice and hand over the Temple to
permanent desolation." By the terms "siim" [ציים] and "chethim" [כתים],
which we have rendered as "triremes" and "Romans," the Hebrews would
have us understand "Italians" and "Romans."[2]

Jerome is here referring to the historical interpretation of the events
described in Dan 11:30-31. We have previously noted that Jerome records
the Hebrew tradition that the ruler mentioned in Dan 11:20 was Trypho.

---

[1]   This seems to be an exception to the general rule stated by Louis F. Hartman in "St.
Jerome as an Exegete," 79, n. 42: "In Jerome's writings, as in ancient Christian literature
generally, 'a Hebrew' (*Hebraeus*) is a respectful term which regards merely the man's race or
language, whereas a 'Jew' (*Judaeus*) is a term of reproach, emphasizing the man's religion,
which from the Christian viewpoint is worthy of reprobation." In his comment on Dan 11:31,
Jerome begins his citation with "Judaei," the Jews, and ends with "Hebraei," the Hebrews,
with no special pejorative context given to the former term. In fact, the two terms seem quite
interchangeable in this passage.

[2]   *PL* 25:569 = *CCSL* 75A, 922, 11. 178-188.

He, in turn, was destroyed and replaced by the "contemptible" ruler mentioned in Dan 11:21. After several battles, this latter ruler will be humbled by the forces described in Dan 11:30.

Jerome has already made clear, several times, that he closely follows Porphyry,[3] the neoplatonist commentator, in his historical interpretation of Dan 11. He parts company with him at vs. 21:

> Up to this point the historical order has been followed and there has been no point of controversy between Porphyry and those of our side. But the rest of the text from here on to the end of the book he interprets as applying to the person of the Antiochus who was surnamed Epiphanes, the brother of Seleucus and the son of Antiochus the Great. He reigned in Syria for eleven years after Seleucus, and he seized Judea, and it is under his reign that the persecution of God's Law is related and also the wars of the Maccabees. But those of our persuasion believe all these things are spoken prophetically of the Antichrist who is to arise at the end of time.[4]

However, it is to Jerome's great credit as a scholar (and to our great fortune) that he continues to cite Porphyry's historical interpretations past vs. 21, even though they disagree with his own views. Ironically, if Jerome had not been so magnanimous, the views of his adversary would not have been preserved.

In his *Commentary on Daniel* 11:30-31, Jerome, following Porphyry, attributes the events in Dan 11:30 to the intervention of the Roman legate

---

[3]   Porphyry was one of the most eminent hostile critics of the OT (c. 232-c. 305). As a youth he met Origen and subsequently condemned the allegorical method of interpretation which Origen used. He studied under the philosophers Longinus and Plotinus in Athens and subsequently wrote a *magnum opus, Against the Christians,* comprising fifteen books. It was suppressed by Constantine, and again condemned by Theodosius and Valentinian (E. Young, *Prophecy of Daniel* [Grand Rapids: Eerdman, 1949] 317-320). Jerome thought it important enough to begin the prologue to his *Commentary on Daniel* with a reference to Porphyry: "Porphyry wrote his twelfth book against the prophecy of Daniel, denying that it was composed by the person to whom it is ascribed in its title, but rather by some individual living in Judea at the time of the Antiochus who was surnamed Epiphanes. He furthermore alleged that 'Daniel' did not foretell the future so much as he related the past, and lastly that whatever he spoke of up till the time of Antiochus contained authentic history, whereas anything he may have conjectured beyond that point was false, inasmuch as he would not have foreknown the future" (*PL* 25:491 = *CCSL* 75A, 771, 1. 1ff.).

Porphyry's object was to show clearly, through a detailed historical interpretation of Dan 11, that the entire book of Daniel was not to be interpreted as a Messianic prophecy, as was done by the Christians in his day. By proving that ch. 11 culminated with Antiochus IV and the Maccabean period, he thought to show that the earlier chapters must also be interpreted similarly. Cf. P. M. Casey, "Porphyry and the Origin of the Book of Daniel," *JTS* n.s. 27 (1976) 15-33.

[4]   *PL* 25:565 = *CCSL* 75A, 914, 11. 3-12.

Marcus Popilius Laenas in the affairs of Antiochus IV. The events in Dan 11:31 are also attributed to Antiochus IV, who after plundering the Temple, sent messengers to exact tribute from the Jews, to eliminate the worship of God, and dedicate the Temple to the worship of Zeus Olympios.

We can now clearly understand the Jewish tradition cited by Jerome. The Jews, Jerome, and Porphyry all agree that the כתים in Dan 11:30 are identified as the Romans. The uniqueness of the "Jewish tradition" cited by Jerome is that the events in Dan 11:31 refer to the Romans as well, and particularly, to Vespasian and Titus who destroyed the Second Temple.[5]

This Jewish historical interpretation of Dan 11:31 can not be found in extant rabbinic literature[6] nor can the identification of צײם with Italians. However, the identification of כתים with Rome, the assumption of Jerome, Porphyry, as well as the Jewish tradition, is well known. We find the word for the first time in Gen 10:4, identifying "Kittim" as the son of Javan, the son of Japheth, the son of Noah: "And the sons of Javan: Elishah, and Tarshish, Kittim,[7] and Dodanim." In Genesis Rabbah 37:1[8] we find the following identification of the above four sons of Javan: "Hellas, Tarsus, Italy, and Dardania." Thus "Kittim" is equated in Genesis Rabbah with "Italy."

The above identification is found even earlier in the *Targumim* on Num 24:24. In the biblical text, we find: "But ships shall come from the coast of Kittim,[9] and they shall afflict Ashur, and shall afflict Eber." In Onkelos' Targum we find: "And ships will come from Rome. . . ." In Targum Jerushalmi I (Pseudo-Jonathan) we find: "And ships armed for war will come forth with great armies from Lombarnia, and from the land of

---

[5] Thus, Jerome's citation of the Jewish tradition, "understand this as referring . . . to the Romans" relating to the events in Dan 11:31. According to the Jewish tradition, the events in Dan 11:31 took place "considerably later" than those in Dan 11:30.

[6] Among the medieval Jewish biblical commentators, Rashi implies that Daniel 11:31 refers to the Roman destruction of the Second Temple; Nachmanides in his *Book of Redemption,* section 3 (Chavel, ed., *The Writings of Nachmanides* vol. 1, p. 287) explicitly states that Daniel 11:31 refers to the destruction of the Second Temple; Abrabanel (1437-1508) in his *Wells of Salvation,* section 11, on Daniel 11:31, explicitly refers this verse to Titus and the destruction of the Second Temple. It seems that there must have been an earlier rabbinic tradition upon which the medieval exegetes based their interpretations.

[7] Krauss in *Monumenta Talmudica* 5, 3, n. 18, corrects the reading in Targum of Pseudo-Jonathan on "Kittim" from אכױא to אכײא and explains that this is Achaia [or Achaea] which was often used, in Roman times, to refer to all of Greece.

[8] (Ed. Theodor-Albeck; Berlin, 1904) 343. Numerous parallels are cited.

[9] The similarity of the phrase "but ships shall come from Kittim," in Num 24:24 and the phrase "for ships of Kittim shall come against him" leads one to the inevitable conclusion that the latter contained an allusion to the former, which was part of Balaam's pregnant prophecies.

Italy. . . ." In the Targum Jerushalmi II (Fragmentary) we find: "And
many troops will come in *Libernae*[10] from the great city and will join with
them many legions of the Romans. . . ." Each of the above *targumim*
identifies "Kittim" with Italy or Rome.[11]

Josephus identified the biblical "Kittim" with the island of Cyprus,
"whence the name Chethim given by the Hebrews to all islands[12] and to
most maritime countries."[13] In Josippon,[14] on the other hand, we find
"Kittim" specifically identified with the Romans who dwelt in the
"Canphania Valley by the Tiber River."

The other early patristic commentators on the book of Daniel do not cite
traditions concerning the identification of "Kittim."[15]

---

[10] *Libernae* were fast sailing vessels, invented by the ancient Libernians, an Illyrian people,
on the northeast coast of the Adriatic, between Istria and Dalmatia, in modern Croatia. Cf. S.
Lieberman, *Tosefta Ki-fshutah* IV (Succa) (New York: Jewish Theological Seminary of
America, 1962).

[11] Krauss in *Monumenta Talmudica* 5, 3, n. 18, points out that the Targum on Ezek 27:6
(where "Kittim" is once more mentioned) has "Apulia" (Lower Italy), but this is not a
contradiction to the other citations since the name "Italy" often implies only Southern Italy.

[12] In 1 Mac 1:1 and 8:5, the term "Kittim" obviously refers to "Macedon."

[13] *Antiquities* 1.128.

[14] The tenth-century Hebrew adaptation and extension of the works of Josephus, Book 1,
ch. 1 (*Sefer Yosippon* [ed. Hominer; Jerusalem, 1956] 2).

[15] It is interesting to note that in the Qumran scroll *Commentary on Habakkuk,* the Kittim
are mentioned. On the verse Hab 1:6a which refers to the Chaldeans as a "cruel and hasty
nation," the commentary notes: "The explanation of this concerns the *Kittim* who are quick
and valiant in battle, causing many to perish" (cf. Dupont-Sommer, 259). Dupont-Sommer
notes (n. 2, p. 259) ". . . the Essene commentator, by means of a bold transposition which is
the very essence of the *pesher,* relates all these biblical sentences concerning the Chaldeans to a
new conquering people, the Kittim. As in the book of Daniel (XI: 30), these Kittim are the
Romans who captured Jerusalem in 63 B.C., and subjected Palestine to their rule. For the
commentator, this event is the prelude to the end of time." Yigael Yadin, *The Scroll of the
War of the Sons of Light Against the Sons of Darkness* 22-23, points out several other places
where "Kittim" are mentioned in various scrolls. He adds to this the places where "Kittim"
are mentioned in the Bible, its versions, and the Apocrypha and Pseudepigrapha (23-24). He
then concludes: "the result of the above consideration of the sources agrees with Josephus
[*Antiquities* 1.128 cited above] that the name *Kittim* could have applied both to the Greeks and
the Romans, depending on the period and the context" (p. 25). While Frank M. Cross, *The
Ancient Library of Qumran,* 92, n. 28 states that "the identification of the *Kittîyîm* . . . with
the Romans . . . appears to me to be established," H. H. Rowley in "The Kittim and the Dead
Sea Scrolls" argues against this identification since the identification of *Kittim* with the
Romans seems to oppose the view that the Essenes pre-dated Roman times.

CHAPTER 16

JEROME'S *COMMENTARY ON DANIEL* 11:33

ומשכילי עם יבינו לרבים ונכשלו בחרב ובלהבה בשבי ובבזה ימים. (דניאל
יא':לג')

And they that are wise among the people shall cause the many to understand;
yet they shall stumble by the sword and by flame, by captivity and by spoil,
many days (Dan 11:33).

In Jerome's *Commentary on Daniel* 11:33 we find:

The Hebrews interpret these things [as taking place] at the final destruction of
the Temple, which took place under Vespasian and Titus; that there were many
of their nation who knew their God and were slain for keeping His law.[1]

Jerome previously referred to this Jewish historical tradition in his
Commentary on Daniel 11:31 as we saw in the preceding Chapter. It follows
that this same Jewish tradition would apply to Dan 11:33 as well. As we
noted previously, this Jewish historical interpretation could not be found in
extant rabbinic literature.[2]

---

[1] *PL* 25:569 = *CCSL* 75A, 923, 11. 205-208.
[2] Cf. Chapter 15, n. 6, where the medieval Jewish commentators which refer Dan 11:31ff.
to the destruction of the Second Temple are noted.

CHAPTER 17

JEROME'S *COMMENTARY ON DANIEL* 11:34

וכהכשלם יעזרו עזר מעט ונלוו עליהם רבים בחלקלקות. (דניאל יא':לד')

Now when they shall stumble, they shall be helped with a little help; but many shall join themselves unto them with blandishments (Dan 11:34).

In Jerome's *Commentary on Daniel* 11:34 we find:

Some of the Hebrews understand these things as applying to the princes Severus and Antoninus, who esteemed the Jews very highly. But others understand the Emperor Julian[1] as the one referred to; for after they had been oppressed by Gallus Caesar and had steadfastly endured much suffering in the afflictions of their captivity he [i.e., Julian] rose up as one who pretended that he loved the Jews, promising that he would offer sacrifice in their Temple. They were to have a little hope of help from him, and a great number of the gentiles were to join themselves to their party, not in truth, but in falsehood. For it would only be for the sake of the worship of idols that they would pretend friendship to them [i.e., the Jews]. And they would do this "in order that those who were approved might be manifest" [1 Cor 11:19]. For the time of their [the Jews'] true salvation and help will be [the coming of] Christ, whom they mistakenly hope is yet to come, for they are going to receive the Antichrist.[2]

There are no extant rabbinic sources which link Severus, Antoninus, or Julian to Dan 11:34.[3] In understanding Jerome's tradition, we must first identify the emperors he mentions. The Emperor Julian is most easy to identify: he is Julian the Apostate who reigned from 361-363 C.E. Severus is most probably *not* Septimius Severus (reigned 193-211), since Reinach points out that he was not favorable toward the Jews.[4] Jerome probably referred to Alexander Severus (reigned 222-235), who was favorable toward the Jews as we shall soon show. We encounter the greatest difficulty,

---

[1] From Jerome's *Commentary on Daniel* 11:36 it seems quite clear that Jerome held the Julian tradition to be the dominant one: "The Hebrews . . . alleging that after the small help of Julian, a king is going to rise up. . . ."
[2] *PL* 25:70 = *CCSL* 75A, 924, 11. 228-240.
[3] Adler, "The Emperor Julian and the Jews," 625 specifically makes this point. Cf. Krauss, *Monumenta Talmudica* 5, 59.
[4] *Textes d'auteurs grecs et romains relatifs au Judaïsme,* 344-346.

however in identifying Antoninus.[5] It is well known that Antoninus is often mentioned in the Talmud together with Rabbi Judah the Prince.[6] An extensive literature has developed concerning the identification of this Talmudic Antoninus.[7]

Alexander Severus was indeed well disposed toward the Jews.[8] Leon points out that he was scornfully given the title "Syrian archisynagogus" by his opposition.[9] In his *lararium* (private shrine) he reportedly had busts of great men, including Abraham.[10] He often called out through a herald, when he was correcting someone: "that which you do not wish to be done to yourself, do not do to another." This indeed is Hillel's famous statement[11] which Jesus later turned into the affirmative rendition of the "golden rule."[12]

Julian was most friendly toward the Jews.[13] In truth it is difficult to assess, at times, whether the motivation for his acts was opposition to

[5] We know that Jerome was very familiar with Roman history. In his continuation of *The Chronicle of Eusebius* he mentions the full name of each Roman Emperor and his dates. The fact that Jerome did not clearly identify the Antoninus and Severus of Jewish tradition shows that he was not sure which emperors the Jews meant. He therefore cited the tradition as he heard it. It also shows that Jerome quoted verbatim the Hebrew tradition, which always refers to the emperor as simply "Antoninus."

[6] Krauss, *Monumenta* 5, 72-74, gives all passages in rabbinic literature pertaining to Antoninus.

[7] Cf. Baron, *Social and Religious History of the Jews,* 400, n. 19. Antoninus has been identified variously as Alexander Severus, Antoninus Pius, Ovidus Passus (the governor of the East during the time of Marcus Aurelius), Lucius Verus Antoninus (a co-regent with Marcus Aurelius), Marcus Aurelius, and Caracalla. The problem of identifying any Roman emperor is compounded by the practice of each Emperor stringing the names of his predecessors before his own. It is most probable that Jerome's Hebrew tradition did not identify Antoninus with Alexander Severus since he mentions "the princes Severus and Antoninus," and, as we have already pointed out, "Severus" was most probably Alexander Severus.

[8] Cf. Reinach, *Textes,* 348-350 for the appropriate texts.

[9] *The Jews of Ancient Rome,* 43.

[10] Ibid. Note, however, that this report comes from the *Historia Augusta,* which is extremely unreliable. Cf. R. Syme, *Ammianus and the Historia Augusta* (Oxford: Clarendon Press, 1968) 61.

[11] Shabbat 3a. It is previously found in Tob 4:15 and *Test. XII Patr.,* Naphtali 1, Heb. (*APOT* 361) and the Proverbs of *Aḥikar* 2,88 (Armenian version: *APOT* 739).

[12] Reinach, *Textes,* 350, points out that Severus' negative rendition of the "golden rule" shows Hillel's influence. Albrecht Dihle, *Die Goldene Regel,* 107, has collected quite a few negative renditions of the "golden rule" in patristic sources. Some Fathers state the rule both positively and negatively. Thus we can not conclude with certainty that a negative rendition of the "golden rule" shows Hillel's influence.

[13] There is disagreement among scholars as to whether Julian is mentioned directly in rabbinic sources. The one source, in Jerusalem Talmud Nedarim 37d, which mentions לוליִנוס מלכא was emended by H. Graetz (*Geschichte der Juden* 4 [Leipzig: O. Leiner, 1897] pt. 2, 492) and others to דוקליטיאנוס [Diocletian] based on the parallel passage in Jerusalem

Christianity or admiration for the Jews.[14] He wanted to restore the preeminence of paganism, specifically of the Mithraic syncretistic creed. Raised as a Christian, he had left the Church, and was thus branded as "Apostate" by the Christians.[15] He enlisted Jewish support in his battle against the Church. Julian formally abolished the *fiscus judaicus,* the special Jewish fiscal tax.[16] He considered abolishing the *aurum coronarium* or *apostolé,* which had been imposed by the Palestinian Patriarchs upon the Diaspora Jews.[17] It seems that he personally knew many Jews[18] and spoke with admiration of Jewish customs and ceremonies.[19]

Without doubt, Julian's most ambitious plan in connection with the Jews was his promise—to which Jerome alludes—to rebuild the Temple. It is generally agreed that Julian did consider rebuilding the Temple in Jerusalem, but his motives are not clear to us.[20] Several conflicting accounts from Syriac and Christian sources tell how he first developed the idea.[21] However, the clearest indication of his intentions come from his Twenty-Fifth Epistle[22] which he sent "To the Community of the Jews" and in which he promised to rebuild Jerusalem and the Temple after his return from the Persian war.[23]

Talmud, Shebuoth 34d. Cf. Krauss, *Monumenta Talmudica* 5, 59, 78-79. On the other hand, S. Lieberman claims that the reading in Jerusalem Talmud Nedarim 37d is correct. In his opinion, the reading in Jerusalem Talmud Shebuoth 34d is an emendation, since the latter is frequently mentioned in rabbinic literature, and the scribes were familiar with this name. Cf. S. Lieberman, "The Martyrs of Caesaria," *Annuaire de l'institut de philologie et d'histoire orientales et slaves* 7 (1939-1946) 436.

[14] Michael Adler, "The Emperor Julian," 595, puts it well: "Whether Julian merely favored Judaism because he was fond of all institutions and customs of antiquity, as some critics assert, or because it was the parent and determined foe of the Christianity he abhorred, or because he approved of the religion as a genuine, pure faith, is a question that each writer must conclude for himself from the evidence before him." It should also be noted that Julian was tolerant of all religions and proclaimed a general religious amnesty upon his succession of Constantius [p. 593]. Marcel Simon, *Verus Israel,* 139-144 also discusses the relationship between Julian's anti-Christian and pro-Jewish programs. Thus, Jerome's remark in his *Commentary on Daniel* 11:34 that Julain "pretended love for the Jews" is quite understandable.

[15] Adler, "The Emperor Julian," 591; Baron, *Social and Religious History,* 151.

[16] Baron, 186, 374, n. 21.

[17] It lasted, however, for another fifty years. Cf. Baron, 194-195, 403, n. 28.

[18] Adler, "The Emperor Julian," 594-595.

[19] Ibid., 603-604.

[20] Cf. Adler, 617-620; Baron, 154, 160, 392, n. 41; Alice Gardner, *Julian: Philosopher and Emperor,* 263-267.

[21] Cf. Adler, 620-622.

[22] On the authenticity of this document, see Adler, 622, n. 2, and Baron, 392, n. 41.

[23] For entire text of letter, see Adler, 622-624.

It is interesting to note the Jewish silence concerning Julian's plan. Rabbinic literature tells us nothing about the proposal. A number of reasons are given for this omission.[24]

Julian's Twenty-Fifth Epistle was written six months before his death.[25] Whether the construction was started at all is disputed.[26] In any event, the rebuilding of the Temple was never completed.

[24] Michael Adler, 625-626, and W. Bacher, "Emperor Julian and the Rebuilding of the Temple at Jerusalem," *JQR* o.s. 10 (1897) 168-172. Bacher does try to show, through citations of the Palestinian Talmud, that a Palestinian *amora,* Rab Acha (4th century), did approve of the rebuilding of the Temple. Cf. E. E. Urbach, "Cyrus and His Proclamation as Viewed by the Rabbis," (Hebrew) *Molad,* 1961, 273, for a further discussion of this matter.

[25] Cf. Adler, 628: "all authorities agree that the famous letter was written about six months before Julian's sudden death."

[26] Cf. Adler, 616-617, 628-651. Adler attempts to disprove arguments that work on the Temple was actually commenced.

CHAPTER 18

JEROME'S *COMMENTARY ON DANIEL* 11:36

ועשה כרצונו המלך ויתרומם ויתגדל על כל אל ועל אל אלים ידבר נפלאות
והצליח עד כלה זעם כי נחרצה נעשתה. (דניאל יא':לו')

And the king shall do according to his will; and he shall exalt himself, and
magnify himself above every god, and shall speak strange things against the
God of gods; and he shall prosper till the indignation be accomplished; for that
which is determined shall be done (Dan 11:36).

In Jerome's *Commentary on Daniel* 11:36 we find:

The Hebrews think that this passage has reference to the Antichrist, alleging
that after the small help of Julian, a king is going to rise up who shall do according to his own will and shall lift himself up "against all that is called god"
[2 Thes 2:4] and shall speak arrogant words against the God of gods. He shall
act in such a way as to "sit in the Temple of God" [2 Thes 2:4] and make
himself out to be God, and so that his will be directed until the wrath of God is
fulfilled, for in him shall be the consummation.[1]

There are no extant rabbinic sources identifying the figure in Dan 11:36
with the Antichrist of Jerome's Jewish tradition. In fact from the wording
of this passage it appears that Jerome was influenced by 2 Thes 2:1-12 and
especially 2 Thes 2:3-4 where it is stated:

Let no one deceive you in any way, for the day of the Lord will not come unless
the apostasy comes first and the man of lawlessness is revealed, the son of
perdition, who opposes and is exalted above all that is called God or that is
worshipped so that he sits in the Temple of God and gives himself out as if he
were God.

The entire passage in Thessalonians is probably based on a Jewish
conception of the Antichrist. The appelations "the man of lawlessness" (2
Thes 2:3) and "the lawless one" (2 Thes 2:8) correspond to the name Belial[2]
found elsewhere as an opponent of the Messiah. The name Belial is ex-

---

[1] *PL* 25:580 = *CCSL* 75A, 925, 11. 246-252.
[2] Cf. 2 Cor 6:15. For other places the name is found, see Bousset, *The Antichrist Legend*,
136-138.

plained by rabbinic texts[3] as a contraction of two Hebrew words which mean "without a yoke," signifying the refusal to bear the yoke of the Law. The death of the Antichrist "with the breath of his [Jesus'] mouth" [2 Thes 2:8] is similar to Targum Jonathan on Isa 11:4: "with the speech of his lips he will kill the evil Armillus." Armillus[4] is the name of the Antichrist and appears often in later Midrashim.[5]

According to the later Midrashim, the Antichrist Armillus is portrayed as a false Messiah.[6] He arises after the coming of the Messiah ben Joseph and kills this Messiah in battle. He himself is then killed by the breath of the Messiah ben David.[7]

[3] Sifré Deuteronomy 93 (ed. Finkelstein) 154, with parallels; Tanna Eliyahu Rabbah 3; Midrash Samuel 6 (ed. Buber) 64. Jerome, *Commentary on the Letter to the Ephesians* 4:27 (*PL* 26 [ed. 1845]:511) explains the name exactly as does the rabbinic tradition: "without a yoke—who casts off from his neck the service of God." Obviously the word is much more ancient than the rabbinic explanation and most probably has mythological origins.

[4] The name Armillus also appears in the Targum Jerushalmi 1 (Pseudo-Jonathan) on Dt 34:3.

[5] The name Armillus is explicitly identified in Othoth ha-Mashiaḥ in the A. Jellinek's *Bet Hamidrash* 2, 60, as that of the Antichrist.

[6] The Mysteries of Simon Ben Yokhai, ibid. 3, 80; Midrash Vayosha on Exodus, ibid. 1, 56; Othoth ha-Mashiaḥ, ibid. 2, 60; the Book of Zerubabel, ibid. 2, 55-57. For a discussion of these and other sources, cf. Bousset, *The Antichrist Legend,* 95-117.

[7] All of the Midrashim cited in n. 6 include this account of the Antichrist's death except Othoth ha-Mashiaḥ. It is to be noted however, that they were written quite later than Jerome, between the 9th and 13th centuries, and therefore Bousset suggests that Christian and Jewish traditions were intertwined in these and other sources. Cf. Bousset, 107, for one example of this.

CHAPTER 19

JEROME'S *COMMENTARY ON DANIEL* 13 (SUSANNA): 5

That year two of the elders of the people were appointed judges — men of the kind of whom the Lord said "Lawlessness came forth from Babylon, from elders who were judges, who were supposed to guide the people" (Susanna [Theodotion version], 5).

In Jerome's *Commentary on Daniel* 13 (Susanna):5, we find:

There was a Hebrew who used to allege that these men[1] [i.e., "two of the elders of the people"] were Achias and Sedeciah of whom Jeremiah wrote: "The Lord do to you as to Achias and Sedeciah[2] whom the king of Babylon roasted in fire because of the iniquity which they had wrought in Israel and because they had committed adultery with the wives of their citizens" [Jer 29:21-23].[3]

Before attempting to analyze this Jewish tradition, we must point out that Jerome prefaces his comments on Susanna with the following:

. . . I shall briefly set forth the comments of Origen concerning the stories of Susanna and of Bel contained in the Tenth Book of his *Stromata*.[4] These are his words.[5]

It is evident from the comments that follow that Jerome did not translate Origen's words verbatim. For example, at the end of the comment on Susanna 8, we find: "Origen says that he has taken this particular passage from the Septuagint." Obviously, this is Jerome speaking. It is not possible to determine the degree to which Jerome injects his own comments.[6]

Assuming that the above comment on Susanna 5 is Origen's, we are

---

[1] Here we learn the significant fact that the apocryphal tradition of Susanna circulated among the Jews during the times of Jerome, and as early as Origen since, as will soon be pointed out, Jerome is here bringing the comments of Origen. This assumes even greater significance in the light of the fact, soon to be noted, that the Susanna story does not enter rabbinic tradition until the eleventh century.

[2] The words "of whom Jeremiah . . . Sedeciah" appear in certain of the manuscripts as noted in the *CCSL* edition.

[3] *PL* 25:580 = *CCSL* 75A, 945, 11. 707-711.

[4] The *Stromata* were composed before 231 C.E. (cf. Eusebius, *Hist. Eccles.* 6, 24.3) and were lost except for fragments which were preserved by Jerome in his *Commentary on Daniel* chs. 13 (Susanna) and 14 (Bel).

[5] *PL* 25:580 = *CCSL* 75A, 945, 11. 698-700.

[6] See Chapter 3, p. 51.

indeed fortunate that we may compare it with a similar statement made by Origen nine years later in his famous *Letter to Africanus* (240 C.E.).

> Moreover I remember hearing from a learned Hebrew, said among themselves to be the son of a wise man and to have been specifically trained to succeed his father, with whom I had intercourse on many subjects, the names of these elders [in Susanna], just as if he did not reject the history of Susanna, as they occur in Jeremiah, as follows: "The Lord make thee like Sedekias and Achiab . . ." [Jer 29:22].[7]

Origen then cites another tradition given to him by another Jew, which vividly describes the adulterous activities of Ahab and Zedekiah:

> And I know another Hebrew who bore such traditions concerning these elders that to those in the captivity, hoping to be freed through the sojourn of the Christ [i.e., the Messiah[8]] from the captivity under the enemy, these elders pretended that they knew how to make clear the things concerning the Christ and each of the two of them, in turn, kept asserting mysteriously to the woman whom he chanced upon and whom he wished to corrupt that indeed it had been given to him from God to sow the seed of the Christ. Then being deceived with the hope of producing the Christ the woman gave herself over to the deceiver, and thus the elders of the citizens, Achiab and Sedekias, had relations with the women. Wherefore it is that the prophet Daniel well calls the one "grown old in evil days" [Susanna 52] and the other heard this: "Thus have you dealt with the daughters of Israel, and they, in fear, had relations with you, but a daughter of Judah [i.e., Susanna] would not abide by your lawlessness" [Susanna 57].[9]

It is not possible to determine whether the tradition of the second Hebrew ends with "had relations with the women" or continues with the verse linking these elders with Susanna. This is indeed a crucial point, since if the former represents this second Jewish tradition, it would contain no connection whatsoever between Ahab and Zedekiah and the book of Susanna. Origen would then have made the link himself. It seems possible that this second tradition of the elders' adulterous activities was independent of Susanna, since Origen takes the trouble to cite it separately, on the authority of another Hebrew, when he could have well fused the two traditions as did his successor, Jerome. Hitherto, this distinction of the *two independent* Jewish traditions cited by Origen has not been pointed out. This becomes important when we shall introduce extant rabbinic traditions.

In his *Commentary on Jeremiah* 29:21-23 written during the last five

---

[7]   *Letter to Africanus* 7 = *PG* 11:61-64.
[8]   See Chapter 13, pp. 106-107 for a discussion on the terms *Christus* and the Messiah.
[9]   *Letter to Africanus* 8 = *PG* 11:64-65.

years of his life, Jerome cites a conglomerate of the two traditions of Origen quoted above. His account is very similar to Origen's presentation of the traditions, and we wonder whether Jerome ever heard this tradition from Jews, or whether he relied completely on Origen's rendition:

The Hebrews say that these are the elders who wrought folly in Israel and committed adultery with the wives of their fellow-citizens, and to one of whom Daniel said: "O you who are grown old in evil days" [Susanna 52] and to the other of whom he said: "You seed of Canaan and not of Judah, beauty has deceived you and lust has perverted your heart! Thus you did with the daughters of Israel and they, in fear, spoke with you; but a daughter of Judah did not abide your iniquity" [Susanna 56-57]. And that which the prophet now says, "And they have spoken a word in my name falsely which I did not command them" [Jer 29:23] they [the Jews] think that this is indicated by the fact that they [Ahab and Zedekiah] thus deceived wretched little women who are carried about by every wind of doctrine by saying to them, because they were of the tribe of Judah, that Christ must be born from their seed, who, having been enticed by desire, furnished their bodies, as if they were future mothers of Christ. But that which is said at present "whom the king of Babylon roasted in fire" [Jer 29:22] seems to contradict the history of Daniel [i.e., Susanna] for he asserts that they were stoned by the people according to the opinion of Daniel [Susanna 61-62]. This indeed has been written [Jer 29:22] that the king of Babylon roasted them in fire. Whence this fable [i.e., the book of Susanna] itself, as it were, is not accepted by very many, including almost all the Hebrews,[10] nor is it read in their synagogues. "For," they say, "how could it be that the captives had the power of stoning their leaders and prophets?" And more than this, they affirm to be true that which Jeremiah writes, that the elders indeed were refuted by Daniel, but that sentence was brought against them by the king of Babylon[11] who had power against the captives as victor and lord.[12]

---

[10] This is another instance where we are indebted to Jerome for his account of Jewish traditions which were popular in his time. It is evident from his statement here that *some* Jews "accepted" the book of Susanna.

[11] Jerome was less concerned with this problem in his *Commentary on Daniel* 13 (Susanna): 60: "If the whole congregation put them to death, the view which we mentioned earlier is apparently refuted, namely that these were the elders, Ahab and Zedekiah, in conformity with Jeremiah's statement [Jer 29:22ff.]. The only other possibility is that instead of taking the statement 'they killed them' [Susanna 60] literally, we interpret it as meaning that they gave them over to the king of Babylon to be put to death." Africanus, in his *Letter to Origen* 2 (*PG* 11:61) was concerned with a similar problem: "How is it that they [the Jews] who were captives among the Chaldeans . . . could pass sentence of death?" Origen answered in his *Letter to Africanus* 14 (*PG* 11:66) ". . . it is no uncommon thing when great nations become subject that the king should allow the captives to use their own laws and courts of justice."

[12] *PL* 24:862-864 = *CCSL* 74, 284, 1.13; 285, 1.15.

When we compare the Jewish traditions preserved in the above patristic sources with rabbinic literature, we are amazed that the Susanna story does not enter rabbinic tradition[13] until the eleventh-century work *The Chronicles of Jerahmeel.*[14] There, this story is presented immediately after the description of the evil deeds of the two false prophets, Ahab and Zedekiah,[15] mentioned in Jer 29:21ff. Jerahmeel makes no attempt to connect and identify the two judges of the Susanna story with Ahab and Zedekiah, as does the Jewish tradition in the patristic sources cited above. Thus, nowhere in extant rabbinic literature do we find this association.

There are however, in rabbinic literature, many versions and variants of the tradition concerning the evil deeds of Ahab and Zedekiah.[16] In Sanhedrin 93a, after the citation of Jer 29:23 we find:

> What did they [Ahab and Zedekiah] do? They went to Nebuchadnezzar's daughter: Ahab said to her, "thus saith God, 'Give thyself to Zedekiah'"; while Zedekiah said to her, "thus saith God, 'Surrender to Ahab.' " So she went and told her father, who said to her, "The God of these hates unchastity; when they again approach thee, send them to me." So when they came to her, she referred them to him. "Who told this to you?" asked he of them. "The Holy One, blessed be He," replied they. "But I have enquired of Hananiah, Mishael, and Azariah, who informed me that it is forbidden." They answered, "We too are prophets, just as they; to them he did not say it, but to us." "Then I desire that ye be tested just as Hananiah, Mishael, and Azariah were," he retorted.

[13] Cf. I. Lévi, "L'histoire de 'Suzanne et les deux Vieillards' dans la littérature juive," especially 158-159. Levi points out that the story of Bel and the Dragon was preserved in rabbinic literature as early as Genesis Rabbah 68:20 (*c.* fifth century). Josippon, the tenth-century Hebrew adaptation and extension of the works of Josephus, tells the stories of Bel and the Dragon, and The Prayers of the Three Children, both apocryphal additions to Daniel, as well as the stories of the apocryphal additions to Esther, but is silent concerning the story of Susanna. Solomon Zeitlin, "Jewish Apocryphal Literature," notes that the book of Susanna presented a contradiction to the adopted Pharasaic halacha concerning the conditions which determine when false witnesses are put to death and that this was a good reason for its exclusion from the canon (p. 236). Sidney Hoenig has pointed out that this would account as well for the exclusion of the Susanna story from rabbinic literature until the eleventh century. See Hoenig, *IDB* 4, 467, where it is pointed out that "the book of Susanna depicts only a contradiction of 'witnesses in fact' and not 'in matter of time.' " Cf. Mishna Makkot, 14.

[14] M. Gaster, *The Chronicles of Jerahmeel,* 202-205. This account essentially follows the popular Theodotion version; Gaster notes, however (p. cv), that in some details the text agrees more with the Syriac version. The dependence of Jerahmeel on Josippon has been noted by Reiner in "The Original Hebrew *Josippon* in the *Chronicle of Jerahmeel.*"

[15] Ibid., 200-202.

[16] Ginzberg, *Legends* 6, 426, n. 106, gives the complete references on this tradition in rabbinic literature.

The king allowed them a third person to accompany them into the furnace. They chose Joshua, the High Priest, thinking his merit would protect them. Ahab and Zedekiah were burned alive while only Joshua's garments were singed.[17] It is interesting to note that in Sanhedrin 93a the story of Ahab and Zedekiah is brought into juxtaposition with citations from the book of Daniel.

In Tanḥuma, Leviticus, 6, we find a similar story. Ahab and Zedekiah were false prophets in Jerusalem and they continued their evils in Babylonia. Each would consort with the wife of a high government official to persuade her, on the word of God, to join the other in order to give birth to prophets, and she consented. Their fame grew in Babylonia. (They even predicted the sex of children, through deceit.) They continued until they came to Semiramis, the *wife* of Nebuchadnezzar, who refused, unless her husband consented. An account follows similar to the one in Sanhedrin 93a but with more details.[18]

Midrash Aggadah, Leviticus, 51, presents a similar story with many more details. They continued their immoral acts in Babylonia for twenty-two years. They continued to prophesy falsely as well, especially in their prediction of the sex of the unborn children.[19]

Pirḳé de Rabbi Eliezer, 33, gives a brief account. Its only new detail is that the elders are presented as false doctors who pretended to heal Babylonian wives and then had sexual relations with them.

The similarities of all the above rabbinic versions of the Ahab and Zedekiah tradition with the Hebrew tradition of Origen and Jerome are indeed self-evident. It is the differences that are more subtle. In the patristic version, Ahab and Zedekiah consort with *Jewish* women in Babylonia, promising to cause them to give birth to the *Messiah*. In extant rabbinic tradition they consort with *Babylonian* women, even Nebuchadnezzar's *daughter and wife,* promising to cause them to give birth to *prophets*. It seems quite plausible that the earlier version of the tradition was preserved by Origen. The seduction of *Jewish* wives in Babylonia by Ahab and Zedekiah sets the scene for the Susanna story, which takes place, according to its opening verses, in Babylonia. Thus it is plausible that in Origen's time a Jewish tradition linking Susanna with Ahab and Zedekiah was current. Perhaps the same motivation and circumstances which caused the Susanna story to be absent from rabbinic records until the eleventh century caused

[17] Note that Joshua in the Talmudic story plays a somewhat similar role to Daniel in Susanna: he brings about the destruction of the scheming elders.

[18] Tanḥuma (Buber), Leviticus, 10 presents a parallel to the above, except that the last part of the story is truncated.

[19] Parallel in Yalḳuṭ, 2, 309.

the tradition concerning the seduction of "Jewish wives" to be changed to read "Babylonian women." In any event, once again we are indebted to Origen and Jerome for the only written record of a Jewish tradition. Our debt to these Fathers of the Church is the greater because none of the other early patristic commentators on Susanna mention this tradition.

N. Brüll in "Das Apokryphische Susanna-Buch" ingeniously points out one rabbinic tradition which may refer to the Susanna story. In Leviticus Rabbah 19:6 we find that when king Jehoiachin was exiled to Babylonia and imprisoned, the Sanhedrin was quite concerned that he would leave no heir and thus the House of David would come to an end. Through the intercession of Queen Semiramis, Nebuchadnezzar permitted Jehoiachin's wife to visit him. When he was about to have marital intercourse with her, she said to him: "I have seen a [menstrual] discharge the color of a red lily (שׁוֹשַׁנָּה)." He then withdrew from her and she "counted [the seven days of separation] and observed the ritual of purification and immersion." The points of tangency between this tradition and the Susanna story are most interesting. First we have the origin of the name Susanna, which in Hebrew means "lily." Next, her husband, Jehoiachin, reminds us of Susanna's husband, Joakim.[20] Last, this rabbinic story ends with Jehoiachin's wife's observance of purification and immersion. Susanna encountered the elders while she was taking a bath in her garden (Susanna 16). On these grounds, Brüll concludes that Susanna = Jehoiachin's wife. Thus even though we do not have the Susanna story preserved in rabbinic tradition, Brüll maintains that we find pieces of it in Leviticus Rabbah 19:6.[21]

---

[20] The history of the confusion of the names Jehoiachin and Jehoiakim has already been discussed in detail. Cf. Chapter 4, n. 53. It should be noted that the most famous patristic critic of Susanna, Africanus, in his *Letter to Origen* 2 identifies Susanna's husband with "King Joacim whom the king of Babylonia had made partner to his throne." Africanus is obviously referring to King Jehoiachin who was so honored according to Jer 52:32. Prior to Africanus, Hippolytus in his *Commentary on Daniel*, 1 (Susanna) also identified Susanna's husband with king Jehoiachin.

[21] It should be noted however, that the major element of the Susanna story is still missing in rabbinic literature, even if we accept Brüll's hypothesis: the elders are not brought to justice by Daniel.

CHAPTER 20

CONCLUSION

We have presented and analyzed the sixteen Hebrew traditions found in Jerome's *Commentary on Daniel*. It is important to summarize the analyses of these sixteen traditions in order to evaluate Jerome's relationship to rabbinic tradition, Josephus, and the earlier patristic commentators on Daniel. We wish to point out in how many cases Jerome relied on Jewish traditions quoted by previous Church Fathers and how many of these Jewish traditions he knew directly. We should also note how many of these Jewish traditions are found in extant rabbinic literature. Finally, we wish to point out the relative degree to which Jerome was aware of Jewish traditions in comparison with other patristic commentators on Daniel.

Out of the sixteen Jewish traditions cited by Jerome, four[1] have definite parallels in extant rabbinic literature. Of these four, two—the eunuch tradition of Dan 1:3 and the role of Noah as a preacher prior to the Flood (Dan 9:2)—are cited both in Josephus and in extant patristic literature. Origen is the only Church Father prior to Jerome that cites the eunuch tradition, although Theodoret cites it later. It is certain that Jerome was well aware that Origen cited this tradition, since Jerome translated *Homily IV on Ezekiel,* one of the places where it appears.[2] However, in *Adversus Jovinianum* 1.25, Jerome states "the Hebrews, up to this day, declare that both he [Daniel] and the three boys were eunuchs."[3] Thus, if we take Jerome at his word, and there is no reason why in this case we should not, the eunuch tradition was prevalent among the Jews in Jerome's time as well. While both Origen and Jerome link Dan 1:3 with Isa 39:7, Josephus, who also mentions the eunuch traditon, does not link these two texts.

Jerome's comment on Dan 9:2, concerning the one hundred and twenty years given to man to repent in Noah's time prior to the Flood, leads us to interesting conclusions. Jerome does not cite this interpretation as a "Hebrew tradition" as he does the other fifteen points. And yet this theme of repentance for one hundred and twenty years is well-known in rabbinic literature, although its connection to Dan 9:2 is not noted there. We thus see that Jerome may cite Hebrew traditions in his writings without even

---

[1]   The traditions on Dan 1:3, 5:2, 7:7, and 9:2.
[2]   See Chapter 4, n. 27.
[3]   See Chapter 4, p. 63.

referring to them as such.[4] Both the Rabbis and Jerome reject a literal interpretation of Gen 6:3 which seems to limit man's life span to one hundred and twenty years.[5] Noah's role as a preacher of repentance is well-known in Josephus, pseudepigraphic, and patristic literature.[6]

Concerning the two other Jewish traditions which have definite parallels in rabbinic literature, the comments on 5:2 and 7:7, we could find no parallels in Josephus or extant patristic literature.

In six of the remaining Jewish traditions of Jerome, we find that although his complete citations are not found in extant rabbinic literature, parts of them or closely related interpretations are today available to us. In Jerome's comment on Dan 13 (Susanna):5, concerning the identification of the two elders with Ahab and Zedekiah of Jer 29:21, we note the unusual phenomenon that the Susanna story does not occur in rabbinic sources until the eleventh century work *The Chronicles of Jeraḥmeel*.[7] Even in this source, the two elders of Susanna are not identified with Ahab and Zedekiah of Jer 29:21ff. In this particular case, Origen cites two distinct Jewish traditions,[8] in the names of two *different* Jews, which could be independent: a) the two elders in Susanna as Ahab and Zedekiah; b) a vivid description of the adulterous activities of Ahab and Zedekiah. Jerome's comments on Susanna are a translation of those in the tenth book of Origen's *Stromata*.[9] Jerome himself, in another work,[10] cites a conglomerate of the two traditions of Origen and does not differentiate between them. We wonder in this case if Jerome relied only on Origen or if he heard this tradition, as well, directly from Jews. In any event, for the second tradition of Origen, which is famous in rabbinic literature, there are many versions and variants.[11] Thus the first tradition, in the time of Origen, could have been current among the Jews although we do not have it in extant rabbinic sources. The above traditions are found neither in other

---

[4] We have another example of this in his *Commentary on Daniel* 8:16 which identifies the angel Michael with the "voice of a man." Although this identification does not occur in extant rabbinic literature, in the next sentence of his commentary on this verse, Jerome adds, "Quite appropriately it was Gabriel, who had been put in charge of battles, to whom this duty was assigned. . . ." Although Jerome does not specifically mention it, this characterization of Gabriel as the angel of war is found in rabbinic literature. Cf. Chapter 11, p. 96. We cannot assume, however, that all traditions mentioned by Jerome (but not identified as "Hebrew traditions") which appear in rabbinic literature must have come to him directly from Jews.

[5] See Chapter 12, pp. 88-89.
[6] See Chapter 12, pp. 101-102.
[7] See Chapter 19, p. 129.
[8] See Chapter 19, p. 127.
[9] See Chapter 19, n. 4.
[10] See Chapter 19, p. 128.
[11] See Chapter 19, pp. 129-131.

patristic literature nor in Josephus.

The tradition mentioned in the *Commentary on Daniel* 7:5 identifies the beast "standing on one side" with a bear representing Persia. The identification of Persia with a bear is well-known in rabbinic literature.[12] Most rabbinic Babylonian traditions seem to be hostile in their evaluation of the Persians while the Palestinian sources, on the whole, are more favorable.[13] Although we can not find rabbinic statements favorable to the Persians derived from Dan 7:5, it seems plausible that such a tradition could have been prevalent in Jerome's time in Palestine. Again we find no record of this tradition either in Josephus or in extant rabbinic literature.

The Hebrew tradition mentioned by Jerome in his *Commentary on Daniel* 9:24-27 concerning the "Seventy Weeks" is the longest one in this book and can not be found, *in toto,* in extant rabbinic literature. Several parts of it are well-known and thus we should be quite ready to accept Jerome's entire tradition on these verses as Jewish were it not that he prefaces his presentation of this tradition with the words "paraphrase, in order to bring out the sense more clearly."[14] This is the only time in his *Commentary on Daniel* when Jerome admits that he is paraphrasing the Jewish interpretation, and we have reasons to doubt that all of his paraphrase represents an indigenous Jewish interpretation.[15] Josephus is evasive regarding his interpretation of the Seventy Weeks and the other patristic commentators do not cite any Jewish traditions on this point.

Although there is no extant rabbinic source for the historical interpretation of Dan 11:31, mentioned by Jerome as a Jewish tradition, we do find the indentification of Kittim with Rome, a basic assumption of Jerome, prevalent in rabbinic literature.[16] We find no other patristic parallel to this; Josephus, on the other hand, identifies Kittim with Cyprus.[17]

Although both the tradition that מצד מלכותא in Dan 6:5 refers to the queen or concubines and the tradition that Daniel could not be accused of lewdness were not found in extant rabbinic literature, one late medieval Jewish tradition could have a common origin with Jerome's tradition.[18] If it actually did, Jerome has uncovered for us an earlier version of a late Jewish tradition. Josephus and the patristic sources are silent concerning this point.

---

[12] See Chapter 9, pp. 86-87.
[13] Ibid.
[14] See Chapter 13, p. 106.
[15] See Chapter 13, pp. 106-107.
[16] See Chapter 15, pp. 117-118.
[17] See Chapter 15, p. 118.
[18] See Chapter 8, pp. 81-82.

Jerome's Jewish tradition on Dan 2:1 which solves the chronological conflict concerning Nebuchadnezzar's dream and "the second year" of his reign has no exact parallel in extant rabbinic literature, although Seder Olam Rabbah seems to be bothered by the same chronological problem.[19] Jerome specifically cites Josephus in his comment on this verse, in addition to the Hebrew tradition; he therefore considered his "Hebrew traditions" as distinct from those in Josephus.

In these six Hebrew traditions of Jerome, we find partial agreement or relationship with extant rabbinic literature, and in five of the six cases we can credit Jerome with helping us recover partially "lost" Jewish traditions.

We have thus accounted for ten out of the sixteen Hebrew traditions of Jerome. To complete the analysis, Jerome's Hebrew traditions recorded in his comments on 2:12-13, 8:16, 11:20, 11:33, 11:34, and 11:36, have no parallel in extant rabbinic literature, nor in Josephus nor patristic literature. Thus we can credit Jerome with the preservation of six more otherwise "lost" Jewish traditions.

It is thus clear that as far as the book of Daniel is concerned, Jerome has cited far more Jewish traditions than any other Church Father or Josephus. With regard to his *Commentary on Daniel,* Jerome has thus fulfilled his promise made in his *Commentary on Zechariah* 6:9:

> I have made it my resolve to make available for Latin readers the hidden treasures of Hebrew erudition and the recondite teachings of the Masters of the Synagogue, as long as these things are in keeping with the Holy Scriptures.[20]

We have taken the words of Samuel Krauss, one of the pioneers in the field of rabbinic and patristic literature, to heart. "Hence such a mass of haggadic material is found in the work of the fathers as to constitute an important part of Jewish theological lore."[21] "This Midrash treasure has unfortunately not yet been fully examined. . . ."[22] We add to this, as a guide, the modest words of Louis Ginzberg: "The large materials culled from the writings of the Church Fathers to illustrate this dependence upon Jewish tradition will be, I hope, of some value to the student of the patristic literature."[23] We add to this Montgomery's evaluation of Jerome's dependence upon rabbinic tradition in his *Commentary on Daniel:* "His commentary is intrinsically valuable for its constant dependence upon the

---

[19] See Chapter 5, p. 73.
[20] *PL* 25:1455.
[21] "Church Fathers," *Jewish Encyclopedia* 4, 80.
[22] Ibid., 86.
[23] *Legends* 5, ix.

tradition of the rabbis under whom he studied. . . ." (p. 107). And thus we offer this work in the hope that it will partially fulfill the promises and evaluations made by the preceding scholars.

Bernard Heller, in his lengthy review of Ginzberg's *Legends of the Jews* devotes one section[24] to the "Relation of the Aggada to the Church." He remarks that "Ginzberg's notes contain many seemingly Jewish Aggadas which were only preserved in church literature."[25] It is this author's hope that his work may offer a modest addendum to Ginzberg's pioneering efforts in this field and help restore, in some small measure, the jewels of lost traditions in the crown of Jewish scholarship.

---

[24] "Ginzberg's *Legends of the Jews," JQR* 24 (1933-1934) 281-307.
[25] Ibid., 284.

BIBLIOGRAPHY

Adler, Michael. "The Emperor Julian and the Jews," *JQR* 5 o.s. (1893) 591-651.

Altaner, Berthold. *Patrology*. Tr. Hilda C. Graef; Freiburg, West Germany: Herder, 1960.

The Apocrypha and the Pseudepigrapha of the Old Testament. Ed. Robert H. Charles. 2 vols. Oxford: Clarendon Press, 1913.

Aptowitzer, Viktor. "Rabbinische Parallelen und Aufschlüsse zur Septuaginta und Vulgata," *ZAW* 29 (1900) 241-252.

Aristeas to Philocrates (Letter of Aristeas). Dropsie College Edition, Jewish Apocryphal Literature. Tr. and Ed. Moses Hadas. New York: Harper and Brothers, 1951.

Bacher, Wilhelm. "Eine angebliche Lücke im hebräischen Wissen des Hieronymus," *ZAW* 22 (1902) 114-116.

Bardy, Gustave. "S. Jérôme et ses maîtres hébreux," *RBén* 46 (1934) 145-164.

_____. "Les traditions juives dans l'oeuvre d'Origène," *RB* 34 (1925) 217-252.

Baron, Salo. *A Social and Religious History of the Jews*. 2nd ed., vol. 2. New York: Columbia University Press, 1952.

Bar Hebraeus, Gregory. *The Chronography of Gregory . . . Bar Hebraeus*. Tr. Ernest A. Wallis Budge. Vol. 1. London: Oxford University Press, 1932.

_____. *Scholien zum Buche Daniel*. Tr. and ed. Jacob Freimann. Bruhn: B. Epstein and Co. 1892.

Barr, J. "St. Jerome's Appreciation of Hebrew," *BJRL* 49 (1966) 280-302.

Berthold, Leonhard. *Daniel aus dem Hebräisch-Aramäischen*. 2 vols. Erlangen: J. J. Palm, 1806-1808.

Biblia Hebraica. Ed. Rudolph Kittel. Stuttgart: Würtembergische Bibelanstalt, 1951.

The Biblical Antiquities of Philo. Ed. Montague R. James. New edition, ed. Louis H. Feldman. New York: Ktav, 1971.

"Bibliographia Selecta." In *S. Hieronymi Presbyteri Opera*: Pars I, I. *CCSL* 72. Turnhout: Brepols, 1959, pp. IX-LII.

Bickerman, Elias J. "The Septuagint as a Translation," *Proceedings of the American Academy of Jewish Research* 28 (1959) 1-39.

Bousset, Wilhelm. *The Antichrist Legend*. Tr. A. H. Keane; London: Hutchinson and Co., 1896.

Brock, S.P. "Origen's Aims as a Textual Critic of the Old Testament," *Studia Patristica* 10, Pt. 1 (1970) 215-218.

Bruce, Frederick F. "Josephus and Daniel," *Annual of the Swedish Theological Institute* 4 (1965) 148-162.

Brüll, N. "Das Apokryphische Susanna-Buch," *Jahrbücher für Jüdische Geschichte und Literatur,* 3 (1877) 1-69.

Cavallera, Ferdinand. *Saint Jérôme: Sa vie et son oeuvre.* 2 vols. Paris: Champion, 1922.

Condamin, Albert. "L'influence de la tradition juive dans la version de S. Jérôme," *RSR* 5 (1914) 1-21.

Cottineau, L. H. "Chronologie des versions bibliques de S. Jérôme." *Miscellanea Geronimiana,* Rome: Tipografia Poliglotta, 1920, pp. 43-68.

Courcelle, Pierre. *Les Lettres grecques en occident de Macrobe à Cassiodore.* Bibliothèque des écoles françaises d'Athènes et de Rome. 2nd ed., Fasc. 159. Paris: E. de Boccard, 1948.

Cross, Frank M. *The Ancient Library of Qumran and Modern Biblical Studies.* New York: Doubleday and Co., 1958.

Daniélou, Jean. *Origen.* Tr. Walter Mitchell; London and New York: Sheed and Ward, 1955.

Daube, David. "Origen and the Punishment of Adultery in Jewish Law," *Studia Patristica* 2, Pt. 1 (1957) 109-113.

Derrett, J. Duncan M. "The Parable of the Prodigal Son: Patristic Allegories and Jewish Midrashim," *Studia Patristica* 2, Pt. 2 (1957) 219-224.

Dihle, Albrecht. *Die Goldene Regel.* Göttingen: Vandenhoeck & Ruprecht, 1962.

Eissfeldt, Otto. *The Old Testament: An Introduction.* Tr. P. R. Ackroyd; New York: Harper and Row, 1965.

Elliot, C. J. "Hebrew Learning Among the Fathers," *Dictionary of Christian Biography.* Edd. William Smith and Henry Wace. Vol. 2. London: John Murray, 1880, pp. 851-872.

The Essene Writings from Qumran. Tr. Géza Vermes; Ed. André Dupont-Sommer; Oxford: Blackwell, 1961.

The Fathers According to Rabbi Nathan. Tr. and ed. Judah Goldin; Yale Judaica Series, 10; New Haven: Yale University Press, 1955.

Field, F. *Origenis Hexaplorum Quae Supersunt sive Veterum Interpretium Graecorum in Totum Vetus Testamentum Fragmenta.* 2 vols. Oxford: Clarendon Press, 1925.

Fischer, Benno. *Daniel und Seine Drei Gefährten in Talmud und Midrasch.* Temesvar: Brüder Moravetz, 1906.

Friedländer, Moriz. *Patristische und Talmudische Studien.* Vienna: Alfred Holden, 1878.

Funk, S. *Die Haggadischen Elemente in den Homilien des Aphraates, des Persischen Weisen.* Vienna: M. Knöpflmacher, 1891.

Gardner, Alice. *Julian: Philosopher and Emperor.* New York: Putnam, 1895.

Gaster, Moses. *The Chronicles of Jerahmeel.* London: Royal Asiatic Society, 1899.

_____. "The Oldest Version of Midrash Megillah," *Semitic Studies in Memory of Rev. Dr. Alexander Kohut* (Ed. George Alexander Kohut; Berlin: S. Calvary and Co., 1897) 167-178.

Gavin, Frank. "Aphraates and the Jews," *Journal of the Society of Oriental Research* 7 (1923) 95-166.

Gerson D. "Die Commentarien des Ephraem Syrus im Verhältnis zur jüdischen Exegese," *MGWJ* 17 (1868) 64-72, 98-109, 141-152.

Ginzberg, Louis. *Die Haggada bei den Kirchenvätern. Erster Theil: Die Haggada in den pseudo-hieronymianischen Quaestiones.* Amsterdam: Levisson Bros., 1899.

_____. *Die Haggada bei den Kirchenvätern und in der apokryphischen Literatur* [2: Genesis]. Berlin: S. Calvary and Co., 1900.

_____. "Die Haggada bei den Kirchenvätern [3] Exodus," *Livre d'hommage à la mémoire du Dr. Samuel Poznanski.* Warsaw: Le Comité de la Grande Synagogue à Varsovie, 1927, pp. 199-216.

_____. "Die Haggada bei den Kirchenvätern. Numeri-Deuteronomium [4]," *Studies in Jewish Bibliography . . . in Memory of Abraham S. Freidus.* New York: The Alexander Kohut Memorial Foundation, 1929, pp. 503-518.

_____. "Die Haggada bei den Kirchenvätern. V. Der Kommentar des Hieronymus zu Koheleth," *Abhandlungen zur Erinnerung an Hirsch Perez Chajes.* Vienna: Alexander Kohut Memorial Foundation, 1933, pp. 22-50.

_____. "Die Haggada bei den Kirchenvätern: VI. Der Kommentar des Hieronymus zu Jesaja," *Jewish Studies in Memory of George A. Kohut.* New York: Alexander Kohut Memorial Foundation, 1935, pp. 279-314.

_____. *The Legends of the Jews.* 7 vols., including Index Volume by Boaz Cohen. Philadelphia: Jewish Publication Society, 1909-1938.

Goldfahn, A. H. *Die Kirchenväter und die Agada. I: Justinus Martyr und die Agada.* Breslau: H. Skutch, 1873.

Gordon, Cyrus H. "Rabbinic Exegesis in the Vulgate of Proverbs," *JBL* 49 (1930) 384-416.

Graetz, H. "Haggadische Elemente bei den Kirchenvätern," *MGWJ* 3 (1854) 311-319, 352-355, 381-387, 428-431; 4 (1855) 187-192.

Hailperin, Herman. *Rashi and the Christian Scholars.* Pittsburgh: University of Pittsburgh Press, 1963.

Hanson, Richard P. C. *Allegory and Event.* London: SCM Press, 1959.

_____. *Origen's Doctrine of Tradition.* London: SPCK, 1954.

Hartman, Louis F. "St. Jerome as an Exegete," *A Monument to St. Jerome.* Ed. Francis X. Murphy; New York: Sheed and Ward, 1952, pp. 37-81.

Hartmann, Phillip D. *Das Buch Ruth in der Midrasch-Literatur.* Leipzig, 1901.

Heller, Bernard. "Ginzberg's *Legends of the Jews,*" *JQR* 24 (1933-1934) 51-66, 165-190, 281-307, 393-408; 25 (1934-1935) 29-52.

Hippolytus. *Commentaire Sur Daniel.* Tr. Maurice le Fèvre; Paris: Editions du Cerf, 1947.

_____. *Die Kommentare zu Daniel.* In *Hippolytus Werke Erster Band: Exe-getische und Homiletische Schriften.* Ed. and tr. G. Nath; Leipzig: Bonwetsch and Hans Achelis, 1897.

Hoenig, Sidney B. "Susanna," *The Interpreter's Dictionary of the Bible.* Vol. 4. N. Y.: Abingdon Press, 1962, pp. 467-468.

Howorth, Henry H. "The Influence of St. Jerome on the Canon of the Western Church," *JTS* 10 (1908-9) 481-496; 11 (1909-1910) 321-347; 13 (1911-12) 1-18.

Jaeger, H. "The Patristic Conception of Wisdom in the Light of Biblical and Rabbinic Research," *Studia Patristica* 4, Pt. 2 (1961) 90-106.

Jellicoe, Sidney. *The Septuagint and Modern Study.* Oxford: Clarendon Press, 1968.

Jephet ibn Ali. *A Commentary on the Book of Daniel.* Edited in the original Arabic and translated into English by David S. Margoliouth. Anecdota Oxoniensa. Semitic Series. vol. 1, pt. 3. Oxford: Clarendon Press, 1889.

Jepsen, A. "Kanon und Text des Alten Testaments," *TLZ* 74 (1949) 65-74.

Jerome. *Commentariorum in Danielem.* In *Corpus Christianorum: Series Latina,* 75A. Turnhout: Brepols, 1964.

_____. *Commentary on Daniel.* Tr. Gleason L. Archer, Jr.; Grand Rapids: Baker Book House, 1958.

John of Damascus. *Writings.* Tr. Frederic H. Chase, Jr.; Fathers of the Church, 37; New York: Fathers of the Church, 1958.

Josephus. *Jewish Antiquities: Books 9-11.* Tr. Ralph Marcus. *LCL.* Josephus, Vol. 6. London: W. Heinemann, 1937.

Kelly, J. N. D. *Jerome: His Life, Writings, and Controversies.* New York: Harper and Row, 1975.

Krauss, Samuel. "Church Fathers," *Jewish Encyclopedia.* Vol. 4. New York: Funk and Wagnalls, 1903, pp. 80-86.

_____. "Jerome," *Jewish Encyclopedia.* Vol. 7. New York: Funk and Wagnalls, 1903, pp. 115-118.

_____. "The Jews in the Works of the Church Fathers," *JQR* o.s. 5 (1893) 122-157; 6 (1894) 82-99, 225-261.

_____. *Monumenta Talmudica.* Vol. 5. Vienna: Orion-Verlag, 1914.

_____. *Persia and Rome in the Talmud and Midrashim* (Hebrew). Jerusalem: Mosad Harav Kook, 1948.

Lagrange, Marie-Joseph. "La revision de la Vulgate par S. Jérôme," *RB* n.s. 15 (1918) 254-257.

_____. "S. Jérôme et la tradition juive dans la Genèse." *RB* 7 (1898) 563-566.

Lamirande, Emilien. "Etude bibliographique sur les pères de l'Eglise et l'Aggadah." *VC* 21 (1967) 1-11.

de Lange, N. R. M. "Origen and the Rabbis on the Hebrew Bible," *Studia Patristica* 14, Pt. 3 (1976) 117-121.

de Langhe, Robert. *Les Textes de Ras Shamra-Ugarit.* 2 vols. Gembloux: J. Duculot, 1945.

Lataix, J. "Le commentaire de S. Jérôme sur Daniel," *Revue d'histoire et de littérature religieuses* 2 (1897) 164-173, 268-277.

Leon, Harry J. *The Jews of Ancient Rome.* Philadelphia: Jewish Publication Society, 1960.

Lévi, I. "L'histoire de 'Suzanne et les deux viellards' dans la littérature juive," *Revue des études juives,* 95 (1933) 157-171.

Lieberman, Saul. *Greek in Jewish Palestine.* New York: Jewish Theological Seminary, 1942.

_____. *Hellenism in Jewish Palestine.* New York: Jewish Theological Seminary, 1950.

_____. *Midrashé Téman* (Hebrew). Jerusalem: Wahrmann Books, 1970.

_____. *Shkiin* (Hebrew). Jerusalem: Wahrmann Books, 1970.

Loewe, Raphael. "The Jewish Midrashim and Patristic and Scholastic Exegesis of the Bible," *Studia Patristica* 1 (1957) 492-514.

Lutz, A. "Die Chronologie des Essias-Kommentars von Hieronymus," *Wiener Studien* 26 (1904) 164-168.

Mann, Jacob. *The Bible as Read and Preached in the Old Synagogue.* Philadelphia: Jewish Publication Society, 1940.

The Midrash on Psalms. Tr. and ed. William G. Braude. 2 vols. Yale Judaica Series, 13; New Haven: Yale University Press, 1959.

Midrash Rabbah. Translated into English. Edd. H. Freedman and Maurice Simon, 10 vols. London: Soncino Press, 1939.

Montgomery, James A. *A Critical and Exegetical Commentary on the Book of Daniel.* *ICC*; New York: Charles Scribner's Sons, 1927.

Neuman (Noy), Dov. *Motif-Index of Talmudic-Midrashic Literature.* Unpublished doctoral dissertation. Bloomington, Indiana; Indiana University, 1954.

Neusner, Jacob. *A History of the Jews in Babylonia.* Vol. 1, 2nd printing, rev. *The Parthian Period.* Leiden: E. J. Brill, 1969. Vol. 2, *The Early Sassanian Period.* Leiden: E. J. Brill, 1966.

Oppel, H. "Kanōn, zur Bedeutungsgeschichte des Wortes und seiner lateinischen Entsprechungen (Regula-Norma)," *Philologus,* Supplement-band 30, Heft 4. Leipzig, 1937.

Patrologiae Cursus Completus: Series Graeca. Ed. J. P. Migne. 162 vols. (incl. index vol. by F. Cavellera; Paris, 1912). Paris: Migne, 1857-1866.

Patrologiae Cursus Completus: Series Latina. Ed. J. P. Migne. 221 vols. (incl. 4 index vols. 218-221). Paris: Migne, 1844-1864; Supplement, ed. Adalbert Hamman, 3 vols. Paris: Garnier Frères, 1958-1966.

Pelletier, André. *Flavius Josèphe Adaptateur de la Lettre d'Aristée.* Paris: C. Klincksieck, 1962.

Pesiķta de-Rab Kahana. Tr. and ed. William G. Braude and Israel Kapstein. Philadelphia: Jewish Publication Society, 1975.

Pesiķta Rabbati. Tr. and ed. William G. Braude. 2 vols. New Haven and London: Yale University Press, 1968.

Pfeiffer, Robert H. *Introduction to the Old Testament.* New York: Harper, 1941.

Pirķé de Rabbi Eliezer. Tr. Gerald Friedlander; London: K. Paul, Trench, Trubner and Co., 1916.

Polychronius. *Commentary on Daniel* (Fragments). In *Scriptorum Veterum Nova Collectio.* Ed. Angelo Mai; Rome, 1825. Vol. 1, part 3, pp. 1-27.

Prophetarum Vitae Fabulosae. Ed. Theodor Schermann. Leipzig: J. C. Hinrichs, 1907.

Quasten, Johannes. *Patrology.* 3 vols. Utrecht, Brussels: Spectrum Publishers, 1950-1960.

Rahmer, Moritz. *Die hebräischen Traditionen in den Werken des Hieronymus: Quaestiones in Genesim.* Breslau: Verlag der Schletterschen Buchhandlung, 1861.

_____. *Die hebräischen Traditionen in den Werken des Hieronymus: Die Commentarien zu den 12 kleinen Propheten.* 2 vols. Berlin: M. Poppelauer, 1902.

Rappaport, Salomo. *Agada und Exegese bei Flavius Josephus.* Vienna: A. Kohut Memorial Foundation, 1930.

Rehm, M. "Die Bedeutung hebräischen Wörter bei Hieronymus," *Bib* 29 (1954) 174-197.

Reinach, Théodore. *Textes d'auteurs grecs et romains relatifs au Judaïsme.* Paris: E. Leroux, 1895.

Reiner, Jacob. "The Original Hebrew *Josippon* in the *Chronicle of Jerahmeel.*" *JQR* 60 (1969-1970) 128-146.

Rohrich, A. *Essai sur S. Jérôme Exégète.* Geneva, 1891.

Rossi, Azariah dei. *Me'or ʿEnayim* (Hebrew). Ed. David Cassel. Vilna: R. M. Romm, 1866. Especially Ch. 7, 129-151.

Rowley, Harold H. *Darius the Mede and the Four World Empires in the Book of Daniel.* Cardiff: University of Wales Press, 1959.

_____. "The Kittim and the Dead Sea Scrolls," *PEQ* 88 (1956) 92-109.

Ruwet, J. "Les Apocryphes dans l'oeuvre d'Origène," *Bib* 25 (1944) 143-166, 311-334.

Ryle, Herbert E. *The Canon of the Old Testament.* 2nd ed. London: Macmillan & Co., 1925.

Schultz, S. "Augustine and the Old Testament Canon," *BS* 112 (1955) 225-234.

Schumpp, Meinrad M. *Das Buch Tobias.* Münster: Achendorff, 1933.

Schürer, Emil. *Geschichte des Jüdischen Volkes im Zeitalter Jesu Christi.* Vol. 1, 4th ed. Leipzig: J. C. Hinrichs, 1901.

Schwarz, W. *Principles and Problems of Biblical Translation.* Cambridge: University Press, 1955.

The Scroll of the War of the Sons of Light Against the Sons of Darkness. Tr. Batya and Chaim Rabin; Ed. Yigael Yadin; London: Oxford University Press, 1962.

Septuaginta. Ed. Alfred Rahlfs. 2 vols. Stuttgart: Würtembergische Bibelanstalt, 1935.

Siegfried, Carl. "Die Aussprache des hebräischen bei Hieronymus," *ZAW* 4 (1884) 34-83.

_____. "Midraschisches zu Hieronymus und Pseudo-Hieronymus," *Jahrbücher für protestantische Theologie* 9 (1883) 346-352.

Silverstone, A. E. *Aquila and Onkelos.* Manchester: University Press, 1931.

Simon, Marcel. *Verus Israel: Etude sur les rélations entre Chrétiens et Juifs dans l'empire romain* (135-425). Paris: E. de Boccard, 1948.

Skehan, Patrick W. "St. Jerome and the Canon of the Holy Scriptures," *A Monument to St. Jerome.* Ed. Francis X. Murphy; New York: Sheed and Ward, 1952, pp. 259-287.

Spanier, Moritz. *Exegetische Beiträge zu Hieronymus' "Onomostikon."* Magdeburg: J. Blumenthal, 1896.

Spiegel, Shalom. "Noah, Daniel and Job touching on Canaanite Relics in the Legends of the Jews," *Louis Ginzberg Jubilee Volume: English Section.* New York: The American Academy for Jewish Research, 1945, pp. 305-355.

Stein, S. "The Dietary Laws in Rabbinic and Patristic Literature," *Studia Patristica* 2, Pt. 2 (1957) 141-154.

Stummer, F. "Beiträge zu dem Problem Hieronymus und die Targumim," *Bib* 18 (1937) 174-181.

_____. "Einige Beobachtungen über die Arbeitsweise des Hieronymus bei den Übersetzung des Alten Testaments aus der hebraica veritas," *Bib* 10 (1929) 1-30.

Sundberg, Albert C. *The Old Testament of the Early Church.* Harvard Theological Studies, 20. Cambridge: Harvard University Press, 1964.

Susanna, Daniel, Bel et Draco. Ed. Joseph Ziegler. *Septuaginta: Vetus Testamentum Graecum, Auctorite Societatis Litterarum Gottingensis editum,* Vol. 16, part 2. Göttingen: Vandenhoeck & Ruprecht, 1954.

Sutcliffe, E. F. "St. Jerome's Hebrew Manuscripts," *Bib* 29 (1948) 195-204.

_____. "St. Jerome's Pronunciation of Hebrew," *Bib* 29 (1948) 112-125.

Swete, Henry Barclay. *An Introduction to the Old Testament in Greek.* 2nd ed., rev. Richard R. Ottley; Cambridge: University Press, 1914.

Tcherikover, Victor. *Hellenistic Civilization and the Jews.* Tr. S. Applebaum; Philadelphia: Jewish Publication Society of America, 1959.

Wiesen, David S. *St. Jerome as a Satirist.* Ithaca, New York: Cornell University Press, 1964.

Wilde, Robert. *The Treatment of the Jews in the Greek Christian Writers of the First Three Centuries.* Catholic University of America Patristic Studies, Vol. 81. Washington, D. C.: Catholic University of America Press, 1949.

Wutz, Franz. *Die Transkriptionen von der Septuaginta bis zu Hieronymus.* Berlin-Stuttgart: W. Kohlhammer, 1933.

Zeitlin, Solomon. "An Historical Study of the Canonization of the Hebrew Scriptures," *Proceedings of the American Academy for Jewish Research* 3 (1931-1932) 121-158.

_____. "Jewish Apocryphal Literature," *JQR* 40 (1949-1950) 223-250.

אבות דרבי נתן. בשתי נוסחאות. הוצאת שניאור זלמן שעכטער, מהדורת צלום. ניו-יורק: פעלדהיים, תש״ה.

לקוטים ממדרש אבכיר. הוצאת שלמה באבער. וויען, תרמ״נ.

מדרש אגדה. על חמשה חומשי תורה. הוצאת שלמה באבער. ווינא, תרנ״ד.

אגדת בראשית. הוצאת שלמה באבער. ווארשא, תרל״י, מהדורת צלום. ניו-יורק: מנורה, תשי״ט.

אוצר מדרשים. יהודה דוד אייזענשטיין, עורך . ב׳ כרכים. ניו-יורק: גראסמאן, תשט״ז.

בית המדרש. אהרן יעללינעק, עורך. (קובץ של מדרשים קטנים). חמישה חדרים. ליפסיא, תרי״נ - ווינא, תרל״נ.

מדרש בראשית רבא. הוצאת יהודה טהעאדר, וחנוך אלבק. ברלין, תרע״ב-תרפ״ז.

מדרש דניאל ומדרש עזרא. ר׳ שמואל מסנות. הוצאת יצחק לנגה ושמואל שורץ. ירושלים: מקיצי נרדמים, תשכ״ח.

מדרש הגדול. ספר בראשית. הוצאת מרדכי מרגליות. ירושלים: מוסד הרב קוק, תש״ז.

מדרש הגדול. ספר שמות. הוצאת מרדכי מרגליות. ירושלים: מוסד הרב קוק, תשט״ז.

מדרש הגדול. ספר ויקרא. הוצאת נחום אליהו ראבינאוויץ. ניו-יורק, תר״צ.

מדרש הגדול. ספר במדבר. הוצאת שלמה פיש. שני חלקים. לונדון, תשי״ח.

מדרש הגדול. ספר במדבר. הוצאת צבי מאיר רבינוביץ. ירושלים: מוסד הרב קוק, תשכ״נ.

מדרש הגדול. ספר דברים. הוצאת שלמה פיש. ירושלים: מוסד הרב קוק, תשל״נ.

מדרש דברים רבה. הוצאת שאול ליברמן. ירושלים, ת״ש.

מדרש ויקרא רבה. הוצאת מרדכי מרגליות. ה׳ כרכים. ירושלים, תשי״נ-תש״ך.

זהר על התורה. נ׳ כרכים, ווארשא, תרכ״ז.

מדרש זוטא. על שיר השירים, רות, איכה, קהלת. הוצאת שלמה באבער. ברלין, תרנ״ד.

ילקוט שמעוני. על התנ״ך. ירושלים: לוין-אפשטיין, תשי״ב.

מדרש לקח טוב. (המכונה פסיקתא זוטרתא) על חמשה חומשי תורה. הוצאת שלמה באבער, ב׳ כרכים, ווילנא, תרמ״ד.

ספרי דאגדתא על מגילת אסתר. כולל: מדרש אבא גוריון, מדרש פנים אחרים, מדרש לקח טוב. שלמה באבער, עורך. ווילנא, תרמ״ז.

מכילתא דרבי ישמעאל. הוצאת חיים שאול האראוויטץ, וישראל אברהם רבין. מהדורת צלום. ירושלים: במברגר את ואהרמן, תש״ן.

מכילתא דרבי שמעון בן יוחאי. הוצאת יעקב נחום אפשטיין ועזרא ציון מלמד. ירושלים: מקיצי נרדמים, תשט״ו.

מדרש משלי. הוצאת שלמה באבער, ווילנא, תרנ״נ.

מעיני הישועה. (The Wellsprings of Salvation) יצחק אברבנאל. פרוש על ספר דניאל. ירושלים, תש״ח. כרך נ׳, פרוש אברבנאל על נביאים וכתובים, דפים רסח - תכא.

סדר אליהו רבה וסדר אליהו זוטא. הוצאת מאיר איש שלום, ווינא, תרס״א. מהדורת צלום, ירושלים: במברגר את ואהרמן, תש״ך.

סדר עולם רבה. הוצאת בער ראטנער. ווילנא, תרנ״ד-תרנ״ז.

ספרא (על ויקרא). הוצאת אייזיק הירש ווייס, עם פרוש הראב״ד. ווינא, תרכ״ב.

ספרי (על במדבר ודברים). הוצאת מאיר איש שלום, ווינא, תרכ״ד.

ספרי על ספר במדבר וספרי זוטא. הוצאת חיים שאול האראוויטץ. ליפצינ, תרע״ו.

ספרי על ספר דברים. הוצאת אליעזר אריה פינקלשטיין. ברלין, ת״ש.

פסיקתא. והיא אגדת ישראל, מיוחסת לרב כהנא, הוצאת שלמה באבער. מהדורת צלום. ירושלים: מקיצי נרדמים, תשכ״ג.

פסיקתא דרב כהנא. הוצאת דוב ב״ר יעקב ישראל מנדלבוים. ב' כרכים. ניו-יורק: הוצאת בית המדרש לרבנים שבאמריקה, תשכ״ב.

פסיקתא רבתי. הוצאת מאיר שלום. ווינא, תר״ס.

פסיקתא רבתי (דרב כהנא). עם פרושי רד״ל, ומהרד״ו. מהדורת צלום. ניו-יורק: מנורה, תשי״ט.

פרקי דר' אליעזר. עם פרוש ר' דוד לוריא. ווארשא, תרי״ב.

ספר קהילות משה. ספר דניאל, עם הפרושים של רש״י, אברהם אבן עזרא, (המיוחס) לר' סעדיה גאון, ויוסף אבן יחייא. אמשטרדם, תפ״ז.

מדרש רבה. על חמשה חומשי תורה וחמש מגילות, עם כל המפרשים, ב' כרכים. מהדורת צלום, ניו-יורק, תשי״ב.

מדרש שוחר טוב על תהילים, שמואל, משלי. עם פרוש מהר״י כהן. ירושלים: מדרש, תש״ך.

מדרש שכל טוב. על בראשית ושמות. הוצאת שלמה באבער. ב' כרכים. ברלין, תר״ס — תרס״א.

מדרש שמואל. הוצאת שלמה באבער. קראקא, תרנ״ג.

מדרש תהילים (המכונה שוחר טוב). הוצאת שלמה באבער. ווילנא, תרנ״א.

מדרש תנחומא. נדפס מחדש. ירושלים: לווין-אפשטיין, תשי״ח.

מדרש תנחומא. על חמשה חומשי תורה. הוצאת שלמה באבער, ב' כרכים. מהדורת צלום. ניו-יורק, תש״ו.

culty in Dan 2:1, 72-73, 74; Daniel, eunuch tradition, references to, 56-57; Daniel, exile of, 64n.; genealogy of, 68; impeccability of, 82-83; Daniel, Nebuchadnezzar's dream and its interpretation, 110-111; Daniel, Seventy-Weeks prophecy in, 109-111; Ezekiel, exile of, 64n.; Jerome, J.'s influence on, 13; Kittim, identification of, 117-118, 118n.; Second Temple, chronology of, 108n.; Septuagint, origin of, 16n., 29, 33; Trypho, account of, 113-114. See also *Index of References*

Joshua, High Priest, accompanies Ahab and Zedekiah, 130, 130n.

Joshua b. Ḥananyah, Rabbi, 85n.

Joshua b. Levi, Rabbi, 85n.

Josippon, apocrypal additions to Daniel and Esther, 129n.; Kittim, identification of, 118

Judah the Prince, association with Antoninus, 121

Julian the Apostate, Dan 11:34 identified with, 120, 124; Jews, friendliness towards, 121-123; Temple, promise to rebuild, 122-123; Twenty-fifth Epistle, 123

Julius Africanus, correspondent of Origen, 18, 22, 40, 47n., 127, 128.; Genesis, 100 years to build Ark before Flood, 101; Susanna, canonicity of, 39-40, 50n.; Susanna, identification of, 131n. See also *Index of References*

Justin Martyr, 24n.-25n., 17n., 32

Justinian, *Novella,* 7n.

Kittim, 115, 117-118

Lactantius, Jews' influence upon, 2

Laodicea, Council of, 36

Levi, Rabbi, 60n.

Levi ben Gerson (Gersonides), Rabbi, 13

Levi b. Sisi, Rabbi, 85n.

Letter of Aristeas, 16n.-17n., 29n.

Libernae (sailing vessels), 18

Longinus, 116n.

Maʿaseh Daniel, genealogy of Daniel, 70-71

Maccabees, wars of, 116

Magi, intolerance toward Jews, 84

Mars, connection with Edom and Rome, 92, 93

Mattathias, rebellion against Greeks, 114

Mazdaism, 84

Mazdean priests, 86

Media, 85

Melito (bishop of Sardis), canon of Old Testament, 36; compared with Origen as a biblical exegete, 22n.

Messiah, birth of, linked with destruction of Temple in rabbinic literature, 107; terms for, in Judaeo-Hellenic tradition, 106-107

Messiah ben David, 125

Messiah ben Joseph, 125

Messiah, false. Cf. Antichrist

Michael (angel), 95-96

Mithraism, advanced by Julian the Apostate, 122

Moses, 91

Nachmanides, Dan 11:31, commentary on, 117n.

Nebuchadnezzar, king, 56, 59n., 64n., 66 (Nabuchadonosor), 72-74, 75-76, 79, 80, 82; daughter of, relations with Ahab and Zedekiah, 129; dream in Daniel interpreted by Josephus, 110-111; permission granted to Johoiachin's wife, 131; reign of, 98

Nehemiah, Second Temple, rebuilding of, 104, 105

New Testament, citations from the Old Testament contained therein, 29, 31n., 31-33

Nicene Synod, 45

Noah: chronology of, 100; Ezek 14:14ff., reference to, 57, 58, 59, 61, 63, 65; preacher of repentance, 101-102

notarikon, 7n.

Old Testament, as cited by the New Testament, 29, 31n., 32, 33

Origen: 13; apocrypha, attitude towards, 37-39, 40-43; biblical exegesis, 22-23, 24n.; canon, Hebrew Bible, definition of, 35, 36-43; controversy concerning, 44n., 65n.; Daniel, eunuch tradition, references to, 57-62, 66, 68, 69; Daniel, identified with Daniel of Ezek 14:14ff., 57-59, 61-62, 65; Enoch, book of, attitude towards, 42-43;

INDEX OF REFERENCES

INDEX OF MODERN AUTHORS

INDEX OF WORDS AND PHRASES